Networks and States

Networks and States

The Global Politics of Internet Governance

Milton L. Mueller

The MIT Press
Cambridge, Massachusetts
London, England

First MIT Press paperback edition, 2013
© 2010 Massachusetts Institute of Technology

This book was set in Stone Sans and Stone Serif by Toppan Best-set Premedia Limited.

Library of Congress Cataloging-in-Publication Data

Mueller, Milton.
   Networks and states : the global politics of internet governance / Milton L. Mueller.
     p.   cm.—(Information revolution and global politics)
   Includes bibliographical references and index.
   ISBN 978-0-262-51857-4 (paperback)
   ISBN 978-0-262-01459-5 (hardcover : alk. paper) 1. Internet—Government policy. 2. Internet—Management. 3. Internet—International cooperation. 4. Internet governance. 5. Telecommunication policy—International cooperation. I. Title.
   TK5105.875.I57M8445   2010
   384.3'3—dc22

                                                                              2010003179

Contents

1 A Battle for the Soul of the Internet

A distinctive global politics is developing around the Internet. Like global trade and environmental policy, Internet governance has become a point of international conflict among states and a target of transnational policy advocates from business and civil society. This book examines Internet governance as a basis for contentious politics and institutional change at the global level. It shows how the problem of governing the Internet has proven to be a disruptive force in international relations and tries to explore where it is leading us.

In 1997 we asked, *can the Net be governed?*[1] By 2008, that question had lost its force. The question now driving discussions of Internet politics is not whether the Net can be governed, but whether there is (or should be) something new and different about the way we do so. Does a globally connected information infrastructure require—or is it already producing—new global institutions? Asking that question leads inexorably to the nation-state and to the relationship between national and global governance. The state, as political scientists insist, is still the predominant supplier of effective public governance and is still an immensely powerful institution. But there is a strong and persistent tension between state sovereignty, which is territorially bounded, and the nonterritorial space for social interaction created by networked computers. This tension puts pressure on the existing nation-centered institutional arrangements in communication and information policy.

Networks and States

Among researchers in Internet governance, the new fashion is to downplay the structural changes wrought by the rise of the Internet, and in some

1. Johnson and Post 1997.

cases even to deny that any exist. This book runs directly counter to that trend. Its central contention is that the problem of Internet governance has produced and will continue to produce institutional innovations in the global regulation of information and communications.

In this book the term *states* carries a very specific meaning. It refers to the nation-state, its claims to sovereignty, and the system of more or less anarchic, conflict-prone relations among nation-states that is an unavoidable consequence of dividing the planet into mutually exclusive territorial monopolies on the use of force. I do not speak of *states* in the more abstract way that Americans tend to use the term *government*: for example, do we want "more" or "less" government. That is really a debate about when or if binding rules or taxes are required to achieve certain public objectives. The focus of discussion here is on *where the rule-making power comes from in the first place*. Where is the capacity to order and make rules institutionalized? Government or governance can take many different forms. One could, for example, have a single world government, or a multiplicity of city-states. It was not so long ago that many functions now performed by states were lodged in the Church. The modern, territorial nation-state is but one particular way of governing. While it has prevailed in Europe and America for a few centuries (and for a much shorter time elsewhere), it is a historically specific answer to the question of who governs and how. It emerged in response to certain economic, political, and technical conditions, and it reflected prevailing ideas about the nature of collective action and community identity. Those conditions and ideas are not immutable. If they can change, the form and nature of government will change, too.

For many years, debates about the role of states in Internet governance have been distorted—disfigured is not too strong a word—by a set of false dichotomies and questionable assumptions. On one side was a way of thinking sometimes referred to as cyber-libertarianism. These early advocates of the Internet supported its freedom and independence but rested their case on a naïve technological determinism. The Internet's freedom, they assumed, was engineered into its protocols. It did not need any particular constitution or political process to maintain its emancipatory capabilities because it was technology, not laws or institutions, that made us free. Technology, they believed, makes the problems of politics and governance go away. It ushers in a world of superabundant resources and self-governing virtual communities that can resolve all problems via consensus or freedom of association. There was in their vision of the world no need for any exercise of compelling authority and no distributional conflicts that generate politics or a need for binding collective action. Nation-states were viewed as dinosaurs, irrelevant distractions—thus there was no need even to discuss governance institutions, policies, or international politics, much less think about how to devise new ones.

Indeed, few adherents to this way of thinking were sophisticated enough to aim their critique at the institution of the nation-state per se. They spoke instead of "government" and "the Internet" in generic terms, as if all governments were the same, as if there was only one government in the world that responded in a uniform fashion to a homogeneous Internet. They did not understand that the Internet had to relate at first to dozens, and later to more than a hundred distinct, autonomous states; that these states have for decades if not centuries engaged in power games over resources and strategic advantage and tended to view Internet governance from within that framework. Indeed, some of the cyber-libertarians turned out, in the end, to be crypto-nationalists, for as soon as the state being challenged was *their own* state, they became apologists for U.S. control and dominance of the Internet.[2] In short, those who have been bold enough to question the status of the nation-state in the age of global communications were simply not up to the task. They had only the most superficial understanding of their enemy. They taunted states with the claim that the Internet rendered them powerless, and were quickly proved wrong.

On the other side of this divide are "realist" political scientists who emphasize the continued power and dominance of states. Existing national governments are assigned "pride of place" in the determination of policy; the influence of other actors is minimized or denied.[3] These scholars assert confidently that nothing fundamentally new is happening around the institutions of communication and information; they praise a "bordered Internet" and claim that "as a practical matter only traditional territorial governments can provide [the] public goods" required for the Internet to work effectively.[4] In addition to these more academically grounded approaches, politicians and practitioners around the world have used the decline of the dream of an ungovernable Internet as a license for unrestrained reassertions of state power over the Internet. If the state is not going to go away automatically, then surely traditional forms of state control must be justified?

2. The CNET news columns of Declan McCullough during the World Summit on the Information Society during 2004 and 2005 provide a good example of this phenomenon. See also Schaefer, Tkacik, and Gattuso 2005.
3. Drezner 2007.
4. Goldsmith and Wu 2006, 142.

But this new *cyber-conservatism* is as unrealistic as its counterpart, and lacking in vision to boot. The Internet's accidental emergence as the dominant standard for global data communications was and remains a major disruption in the way we regulate communication and information technology. Yes, there has been a counter-revolution, as states and other incumbent powers have fought back against these disruptions and innovations, asserting their sovereignty and coming up with new ways to border or regulate the Internet. But we need to understand this dynamic interplay of control and escape from control as a process of evolution and change, not as "business as usual."

Internet vs. the Nation-State

The Internet puts pressure on the nation-state in five distinct ways.

First, it globalizes the *scope* of communication. Its distance-insensitive cost structure and nonterritorial addressing and routing architecture make borderless communication the default; any attempt to impose a jurisdictional overlay on it requires additional (costly) interventions.

Second, it facilitates a quantum jump in the *scale* of communication. It massively enlarges our capacity for message generation, duplication, and storage. As a programmable environment, it industrializes information services, information collection, and information retrieval. The sheer volume of transactions and content on the Internet often overwhelms the capacity of traditional governmental processes to respond—and can transform governmental processes as well.

Third, it *distributes control*. Combined with liberalization of the telecommunications sector, the Internet protocols decentralized and distributed participation in and authority over networking and ensured that the decision-making units over network operations are no longer closely aligned with political units.

Fourth, it *grew new institutions*. Decision-making authority over standards and critical Internet resources rests in the hands of a transnational network of actors that emerged organically alongside the Internet, outside of the nation-state system. These relatively young but maturing institutions, such as the Internet Engineering Task Force (IETF), the Regional Internet Address Registries, and the Internet Corporation for Assigned Names and Numbers (ICANN), provide a new locus of authority for key decisions about standards and critical resources. We are just beginning to confront the problem of how national governments should relate to these "native" institutions.

Finally, it *changes the polity*. By converging different media forms and facilitating fully interactive communication, the Internet dramatically alters the cost and capabilities of group action. As a result, radically new forms of collaboration, discourse, and organization are emerging. This makes it possible to mobilize new transnational policy networks and enables new forms of governance as a solution to some of the problems of Internet governance itself.

Transnational scope; boundless scale; distributed control; new institutions; radical changes in collective action capabilities—this book will document the way these factors are transforming national control and sovereignty over communication and information policy.

The Ideal and the Real

This is a work of social science, but a strong normative stance underlies and informs its analytical approach. The author's normative stance is rooted in the Internet's early promise of unfettered and borderless global communication, and its largely accidental and temporary escape from traditional institutional mechanisms of control. The expectations and norms created by the early Internet were radically liberal in nature, and gave new vitality to ideals of freedom of expression in politics and culture, and to concepts of freedom of exchange and open, competitive entry into information and communication markets in the economic sphere. While acknowledging the flaws in the early, apolitical visions of Internet freedom, we need not categorically dismiss them. We can, instead, embrace the way they opened our eyes to new possibilities. In analyzing and pursuing the global politics of Internet governance, we must be aware of the revolutionary potential of the new social relations fostered by the Internet and digital media; but at the same time we must be unblinkingly realistic about the political, legal, institutional, economic, and cultural forces that shape and constrain any changes. The book strives to occupy this creative space between the ideal and the real. The challenge, as one critical scholar puts it, is to "locate normative standards and emancipatory political possibilities precisely within the historically unfolding constellation."[5]

At this time there are four main drivers of change in global Internet governance: contention over intellectual property protection, cybersecurity, content regulation, and critical Internet resources. About half of the book is devoted to exploring those policy domains, with a chapter devoted

5. Fraser 2007, 8. See also Ruggie 2004.

to each one. These four arenas are not intended to be static categories into which various policy problems can be dropped; they are an attempt to identify the critical areas of conflict and coordination that are generating a global politics of Internet governance. There is a family resemblance across each of these domains, observable in the acute conflict between the capabilities of open, global networking and the problem of maintaining boundaries and control. That conflict can only be resolved through changes in the existing institutions governing communication and information. In each of these arenas we see new forms of governance organized around peer production or transnational networks, as well as efforts by territorial states to reclaim the Internet in ways that make it conform to their authority. Readers who do not find their favorite policy issue in that list should bear in mind that the list does not purport to describe what should be or could be driving change; the issues covered are an attempt to explain what *is* driving change.

Networks and "Networked Governance"

In line with this agenda, the book highlights the critical role that transnational institutions play, or could play, in fostering global governance and political activity. It calls attention to the positive-feedback relationship between institutional structures at the transnational level and the globalization of the politics of communication and information. The book also draws on empirical evidence to explore the meaning and validity of ideas about global governance that are influencing actors in the Internet governance debates.

Networked governance provides one possible way of bridging the gap between national institutions and global connectivity. Governance networks are defined as relatively stable articulations of interdependent but operationally autonomous actors.[6] Networked forms of organization are said to consist of looser affiliations of organizations and individuals that rely on regularized interaction to pursue cooperative goals. The bonds that hold the nodes together, so the theory asserts, are based on the reciprocal benefits that can be achieved by affiliation and cooperation—not on a division of labor defined and enforced from above.[7] The concepts *network organization* and *global public policy networks* are widely used by international relations scholars to describe, for example, civil society advocacy

6. Sørenson and Torfing 2007.
7. Powell 1990.

groups involved in global governance[8] and new forms of transnational cooperation by government agencies.[9]

Ideas about governance networks are relevant in this context because networks that combine state and nonstate actors can overcome some of the limitations of government based on territorial sovereignty. More importantly, the practices of the operators of the Internet itself can be conceptualized as a kind of networked governance. Through bilateral and sometimes multilateral interactions and agreements, Internet service providers establish their own policies and negotiate among themselves what is blocked and what is passed, what is authenticated and what is not; how to respond to threats, and so on. Because of the way the Internet has dispersed control over operations and resources, those with a stake in Internet governance rely heavily on network forms of organization. Those who wish to govern the Internet, therefore, may be required to mirror its transnational, networked relations. In this respect, there is evidence that the problem of Internet governance *is* changing governance via the nation-state, at least in the domain of communication and information policy.

The literature about *commons-based peer production* provides another relevant and closely related strand of thinking about new governance forms. This idea was first conceived by free/open source software developers and given theoretical elaboration by Yochai Benkler.[10] Similar in some respects to the concept of network organizations, *peer production* describes how producers of open source software or content such as Wikipedia rely on nonhierarchical, largely voluntary collaboration techniques within a nonproprietary legal framework and a ubiquitous networked infrastructure. David Johnson, Susan Crawford, and John Palfrey have explicitly applied the concept of peer production to Internet governance in discussing how Internet service providers might respond to security threats.[11] As we shall see, peer production practices already play an important role in Internet governance.

There is yet another "ism" to contend with: the idea of *multistakeholderism*, or the opening up of state-based international organizations to participation by "stakeholders" besides governments. Multistakeholder governance means that representatives of public interest advocacy groups, business associations, and other interested parties can participate in

8. Keck and Sikkink 1998.
9. Slaughter 2004; Eilstrup-Sangiovanni 2009.
10. Raymond 2001; Benkler 2006.
11. Johnson, Crawford, and Palfrey 2004.

intergovernmental policy deliberations alongside governments. It might be described as the *pluralization* of international institutions. Most discussions of networked governance and of global public policy networks recognize the presence of different stakeholder groups in governance networks.

While these new ideas are useful, this book will approach them critically. The mere act of forging networked relations across organizational boundaries does not by itself resolve questions about how much authority the organizations have and what rights the "citizens" of cyberspace can claim against them. Likewise, the participation of multiple stakeholder groups in a governance institution does not determine how power is distributed among these groups or how much weight they are given in decision-making processes. There are still vital questions regarding the status of individual rights in such schemes, and about how conflicts over the distribution of benefits and costs will be resolved. It is important, therefore, to understand how the new networks of actors thrown together by the problems of Internet governance are answering questions about rights, authority, and distributional conflict. What is a loose network today may become a more institutionalized—and possibly hierarchical—form of interaction tomorrow.

Networked governance, peer production, multistakeholder models, and transnational civil society are all related concepts. They pertain to the way the institutions and processes of global governance are organized, and speak to who can participate, who is represented, and how "stakeholders" interact. A study of Internet governance provides an opportunity to observe how these ideas are translated into action (or not) in a real political context, and to assess whether they provide viable alternatives. This book will explore those ideas both at the conceptual level and by relating them to the empirical facts about the progress of Internet governance in recent years.

Internet Governance's Defining Moment

Why do I use the term *Internet governance* as the label for the main topic of this book? The term is repellant to many because it is often (mis)interpreted as implying a kind of top-down regulation or control of the Internet. The term *governance,* however, gained currency in international relations precisely because it was weaker than *government*; it denotes the coordination and regulation of interdependent actors in the *absence* of an overarching political authority.[12] In international relations the term *global governance*

12. Rosenau and Czempiel 1992.

suggests that some steering and shaping function exists, but is less hierarchical and authoritative. Thus, *Internet governance* is the simplest, most direct, and inclusive label for the ongoing set of disputes and deliberations over how the Internet is coordinated, managed, and shaped to reflect policies.

Internet governance used to refer to a vital but relatively narrow set of policy issues related to the global coordination of Internet domain names and addresses. The encounter with those problems from 1994 to 1998 culminated in a notable institutional innovation, the Internet Corporation for Assigned Names and Numbers (ICANN).[13] Since then, the meaning of the term has expanded. A United Nations Working Group charged with developing a definition of Internet governance included a much wider range of policy issues,[14] applying the term to any and all "shared principles, norms, rules, decision-making procedures, and programmes that shape the evolution and use of the Internet." The definition noted that these shared processes involve not just governments but business and civil society as well.[15] That definition at once ratified the position of nonstate actors in Internet governance and put practically all of the traditional problems of communication and information policy within its frame. And yet that definition, too, was still too narrow in one important respect. It saw "governance" as taking place primarily in formal policy-making institutions like the UN or ICANN. In fact, as noted before, most of the real-world governance of the Internet is decentralized and emergent; it comes from the interactions of tens of thousands of network operators and service providers—and sometimes users themselves—who are connected through the Internet protocols.

Broadening our understanding of what constitutes Internet governance has profound consequences. A technological trend known as digital convergence has made the Internet a unified platform for all forms of information and media. We use it to place telephone calls, watch live or recorded video, browse libraries, and download or play music. We use it to exchange email, buy products, do social networking, and construct shared scientific data sets. All these media, which used to be delivered through separate technologies governed by separate legal and regulatory regimes, have

13. The origin of this global governance scheme was documented in my prior book *Ruling the Root: Internet Governance and the Taming of Cyberspace* (Mueller 2002).
14. See chapter 4 for a more thorough discussion of the UN Working Group on Internet Governance (WGIG) and its report.
15. WGIG Report 2005, paragraph 10.

converged on the Internet protocols. So the things that "shape the evolution and use of the Internet" would now include the policies, laws, and regulations that once were applied to the broadcast media, the print media, government information policy, intellectual property, telecommunications policy, and privacy. The range of issues raised by the governance of the Internet is huge: it includes contention over censorship and content regulation; battles over the protection of trademarks and copyrights; privacy and surveillance policies; economic regulation of communication services; and technical standards formation. And of course, there are also a host of policy problems unique to the Internet or the Internet era, such as cybersecurity and cyberattacks; the resource assignment and coordination policies of ICANN; the control of spam; or the promise and pitfalls of social networking sites and other forms of user-generated content. In short, the Internet has become the preeminent platform for contention over the entirety of communication and information policy. These broader debates need to be connected and properly conceived as Internet governance.

Two landmarks stand out in the evolution of Internet governance as a focal point of international political contention. One was the creation of ICANN in 1998. ICANN arose from a unilateral construction of a global regime by the United States, and was based on a new, nongovernmental model. The other was the United Nations' World Summit on the Information Society (WSIS)—an emphatically *multilateral*, state-centric series of diplomatic conferences held from 2002 to 2005 that attempted to "address the whole range of relevant issues related to the information society."[16]

Significantly—and unexpectedly—the World Summit on the Information Society morphed into the World Summit on Internet Governance. It was here that what some called a "battle over the soul of the Internet" took place.[17] WSIS could be characterized as a collision between those who saw national governments as the proper agents for defining and implementing international communication and information policy, and those who pursued a more open, pluralistic, and transnational policy-making framework. The decision to focus on Internet governance was the international system's first major adjustment to the initial disturbance created

16. UN General Assembly Resolution 56/183, December 21, 2001, http://www.itu.int/wsis/docs/background/resolutions/56_183_unga_2002.pdf.
17. Elliot Noss, "Perspective: A battle for the soul of the Internet," *CNET News*, June 8, 2005, http://news.cnet.com/A-battle-for-the-soul-of-the-Internet/2010-1071_3-5737647.html.

by the United States' creation of ICANN. The WSIS process provided a platform for developing country governments and the European Union to challenge the preeminence of the United States in the prevailing governance regime. But WSIS also mobilized a broad range of advocacy networks around issues of communication-information policy, deepening the involvement of civil society groups. The norm of "multistakeholder" participation became one of the rallying cries of both civil society and private business-sector participants.

WSIS was an important inflection point in global Internet governance, as chapters 4 and 5 explain. Nevertheless, few of the issues that animated the summit were resolved decisively. Thus, global governance of the Internet has not reached equilibrium; the process of institutional change continues.

Sectors and Institutions

The beginning of this chapter compared contention over Internet governance to the struggles over global trade and environmental policy. That comparison was not a casual one. It was intended to flag the importance of the topic while simultaneously constraining our conception of it to realistic and manageable proportions.

As with trade and environmental policy, the globalization of communication and information affects ordinary people in significant ways. But the strongest effects are confined to a specific sector of public policy, and hence to specific institutional arenas. The changes wrought by the Internet are not boundless; they have their most concentrated impact on the way states regulate and control communication and information systems and the behaviors and businesses built around them. By putting Internet governance in the same class as trade and environmental policy, we can rescue the topic from ethereal theories that attribute to digital networks an undifferentiated transformation of anything and everything. We can speak of change in, even the erosion of sovereignty over, communication-information policy; but it is hard to make a case that the inability of states to regulate the Internet in traditional ways also revolutionizes the way they exercise domestic police powers, run prisons, handle marriage law, or regulate landing rights for airplanes. Perhaps, over a longer period of time, the emergence of an Internet-enabled transnational public sphere and the continued expansion of e-commerce will produce more far-reaching changes. In the intermediate term addressed by this book, we focus on public policy in the communication-information sector alone.

The problems of trade and environmental policy have produced international regimes, treaties, and organizations *specific to those sectors,* such as the World Trade Organization or the negotiation of the Kyoto Treaty on climate change. Political movements also follow a pattern of sectoral clustering. Advocacy around environmental and trade issues are distinct movements, with their own identities, specialized social networks, and leading organizations. The same is becoming true of Internet governance. Communication-information policy constitutes a domain of public policy that should be considered equal in status to trade and the environment.

Now-clichéd references to an "information society" reflect widespread acceptance of the centrality of communication and information in the contemporary world. Despite this, the scholarly literature on global governance and social movements has all but failed to notice this sector. A glance at the literature on transnational advocacy networks, social movements, and global civil society will invariably turn up massive numbers of references to environmental, trade, and human rights advocacy networks. A more extended search might also find mention of advocacy around debt and international financial institutions, corruption, child labor, gender issues, corporate social responsibility, climate change, biotechnology, land mines, or the arms trade. Communication-information policy, however, has not achieved widespread recognition as a domain around which a transnational advocacy network or social movement might form.[18] This is odd, because such networks and movements do exist. Around intellectual property and "access to knowledge" issues there is something that qualifies as a transnational social movement—a fact that the book will document and explore.

One reason for this oversight is the tendency to think of the Internet as a *tool* that enables policy advocacy rather than as an *object* or *target* of political action. Much of the literature on global civil society has focused on the Internet as a *resource* used by stakeholders to network and to mobilize people.[19] This book, in contrast, is concerned with how transnational politics are fostered by contention over the substantive policy issues raised by the growth of the global Internet itself. Electronic networks and digital information are not exogenous, taken-for-granted features of the international environment. The prices, policies, and practices of networking are the target of interest groups, public policy makers, and policy activists. The substantive issues raised by efforts to govern the Internet are important,

18. But see Bennett 2003 and 2004.
19. Hajnal 2002; Smith 2001.

and as the visibility and importance of information and communication technologies have grown, the stakes of these policy issues have risen.

Outline of the Book

The book is divided into three parts. Part I takes up the concept of networks and networked governance. It begins by describing three incidents: the takedown of Indymedia in 2004, the Estonian "cyber riot" in 2007, and the UK attempt to censor Wikipedia in 2009. Each illustrates the unique governance problems posed by the Internet. The next chapter moves to a more theoretical discussion of ideas about network organizations, peer production, and networked governance and how they apply to Internet governance. That discussion provides the conceptual basis for understanding what is different about Internet governance and how those differences are shaped and constrained by states.

Part II provides a narrative on the historical evolution of the institutions of global Internet governance. Chapter 4 describes the World Summit on the Information Society as an exercise in interstate politics and explains why it was a significant inflection point in the evolution of Internet governance. Chapter 5 describes the mobilization of civil society groups around the WSIS process and documents some fundamental problems associated with multistakeholder governance arrangements. Chapter 6 focuses upon the new UN Internet Governance Forum, noting how it consolidated the new transnational policy network formed around WSIS. It explores the strengths and weaknesses of the experiment.

Part III examines what I have called the four main drivers of change in Internet governance. Battles between Internet users and copyright-trademark holders are analyzed in chapter 7. Chapter 8 handles the response to cybercrime and the linkage of Internet security to national security. Chapter 9 covers the efforts to regulate and censor Internet content. The public policy issues and institutional dilemmas posed by transnational management of critical Internet resources are addressed in chapter 10. The book concludes with a conceptual essay that analyzes the new global governance concepts and ideologies and their relevance to the governance of the Internet.

I Networks and Governance

2 Networks in Action: Three Case Studies

Network has become a trendy term. We are said to live in a networked society or, even more grandly, *the* network society.[1] Instead of the wealth of nations, we read about the wealth of networks.[2] Political scientists searching for new labels to describe the ferment in global governance have joined this parade. We hear of global public policy networks,[3] transgovernmental networks,[4] transnational advocacy networks,[5] and networked governance.[6]

Like all pregnant metaphors, the network concept can be stretched too far or applied indiscriminately. The potential for insight—and confusion— is magnified in discussions of Internet governance because there we are addressing the very technological networks that have stimulated much of the theorizing. This has led to a profusion of overlapping and sometimes confusing applications.[7] When we talk about "networks" are we talking about technologies, or societal organization, or both? Or are we simply projecting the latest metaphor into any and every kind of social relationship we can see? The recursive relationship between technological

---

1. Castells 1996.
2. Benkler 2006.
3. Reinicke 1997 and 1999–2000; Benner, Reinicke, and Witte 2000.
4. Eilstrup-Sangivanni 2009; Slaughter 2004; Raustiala 2002.
5. Keck and Sikkink 1998.
6. Sørenson and Torfing 2007; Kooiman 2003.
7. A selection from an academic work (Hudson 2001, 334) provides a typical example of the cascading application of the concept: "Castells (1996) argues that networks are central to the information age, while Moghadam (2000: 80) suggests that 'the network form of transnational organizing may be the one most conducive to the era of globalization'. Although this may be a premature conclusion, many commentators would seem to concur, talking about digital networks (Sassen 2000), transnational business networks (Yeung 2000), knowledge networks (Sinclair 2000), citizens networks (Deibert 2000), transnational feminist networks (Moghadam

networks, networks of actors, organizational networks, and governance institutions becomes an unavoidable theme in any discussion of what's different about the Internet.

Instead of beginning the book with a complicated and abstract discussion of networks in social science theory, I start with three concrete case studies. The incidents discussed in the following pages provide potent examples of the relationship between the Internet's ability to connect information and people and how that can transform the political economy of communication and information. I have deliberately chosen messy examples, not simple ones. They are cases in which Internet-based activities overlap, intersect, or clash with governments and international governance processes in the kind of unformed spaces where new organizational models and practices can take root.

Indymedia and the "Guantanamo Bay for 'Terrorist' Computer Hard Drives"

The Independent Media Center (Indymedia) is an Internet-based news network. It produces news for antiglobalization protest-oriented activists and their supporters. Born in Seattle at the 1999 World Trade Organization (WTO) protests, it provided an alternative to what movement activists perceived as the biased coverage of events by the commercial mass media. From these origins Indymedia grew into a transnational network of autonomous media collectives, interlinked via the Web and a shared publishing platform. *Be your own media* is their motto. Indymedia epitomizes what some people like to refer to as the network form of organization: loosely structured, noncommercial, and nonhierarchical. With no central managers, no advertisers, a lot of volunteer labor, and some donations it has grown to 150 local centers in more than thirty different countries.

This is where most stories about networks stop. But a thorough and realistic assessment of the global governance implications of this kind of networking can't stop there. For it did not take long for Indymedia's success at growing a network to collide with the demands of states. On

---

2000)." In this paragraph we see thrown into one gigantic pot the physical infrastructure for processing and transmitting information, Manuel Castells's macrosocial characterization of a type of society, a generic technology of networking (digital networks), an organizational form, a coalition of activists around a particular ideology or issues, and business relationships among suppliers.

October 7, 2004, its Internet hosting provider, acting in response to a request from the U.S. Federal Bureau of Investigation (FBI), removed two hard drives from Indymedia servers. As a result, twenty Indymedia Web sites in thirteen different nations were suddenly offline. Confusion, secrecy, and a tangle of transnational connections surrounded the event. The hard drive removal disabled the Web sites of local media collectives in Uruguay, Andorra, Poland, France, Basque Country, Belgium, Serbia, Portugal, the Czech Republic, Italy, Brazil, the United Kingdom, and Germany. The global radio service of Indymedia also went down.

The multinational company that operated the affected Indymedia servers, Rackspace Managed Hosting, was based in Texas. Its servers containing the Indymedia sites were in London. Yet the British government and British law never played a role in the takedown.[8] And while the shutdown was prompted by a subpoena issued by the U.S. government, the FBI claimed that it was "not an FBI operation" but merely a response to requests by Italian and Swiss authorities under Mutual Legal Assistance Treaties (MLATs).[9] Rackspace would say only that it was "cooperating with international law enforcement authorities" and that "the court prohibits Rackspace from commenting further on this matter." The U.S. court documents were sealed. One angry Indymedia volunteer opined that "the equipment that we use to help people *be their own media* has been spirited away to some sort of Guantanamo Bay for 'terrorist' computer hard drives."[10]

More facts eventually came out, thanks in large part to the Electronic Frontier Foundation's successful lawsuit to unseal court documents.[11] It turned out that in April 2004—a full six months before the takedown—the United States had received an MLAT request from the Public Prosecutor's

8. When asked which UK law-enforcement agency was involved in the seizure of Indymedia servers in London, the Home Office Minister responded: "I can confirm that no UK law-enforcement agencies were involved in the matter referred to in the question posed by the Hon. Member for Sheffield, Hallam." *Statewatch News*, October 2004, http://www.statewatch.org/news/2004/oct/04uk-usa-indymedia.htm.
9. MLATs are agreements between states to assist each other in prosecuting criminals. The agreements give their parties the power to summon witnesses, compel the production of documents and other evidence, issue search warrants, and serve process across boundaries. These and other tools constitute an extensive and growing skein. The first U.S. MLAT was concluded in 1977; there are more than fifty of them now. Underscoring their relationship to recent globalization trends, all but four of them were signed after 1990 and twenty-seven of them were signed in 1999 or later.
10. http://www.indymedia.org.uk/en/2004/10/298884.html.
11. http://www.eff.org/cases/indymedia-server-takedown.

Office in Bologna, Italy. The request originated from the investigation of a violent anarchist group in Italy that had planted bombs or mailed incendiary packages to European politicians, including Italian Prime Minister Romano Prodi, in December 2003 and January 2004. Describing Indymedia as "politically near to the extremist milieu," the Italian police claimed that a document claiming responsibility for the attack on Prodi had been posted on the Indymedia newswire section. Indymedia's "open publishing" newswire platform allows anyone to post and syndicate a story, anonymously and unedited. In order to identify the Internet user who published the Web version of the document, the Italian officials used their treaty with the United States to ask the U.S. Justice Department to obtain log files of the creation and updating of various URLs under the Indymedia domain.

The Italian request for log files did not require removing the hard drives or shutting down Web sites.[12] So why did the shutdown occur? The only available explanation highlights the tenuousness of the governance processes at play. A Rackspace spokeswoman asserted that an employee mistakenly used the word *hardware* to describe what the FBI was asking for, and therefore agents removed the two hard drives rather than copy the log files sought by the Italian prosecutors. A number of other questions about this incident remain unanswered. Why did Rackspace tell the world that it was under a gag order, when subsequent documents revealed that it was not? Was the confusion about hardware real, or did law enforcement pressure the hosting provider to hand over more than the FBI was legally entitled to? Or was Rackspace overzealous in its cooperation? If this was an urgent, terrorism-related MLAT request, what accounts for the six-month delay between the Italian prosecutors' request and the FBI's delivery of the subpoena to Rackspace?

Regardless of how those questions are answered, the Indymedia shutdown concretizes some initial insights into the relationship between networks and global governance. We see in this case the ability of a technological network to provide open, lightweight forms of organization capable of supporting rich communication and collaboration among transnational networks of political actors. We even see something of the self-healing capability of these networked relationships when disrupted by

12. Indeed, because the Independent Media Center (IMC) policy was never to log the specific IP address of the computer that reads or posts information to their sites, it might have been possible for Rackspace to resist or delay the request on the grounds that it would not yield the desired information.

external forces.[13] But we also see how this openness exposed Indymedia to the use of its network by violent groups, bringing with it surveillance and subpoenas. We see discussion and debate within the network about how much openness it should tolerate.[14] We see that far from being helpless in the face of transnational networking, state actors were able to draw on well-established transboundary law enforcement tools—but we also see how uncertain, nontransparent, and ad hoc the application of those mechanisms can be. We see the appalling weakness of the legal rights and procedural protections afforded to Indymedia because of its status as a loose transnational network without the organizational overhead of lawyers and managers. We see too the intimidation or complicity—we don't know which—of Rackspace, the multinational business that operated the physical facilities. Its legal exposure and obligations under the skein of MLATs was unclear,[15] which made it all too easy for a risk-averse, bottom-line-oriented business to abandon its customers' interests. Last but not least, we see that the UK national privacy law that one might think applicable had utterly no impact on the action, despite the server's location in that jurisdiction. Whatever legal rights the parties thought they had disappeared into the cloud of a multinational network.

13. One Indymedia technical support person wrote: "Support from IMCistas and the 'net in general has been amazing. Indy journos, lawyers, & geeks have been working 24/7 ever since. Even the trolls on slashdot can't back the governments on this. Everyone has been rallying and quickly making more mirrors of sites. We have renewed efforts to get better code which allows for faster & wider site replication. It has pulled everyone together to work for more robust and decentralized servers." —Jebba, indymedia tech, imc-press list, October 11, http://www.indymedia.org.uk/en/2004/11/300886.html.
14. An Indymedia supporter noted "there have been many discussions about the open nature of the news wire. Many of the web sites are besieged with crank posts, occasional racist slurs and even a sort of 'left spamming'. There have been calls for heavy moderation and censorship of racist and offensive material. Most IMCs have resisted any censorship of the open newswire." Halleck 2003.
15. Two legal scholars cite the case of *United States v. Bank of Nova Scotia*, wherein the Bank of Nova Scotia refused to respond to a request from the U.S. authorities for banking information kept in the Bahamas, because divulging the information would violate Bahamian banking secrecy laws. In this case the courts decided against the Bank of Nova Scotia. "Rackspace is left in the situation where it is complying with U.S. law and yet possibly breaking UK law, and this is entirely legal because Rackspace elected to do business in the UK." Koops and Brenner 2006, excerpt cited by Privacy International, "International cooperation gone awry," http://www.privacyinternational.org/article.shtml?cmd[347]=x-347-530312.

What we do not see is the "business as usual" predicted by realist legal theorists.

The Cyber-Riot in Estonia

Estonia is a small Eastern European nation that borders Russia. In the last days of April 2007, Web sites of banks, the ruling political party, and government ministries in Estonia were hit by a series of coordinated attacks. The incident proved to be a politically motivated assault on the country's information infrastructure, one that succeeded in seriously disrupting Internet usage inside the country for nearly two weeks. The attack effectively defaced and crashed the Web site of the ruling political party, disabled several government ministries' online presence, crippled electronic interactions with the country's two largest banks, and disrupted the sites of the two national newspapers. The attacks were especially noteworthy because Estonia had made it a point of national policy to put as much of its essential public functions as possible online, increasing its dependence on the Internet.[16]

The weapon used in this case was the distributed denial of service (DDoS) attack. DDoS attacks bombard targeted computers with so many bogus requests for information that they become overloaded and crash. While DDoS attacks can come from individuals using relatively simple methods, in Estonia there was, in addition to individual attacks, evidence of a more sophisticated technique: the rental of commercial botnets.[17] Botnets are composed of hundreds of computers on the Internet, which unbeknownst to their owners are infected with malicious software that puts them at the disposal of some remote operator. Once control of these "zombie" computers falls into the hands of botnet operators, their capabilities can be sold in a black market and used to distribute spam or engage in phishing (a way of tricking people into revealing their bank account numbers or passwords) or other illegal but profitable Internet activities.

The Estonian incident was not, however, a simple story of cybercrime. It was an outgrowth of political tensions among Estonians, the sizable minority of ethnic Russians residing in Estonia, and the Russian government. The trigger was a fierce controversy over the removal of a Soviet-era war monument. When the Estonian president proposed to move a statue of a Soviet soldier out of the center of the capital city to the outskirts of

16. For a comprehensive description of the e-Estonia efforts, see Odrats 2007.
17. Evron 2008; Kaeo 2007.

town, ethnic Russians reacted with outrage. The Russian government fanned these flames by propagating anti-Estonian messages through its state-controlled media.[18] When the statue was actually moved, there was some old-fashioned physical rioting and looting in the capital city of Tallinn. In addition, however, Russian-language Web sites' online forums and blogs (both inside and outside Estonia) lit up with angry discussions. Some messages outlined potential Internet targets associated with the Estonian government to attack and provided instructions for how to do it. As the incident progressed, dialogue on these sites sometimes identified new targets and offered new instructions. The attacks came in waves, which suggested to some that there was a coordinated effort to respond to Estonian defenses.

In the aftermath a critical question surfaced. Was this the world's first instance of a true "cyberwar?" The answer to this question hinged on the answer to another one: what was the role of the Russian government in supporting and carrying out the attacks? In the immediate aftermath of the attacks, a flustered Estonian government blamed the Russian government and even considered invoking NATO Article 5 to marshal a multinational military counterattack against Russia. Fueling these suspicions, Estonian attempts to use an Estonia-Russia Mutual Legal Assistance Treaty to identify and prosecute attackers in the jurisdiction of the Russian Federation were rebuffed.[19]

Later, Estonia's director of e-governance relabeled the event a mass "cyber-riot" and discounted theories about the direct involvement of the Russian government. In January 2008 a twenty-year-old ethnic Russian citizen, who lived in Estonia, was convicted of participation in the cyber-riot. In what proved to be the only successful conviction so far, he was fined about $1,600. Many foreign observers and journalists misinterpreted the announcement of the young man's conviction as an admission that a

18. Anton Nossik, one of the pioneers of the Russian Internet, said, "There were anti-Estonian sentiments, fuelled by Russian state propaganda, and the sentiments were voiced in articles, blogs, forums and the press, so it's natural that hackers were part of the sentiment and acted accordingly." Quoted in *BBC News*, May 17, 2007, http://news.bbc.co.uk/1/hi/world/europe/6665195.stm.

19. On May 10, 2007, the Estonian Public Prosecutor's Office made a formal request for assistance to the Russian Federation's Supreme Procurature. But Russian authorities declined the request, claiming that the proposed investigative processes were not covered by the applicable MLAT. The Estonian authorities rejected this legal claim and interpreted the refusal as an indication of Russia's complicity in the attacks.

single individual was responsible for the entire incident.[20] Prominent technical security experts such as Ross Anderson and Bruce Schneier, (over) reacting against media framing of the incident as a cyberwar, lent their support to this hasty interpretation.[21]

The journalists and security experts were locked into a false dichotomy. They thought that either the attacks had to be centrally coordinated by a hierarchical organization such as the Russian government and so fit into traditional notions of organized war, or they had to be a garden-variety DDoS attack attributable to a few hacker kids inside Estonia. In fact, the attacks were the product of a large-scale, transnational, spontaneously organized collective action. It was made possible by the Internet and its capacity for quickly sharing information and software tools and for mobilizing like-minded but dispersed and mostly anonymous groups of people. While describing the incident as cyberwar exaggerated the situation, framing it as a plain vanilla DDoS attack unjustly trivialized it. The Estonians' own official term, *cyber-riot*, was both accurate and pointed.

There are three distinct "network" stories to be drawn from the Estonian incident. The first relates to the loosely organized network of Russians who participated in the attacks. Mob actions animated by ethnic tensions are nothing new. Prior forms of mass communication, ranging from newspapers to the combination of fixed and mobile telephones, radio, and television have made it possible to mobilize a cascade of dispersed social networks into spontaneous collective action. What's different here is that the mass riot took place *within the network*. The software tools and protocols of the Internet itself were used to attack other nodes in the network, and the society involved was so Internet-dependent that the attacks had a major impact outside as well as inside the Internet. The capability for engaging in such disruptive action was not confined to states and a few specialized corporations who operate the infrastructure, but broadly diffused across civil society.

20. Kevin Poulsen, "We traced the cyberwar—It's coming from inside the country!" *Threat Level* blog, *Wired*, January 24, 2008, http://www.wired.com/threatlevel/2008/01/we-traced-the-c/.
21. In his *Schneier on Security* blog, January 28, 2008, Bruce Schneier noted the conviction of the local hacker and dismissed the entire incident with the line "so much for all that hype," http://www.schneier.com/blog/archives/2008/01/the_estonia_cyb.html. The discussion of the Estonia incident in Anderson et al. (2008, 76) confuses Estonia's inability to locate and prosecute anyone else outside its borders with the conclusion that there were no other suspects in the case.

This important difference has major implications for Internet governance. It underscores the oft-contested point that cyberspace is indeed a place of its own, with its own native version of riots, crime, street barricades, defacement, and even war. This in turn means that—despite the huge and generally positive potential for open and universal networking—there remains a need to maintain boundaries and to construct defenses within that new space. But the need to construct virtual boundaries on the Internet constitutes a massive shift in the nature of the institutional problem of "security." Despite the presence of traditional actors like national governments, NATO,[22] and the EU in this story, the methods for maintaining and enforcing such defenses and boundaries are bound to result in new policies, practices, organizations, and institutions. That is because the defenses must be constructed within a distributed, transnational network of tens of thousands of autonomous systems, most of which are privately owned.

We can find evidence of such new practices and institutions in the role of computer emergency response teams (CERTS) and computer security incident response teams (CSIRTS) in the Estonian incident, which is the second network story. CERTS/CSIRTS are new institutional forms focused on monitoring and maintaining the security of information and communication technology networks. They have grown up alongside the Internet. Some are formally organized, even government-supported; others are more like informal expert community networks. At the core of these CERTS is a transnational, cosmopolitan network of reciprocally trusted Internet technical experts. In the case of Estonia, global cooperation with these people around the world helped synchronize a multilateral response. According to Evron (2008), the Estonian CERT, "in cooperation with local providers and volunteer networks of IT professionals in industry and government, coordinated the emergency defense program." CERT organizations from Germany, Finland, and Slovenia also filed abuse reports documenting the incidents. American Internet experts boasted of their participation in the defense of Estonia the way prior generations told tales about their service in World War II.

The third network story relates to the topic of cyberwar. Whether or not Russian officials were involved in the previous case, it should be obvious that they *could* have been. Nothing prevents states, as a general principle, from encouraging, benefiting from, or manipulating cyber-riots

22. Starting in August 2008 NATO's Cooperative Cyber Defense Center of Excellence operates in Tallinn.

and other forms of Internet-based collective action while keeping their presence obscure. (For example, if commercial botnets were involved, where did the money to hire them come from?) That same debate now pervades discussions of cyberattacks on the United States coming from China.[23] Are these private actions motivated by anti-Americanism, are they subtly encouraged by the Chinese state, or are they directly contracted and funded by the government? Are the Americans doing the same thing to the Chinese? The Estonian incident underscored the absence of a clean division between state and nonstate actors in the networked environment. As one U.S. report on cyberspace security noted, "Deterrence in cyberspace is particularly complicated because of the problems with attribution and identification. If a country does not know who is attacking, it is difficult to create appropriate and proportionate responses in ways that reduce the chance of escalation." Noting that the Estonian attacks used captive computers in Europe, China, and the United States, the report noted that "a counterstrike against the attacking computers would have damaged innocent networks in many countries and might not have affected the attackers at all."[24]

Wikipedia and the "Virgin Killer"

On December 4, 2008, an Internet user in England submitted a complaint to the Internet Watch Foundation (IWF). IWF is a British hotline for reporting and taking "potentially illegal" content off the Internet, especially child pornography.

The complaint was about an image, a digital scan of an album cover from the German rock band Scorpions. A nude adolescent girl sits confidently in a centerfold-type posture, while a cracked-glass effect obscures a direct view of her genital area. The image comprised the cover art for the Scorpions' 1976 album, named *Virgin Killer*. It was widely distributed by RCA at that time and can still be found in shops and online.

The complaint to the IWF referred not to the trade in Scorpions albums but to a Wikipedia article. Wikipedia.org is one of the most heavily trafficked sites on the Internet. It is a massive online encyclopedia, the content

23. "Chinese cyber attacks," *Schneier on Security* blog, July 14, 2008, http://www .schneier.com/blog/archives/2008/07/chinese_cyber_a.html. For a more recent and more empirical discussion of the role of Chinese-controlled cyber-intrusions, see Deibert and Rohozinski 2009a.
24. Lewis 2008.

of which is generated and edited by millions of Internet users. For three and a half years, there had been an encyclopedia entry about the Scorpions' *Virgin Killer* album. It had originated in April 2005 as a short definition of the slang term *virgin killer*. The contributor of this piece of ephemera made a passing reference to the Scorpions' album at the end. In an example of the constantly evolving nature of user-generated content, the slang term quickly fell out of the article altogether, and over the next three years the entry became a lengthy discussion of the album itself, especially the controversy surrounding the cover art. One of the band members was quoted in the article as saying he thought "the cover art was a 'great thing' and that he had 'pushed the band to really stay behind it.'" Another band member countered, "The picture today makes me cringe. It was done in the worst possible taste. Back then I was too immature to see that."

A digitized image of the original album cover was added to the Wikipedia article in late June 2005. Wikipedians themselves debated whether the image should be removed. In November 2007, a decision was made to take it down for fear that it was illegal in Florida, where Wikipedia's servers are located. A few weeks later it was put back up, based on a determination that the album cover had been circulating legally for years and was still being sold in U.S. stores—and because of the principle that "Wikipedia doesn't censor."[25] In 2008 there were complaints about the image from conservative Christian media-monitoring groups in the United States. The FBI reportedly investigated but took no action.

The IWF apparently was unaware of this background. After receiving the complaint, the British content watchdog ran the image through its routine assessment procedures. It determined that the image was a "potentially illegal indecent image of a child under the age of 18."[26] Had the servers containing the image been located in the United Kingdom, the IWF would then have notified the local hosting company and UK law enforcement agencies, and the image probably would have been taken down.

25. Archives of these discussions can be found here: http://en.wikipedia.org/wiki/ Wikipedia:Images_and_media_for_deletion/2007_November_27#Image:Virgin _Killer.jpg. For a general discussion of Wikipedia's policy regarding self-censorship and the strengths and weaknesses of its approach, see http://en.wikipedia.org/wiki/ Wikipedia:About.

26. IWF rated the image "1 on a scale of 1 to 5, where 1 is the least offensive" because it involved "erotic posing with no sexual activity." J. R. Raphael, "Wikipedia censorship sparks free speech debate," *PC World*, December 8, 2008, http://www .pcworld.com/article/155156/wikipedia_censorship_sparks_free_speech_debate .html (accessed May 19, 2009).

Wikipedia, however, hosts its content in the United States. That triggered a different response. IWF no longer just facilitates the takedown of content in British territory. It now tries to *block access* to "potentially illegal" content hosted in other countries as well. The maintenance of a blacklist of censored sites has become an increasingly prominent—and controversial—feature of Internet governance, not only in authoritarian countries like China but also in the West. The IWF's "Child Sexual Abuse Content URL List" is compiled from its local hotline and distributed twice a day to most UK Internet service providers (ISPs). Participating ISPs are then expected to prevent their users from viewing these sites.

And so on December 5, 2008—only a day after the complaint—the IWF added two URLs to its blacklist. One pointed to the web page with the "Virgin Killer" Wikipedia article; the other to the image itself. IWF had done this, so its staff thought, many times before for hundreds of URLs containing "potentially illegal" images. But this time the process blew up in their faces.

The first problem was that the blocking had unintended and destructive technical consequences. The blocking regime in Great Britain does not block entire domains; in an attempt to be more precise it first passes requests for IP addresses with blacklisted content to a web proxy server. The proxy compares the users' URL request to the URLs on the forbidden list. If it is on the list, the request is blocked; if it is not, it goes through. In this case, the two-step procedure had unforeseen consequences. One was that it didn't scale. Some of the ISPs' proxy servers were unable to handle the huge volume of traffic Wikipedia attracts. This made *all* of Wikipedia unavailable to its users. The procedure also imposed collateral damage on Wikipedia's security procedures. Wikipedia allows anyone to edit an article by clicking an "edit" button, changing the text, and clicking "save." This open arena for user-generated content, however, attracts its share of abusers, who regularly try to use the editing process to deface pages. Wikipedia responds to repeated attempts at vandalism by blacklisting the IP addresses identified as the source of defacing edits. The UK's blacklist procedure, which forced all British users of Wikipedia to pass through a small number of proxy servers, meant that all users appeared to come from a few IP addresses. As the Electronic Frontier Foundation's Peter Eckersley wrote, "ordinary British Internet users could no longer edit Wikipedia, because technical decisions by Internet censors suddenly caused them to be sharing IP addresses with a horde of vandals." As complaints from Wikipedia users poured in, then and only then did Wikipedia learn that it had been blacklisted by the IWF.

Ironically, the IWF's choice of URLs to block did not reflect a recent movement of the Virgin Killer image file. This meant that for many users, the block didn't even work.[27] IWF's censorship effort backfired substantively as well. It fell victim to what is often called the "Streisand effect," in which an attempt to repress information attracts more attention to it. The controversy over the album cover sparked millions of downloads and distributions of the Virgin Killer image from other sources. Not only had they failed to block it, but they had also advertised it. The IWF itself admitted defeat in a December 9, 2008, news release: "IWF's overriding objective is to minimise the availability of indecent images of children on the Internet, however, on this occasion our efforts have had the opposite effect."[28]

And so a chastened IWF reversed its decision and removed the block on the Wikipedia URLs. "Any further reported instances of this image which are hosted abroad, will not be added to the list. Any further reported instances of this image which are hosted in the UK will be assessed in line with IWF procedures."[29]

The attempt by the IWF to censor a Wikipedia article contains, in microcosm, many of the key elements of networked governance of the Internet. Both IWF and Wikipedia are organized as private foundations and execute self-regulatory functions. What is most notable about this case is that both Wikipedia and IWF are in the business of leveraging the capabilities of the population through networking. This is obvious in Wikipedia's case: it is the example par excellence of user-generated content production. But IWF also relies on informal, unpaid networks of Internet users to voluntarily

27. Richard Clayton's blog analyzed the technical issues in detail: "[IWF] had failed to notice that this URL had returned a 301 'moved permanently' response and redirected [users] to a 'Virgin_killer' URL (with a capital V). Wikipedia treats page names as case sensitive except for the first letter. In fact, Wikipedia also returns identical content for 'Virgin_Killer' (with capital V and K) but without a redirection. Their index lists both the 'Virgin_Killer' and 'Virgin_killer' variants, but not the 'virgin_killer' URL that the IWF were considering. This meant that when people tried to access the page either by following a URL cut and pasted from a browser, or by looking up the topic in the Wikipedia index, they were not accessing the URL that was being listed by the IWF." In other words, they could access the image without any block. Richard Clayton, "Technical aspects of the censoring of Wikipedia," *Light Blue Touchpaper* blog, December 11, 2008, at 02:00 UTC, http://www.lightbluetouchpaper.org/2008/12/11/technical-aspects-of-the-censoring-of-wikipedia/.
28. IWF News release, December 9, 2008.
29. Ibid.

identify and report "potentially illegal images." (This will be examined in greater detail in chapter 9.) With significant government funding, IWF assumes the role of censor without being a formal police agency, which calls attention to the shifting roles of state and nonstate actors in the networked environment.

The status of Wikipedia is not all that different, although it lacks any direct support or control by governments. It started as an entirely open system but was gradually forced to adopt more rules and governance procedures to prevent vandalism and to respond to policy issues such as illegal content and defamation. While it is easy to paint IWF as the one with the restrictive blacklist, the incident was in large part a clash of blacklists. Wikipedia had its own list of blocked IP addresses, targeted at vandals and abusers of its system.[30] It was also a clash of different community standards. Who has the more legitimate right to govern what goes up on the globally accessible Wikipedia encyclopedia: the community of Wikipedia editors, or the IWF?

In the three cases discussed in this chapter, there is one common thread: all of these are unique, historically unprecedented governance problems, and all of them point to major shifts in the role of states. Stories like these could be multiplied. The Internet creates many new challenges to traditional forms of national and international regulation of communication and information.

30. Unlike IWF, however, Wikipedia's blacklisting was confined to its own users and its own Web site.

3 Do Networks Govern?

The cases in chapter 2 provided concrete demonstrations of ways in which networks of actors leveraging the capabilities of the Internet can create issues of Internet governance. We now delve deeper into the concepts of network organization and networked governance as they have developed in the social sciences. This chapter looks at *network organization* as a theoretical construct and attempts to clarify what this kind of thinking really can (and cannot) do for the analysis of Internet governance.

The discussion is especially concerned with the claim that networking is itself a form of governance. We will find much that is useful in social science network theories, but also many problems and ambiguities. If the network is a form of governance, can it replace other organizational forms or does it merely complement them? To what extent does networked governance provide an alternative to traditional state-based governance? To what extent does it provide answers to some of the global governance problems posed by the Internet? Can we "choose" to govern the Internet via networked forms, or is it only an emergent form of organization that thrives in the vacuum left by the absence of other, more formal or hierarchical forms? A critical review of the literature provides the foundation for answering these questions.

The Meanings of "Network"

There are two easily distinguishable ways in which the concept "network" appears in the social sciences. First, it can refer to a formal, mathematical tool for representing and analyzing social relations. I will call this *network analysis*. Second, and more problematically, it is used as a theory (or sometimes only a metaphor) of social organization. I refer to this meaning of network as *organizational form*. Network analysis and network as organizational form can interact with each other in a powerful way, as we shall see. But this interdependence can also lead to confusion. Likewise, there are many different conceptions and definitions of what constitutes *network organization*, derived from economics, political science, anthropology, and sociology. These different notions are often conflated or defined in a way that blurs important distinctions between them. To make use of these concepts for the analysis of Internet governance one needs to cut one's way through a thicket of distinct but overlapping literatures developed over fifty years. We will discover that all of these network concepts can be useful, but also that they need to be carefully differentiated and kept distinct.

Network as Analytical Technique

Network analysis is probably the most well-defined and least-confusing piece of the puzzle, so we begin there. The study of network relationships has been formalized into a set of mathematical techniques grounded in graph theory.[1] This mode of analysis strips networks down to two simple elements, links and nodes (figure 3.1). Networks are defined as a set of interconnections among nodes. By virtue of its simplicity and abstraction, this analytical tool is very flexible and powerful. Anything can be a con-

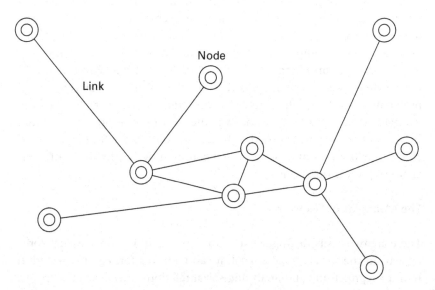

Figure 3.1
Links and nodes: The components of network analysis

1. Barabási 2002; Dorogovtsev and Mendes 2003; Monge and Contractor 2003.

ceptualized as a node: humans, airports, scholarly articles, cells. Any kind of relationship between nodes can be treated as a link. Physical proximity among humans, for example, can be the links and humans the nodes in a network describing exposure to a disease. Citations in journal articles can be considered links and scholarly articles nodes; chemical bonds can be the links in a network of cells; and so on. The utility of network analysis comes from its ability to provide a precise vocabulary for describing relationships, and its ability to quantify their structural properties. The mathematical techniques can be used to derive measures of the centrality of certain actors in a social network, for example, or to differentiate between the types and properties of networks.

Note that this method finds "networks" anywhere and everywhere. Handwritten correspondence among Jesuit missionaries in the fifteenth-century would be as suitable as twenty-first-century Web sites as a subject of the techniques. The network model is *imposed* on physical and social phenomena by the application of the link-node construct to them. The fact that this analytical method can be applied to anything does not mean that the world is more networked than it used to be, nor does it necessarily herald the existence of some new kind of society or organizational form. Our ability to apply and utilize network analysis, in other words, is completely independent of the type of society or organization studied.

Network analysis is thus a technique for representing and mathematically analyzing social relations and not a sociological or economic theory of organization. In applying the technique, it is important not to confuse the ability to *represent* social arrangements as networks with their status as organizational forms, institutions, or governance mechanisms.[2] Network analysis is not a substitute for social theory; it is merely a way to structure and analyze relational data that must be interpreted using theory from some other discipline, such as political science, economics, or sociology.[3] In this book, when network analysis techniques are used (in chapter 5), they are grounded in theories of policy networks that are drawn from political science/international relations.

2. Sociologists such as Wellman and Berkowitz (1988) go the farthest down the road of attempting to interpret behavior entirely in terms of structural constraints created by the relations between units, but even this requires an additional layer of theory regarding what kind of a relationship constitutes a link, the nature of individuals and family units, and so on.
3. Some experts in network analysis believe that distinctive types of social processes leave a "signature" that can be decoded using mathematical network analysis techniques (Monge and Contractor 2003).

Network as Organizational Form

The discussion of network organization is more complicated. Its disciplinary roots are varied and multifarious, and it is beyond the scope of this chapter to do a comprehensive review. I will concentrate on concepts of network organization as they have evolved out of the literature on economic organization and political science.

Production Networks In economics and economic sociology, *network* has come to mean a mode of governance that differs from managerial hierarchies or markets.[4] This concept emerged within the framework of transactions-cost economics and was originally intended to explain the organization of economic production.[5] Business firms, also called hierarchies, were defined as formal organizations with a managerially imposed division of labor. Markets were defined as transactions with external firms or individuals governed by the price system. The transactions-cost theory of economic organization attempted to explain which aspects of economic production were conducted internally by firms (hierarchies) and which were handled externally, by means of the market transactions among firms. Note the inherent interdependence of markets and hierarchies as organizational forms; the mode of governance selected responds to the same stimulus (transaction costs) and an efficient economy finds an optimal mix of the two modes.

In the 1980s, theorists began to observe looser affiliations among multiple firms—outsourcing, franchising, research alliances, and other semi-autonomous relations—and to discuss how this phenomenon fit into the market-hierarchy dichotomy. The initial tendency was to describe them as hybrid organizational forms located somewhere "between markets and hierarchies."[6] But in 1990 sociologist Walter Powell published a famous paper advocating a clean break with transactions-cost theory. Powell contended that *networks* constituted a distinctive "organizational form" or "type of governance" that was "neither market nor hierarchy." A network was said to be based on *the relationship* rather than *the transaction*; it was composed of longer-term bonds of reciprocity and trust among economic actors that were too stable to be classified as market transactions and too loose to be classified as formal hierarchies.

4. Powell 1990; Podolny and Page 1998.
5. Coase 1937 and 1960; Williamson 1975 and 1985.
6. For example, Thorelli 1986.

Many of the advantages attributed to this form of organization were related to its efficiency in sharing and processing information and knowledge. Networks were characterized as relying on lateral as opposed to hierarchical channels of communication, which made it possible to more efficiently exploit complementary skills and knowledge dispersed among multiple actors. As learning and innovation vehicles, network organizations compared favorably to "passing information up and down a corporate hierarchy or purchasing information in the marketplace" because they facilitated the development of "new interpretations" and "novel linkages,"[7] and took advantage of the unique economics of information, in that sharing information does not deplete it.

Peer Production A more contemporary, Internet-related argument about networks as a form of organization for production is put forward by scholars such as Paul Adler and Yochai Benkler, and by practitioners and futurists like Erik Raymond, Howard Rheingold, and Clay Shirkey.[8] Their point of departure is the presence of ubiquitous, powerful networked information technology. The availability of this infrastructure dramatically reduces the cost and magnifies the scope of establishing relationships based on the reciprocal benefits of association. According to Benkler, the networked information economy "improves the practical capacities of individuals . . . to do more in loose commonality with others, without being constrained to organize their relationship through a price system or in traditional hierarchical models of social and economic organization." Using free software and Wikipedia as his chief exemplars, he claims that networked relations are nothing less than a new "mode of production" he calls "commons-based peer production."[9]

Peer-to-peer (p2p) file sharing exemplifies a technologically-based network organization. Individuals join a p2p network by downloading and

7. Powell 1990, 325. Adler (2001) makes a similar argument on a macro scale.

8. Adler 2001; Benkler 2006. The original inspiration for the peer production concept was the analysis of collaboration in free/open source software developer communities by Erik Raymond (2001). Related ideas are given popular treatment by writers such as Clay Shirkey (2008) and Howard Rheingold (2002). See also Watson et al. 2005.

9. "The networked environment makes possible a new modality of organizing production: radically decentralized, collaborative, and nonproprietary; based on sharing resources and outputs among widely distributed, loosely connected individuals who cooperate with each other without relying on either market signals or managerial commands" (Benkler 2006, 60).

installing software (e.g., BitTorrent, Morpheus, Limewire, Nodezilla) on their computers. Once connected to the Internet, the software automatically puts them into resource-sharing relationships with (potentially) millions of others. Rather than relying on a central file server, a p2p network uses a series of direct, ad hoc connections between participants in a network and the cumulative bandwidth of all the network participants. The technical advantage of a p2p network is that all users contribute resources, including bandwidth, storage space, and computing power. As additional users arrive and demand on the system increases, the total capacity of the system also increases. In other words there are strong positive network externalities associated with the performance of the system.[10]

With its emphasis on the absence of market and hierarchy and the reciprocal benefits of association, Benkler's concept of peer production sounds very similar to Powell's network organization.[11] But there is an important difference. While both organizational types are based on reciprocal benefits obtained without a market or a hierarchy, the linkages among participants in a peer production network are usually not based on what Powell called *the relationship*; in other words, interpersonal familiarity and trust. The relationship can be relatively anonymous and automated. In a p2p network or communities like Wikipedia one does not know very much, if anything, about with whom one is collaborating or sharing information; what matters are the benefits of sharing, the satisfaction one derives from making a contribution, and a basic level of trust in the workings of the system. The essential feature of the relationship is simply the decision to join the network itself. One can think of peer-to-peer networks as a massively scaled-up, technologically driven version of the network organizational form—Powell on steroids. And because they are Internet-based, such networks can easily be transnational; any attempt to make them conform to jurisdictional or organizational boundaries requires extra work and cost.

10. Client-server architectures, in contrast, rely on a fixed set of servers to meet whatever level of demand exists. In the client-server mode adding more users can often mean slower data transfer for all users.
11. Oddly, Benkler does not cite Powell (1990) in *The Wealth of Networks*. Also, other scholars have used the term *community* rather than *network organization* to describe peer production networks. See, for example, Adler 2001 and Watson et al. 2005. Watson et al. consider peer production communities to be a fourth organizational form in addition to networks—underscoring the terminological and theoretical confusion that prevails in this area.

Peer-to-peer networks occupy an extreme space in any typology of network organizations. They might be considered a pure form or ideal type that reflects the full capabilities of the Internet. Other kinds of loose, smaller-scale network organizations are pervasive on the Internet. They can be found among the operators of the Internet itself and the entities involved in its governance. The interconnections among Internet service providers, for example, are based on a kind of loose cooperation enabled by the routing protocol BGP. ISPs negotiate bilateral agreements to accept each others' traffic, while the BGP protocol provides a common method for all ISPs to announce to each other which service providers can be reached through which routes. ISPs of equivalent size and traffic volumes "peer" with each other; meaning they accept each other's traffic without charging for it.

Perhaps the most common form of network organization on the Internet is the email discussion list, around which communities of discourse form. Email lists are central features of the contemporary political environment. They are used by standards organizations, governance agencies such as ICANN and the Regional Internet IP address Registries (RIRs), advocacy groups, and expert communities interested in the same issues. The relationships among actors are usually based entirely on free association; joining a list is voluntary and network members neither pay, nor get paid, to participate. Such lists or Web sites can generate an enormous amount of value.

Email lists are very lightweight organizations, with little overhead and no ability to impose a division of labor on the participants. It is useful and important to emphasize, as Benkler does, that the setup costs of such an organization are such a tiny increment on top of the preexisting infrastructure that group members can usually dispense with problems of payment or fundraising. The ease with which these lists can be created or eliminated, and the flexibility with which people can join them, abandon them, or set up alternative lists often means that there may be no need for a formal legal or hierarchical relationship between the group and the list administrator. As a consequence of this ability to vote with their virtual "feet," normative and interpersonal interactions among the participants, rather than formally specified rules, do most of the real governance work. Nevertheless, they are still bounded organizations. Their existence depends on an individual or group making (or accepting) binding, mutually exclusive decisions about who will administer the email list and where the infrastructure resides. An administrator has the power to add or remove people from the list; hence, there is a point of control and management. The network organization is a mode of governance, in which hierarchy is minimized but not entirely absent.

Political Networks Moving from production to politics, the narrative gets more complicated. The literature on networks in political science is quite old and developed. Prior to Powell, it examined actor networks in a manner fundamentally different from that of the economic sociologists. Research on policy networks emerged in the 1950s around the study of interest-group interaction with government.[12] Originally, policy networks were conceived as relatively small and stable sets of corporate actors drawn into regularized interaction around a set of laws and regulations in a specific sector.[13] So strong and institutionalized were the links among these actors that they were sometimes referred to as "subgovernments" or "iron triangles."[14]

Policy networks were not described by political scientists as a consciously chosen organizational arrangement, but as an unconsciously formed clustering pattern. These clusters were formed via an ongoing process of interpersonal or interorganizational contacts that produced regularized associations within a community. Characterizing these clusters as a network fostered a relational perspective that exposed the links among formal state institutions and the organized groups that influenced them. It also shed light on the participation (and exclusion) of specific actors.[15] The incentive to gain and exchange influence over the decisions and resource allocations made by an authoritative institution was the primary cause of the clustering pattern. The study of policy networks lent itself to

12. Worthwhile reviews of the evolution of this literature are in Jordan 1990, Rhodes 1990, and Boerzel 1998.
13. Policy networks as Scharpf (1997) describes them are operating in "the shadow of hierarchy" and the presumptive context of his discussion is national politics. Such networks involve a process of arriving at a negotiated bargain or decision acceptable to the diverse interests involved, but only within an institutional framework of laws and regulatory agencies established by national governments.
14. Bernstein 1955. See also Jordan 1990 and Tichenor and Harris 2005 for more contemporary discussions of the subgovernment concept.
15. As Peter John (2001) put it: "Writers on policy networks stress the blurred boundary between the state and society, and it is networks that fuse the public and private. By studying these partially institutionalized relationships, researchers may observe topics like the power of economic elites in policy and the socialization of professional groups."

the application of the network analysis techniques previously described. Researchers could map out the concrete configuration of links among interest groups, policy advocates, and government agencies to assess or quantify actors' centrality or isolation.[16]

The policy network concept was later broadened to include looser kinds of relationships, known as *issue networks*.[17] In his seminal work introducing this term, Hugh Heclo defined issue networks as "a shared-knowledge group having to do with some aspect (or, as defined by the network, some problem) of public policy. [They are likely to have] a common base of information or understanding of how one knows about policy and identifies its problems."[18] Issue networks were less tied to specific legal and regulatory regimes than policy networks were, but involved an open system of sometimes contentious, sometimes cooperative actors seeking to define and influence policy around specific public policy domains.

A recent and important application and extension of the issue network concept was Keck and Sikkink's research on transnational advocacy networks (TANs), a concept central to the subject matter of this book. TANs were defined as transborder "networks of activists, distinguishable largely by the centrality of principled ideas or values in motivating their formation."[19] From an international relations perspective, TANs are linked to the concept of "global civil society," which views international politics as driven not entirely by the security needs and self-interest of sovereign states, but also by internationally accepted norms and conceptions of the public good promoted by "sovereignty-free" actors. Networks of civil society advocacy groups create a space for the negotiation and development of these norms and a vehicle for pressuring states and businesses to conform to them.

Just as the Internet magnifies the opportunities for forming network organizations, so it also enhances the ability to form larger-scale, transnational policy networks as well. The literature on TANs and global civil society routinely calls attention to the ability of the Internet to catalyze policy communities on a larger, transnational scale.[20]

16. In the 1980s, quantitative network analysis techniques were applied to policy domains such as telecommunications, labor, and agriculture (e.g., Heinz et al. 1990; Knoke 1990; Knoke and Boli 1997; Knoke et al. 1997; Schneider and Werle 1991; Marin and Mayntz 1991).
17. Marres 2006, 8.
18. Heclo 1978, 103–104.
19. Keck and Sikkink 1998, 1.
20. Hajnal 2002.

The Melding of Network Organization and Policy Networks   Until the
1990s, theories of economic organization based on transaction costs and
the literature on policy networks were separate and distinct. Powell's
concept of a new organizational form, however, jumped the gap between
production and politics. As his seminal conception of the network organization made its way into political science, a growing number of scholars
in that field began to conceive of policy networks as network organizations.[21] The linkages among actors in policy networks were reconceived as
bonds of reciprocity and trust. In formulating the concept of the transnational advocacy network, Keck and Sikkink cited Powell and classified TANs
as a "network form of organization."[22]

The clearest conception came from German political scientist Fritz
Scharpf, who characterized networks "as a semi-permanent structure
within which individual interactions are embedded"; they involve the
"memory of past encounters" and the "expectation of future dealings."[23]
To Scharpf, networks were "voluntary negotiation systems in which partners are free to choose between negotiations and unilateral action."[24] The
argument for "network governance" was especially applicable to transnational governance because of the weakness of simple command hierarchies
or clear principal-agent relations among the actors at that level.[25]

American scholars inaugurated a growing literature on international
links among lower-level government agencies—so-called *transgovernmental
networks* (TGNs)—that share information and ideas and coordinate policies
across borders without formally negotiated treaties.[26] European writers
claimed that "governance networks play a central role as a medium for vertical and horizontal coordination between multiple units of governance."[27]
European scholars tracked TGNs to show how networking among ministries
contributed to the integration of nation-states into the European Union.[28]

The notion of networked governance moved easily from the positive to
the normative. Wolfgang Reinicke and his colleagues promoted "global
public policy networks" (GPPNs) as a response to contemporary transna-

21. Boerzel 1998; Schneider and Werle 1991.
22. Keck and Sikkink 1998, 8.
23. Scharpf 1997, 137.
24. Ibid., 143. See also Scharpf 1993.
25. Schneider and Werle 1991; Dean, Anderson, and Lovink 2006.
26. Picciotto 1997; Slaughter 2004; Raustiala 2002.
27. Sørenson and Torfing 2007, 19; Kooiman 2003, 139.
28. Thurner and Binder (2008, 97) use network analysis to find an "institutionalization of transborder interactions among national bureaucracies."

tional governance problems.[29] GPPNs were understood to be arranged organizations that bring stakeholders from government, business, and civil society together in order to capitalize on the superior ability of the network form to "manage knowledge" and leverage dispersed forms of expertise. Here the concept of networked governance overlaps directly with the concept of "multistakeholder" governance. There was also, during this period, a tendency to idealize networks as intrinsically egalitarian and democratic.

While this melding of network organization and policy networks was taking place, the use of network analysis techniques in political science grew rapidly.[30] While many valuable contributions were and are being made, the application of network analysis to political phenomena often led to indiscriminate characterizations of organizations and institutions as "networks." Many applications of the technique were completely orthogonal to the study of organizational form. Network diagrams mapped membership in traditional hierarchical organizations, for example.[31] Or the technique was used to map relationships that were not based on trust and reciprocity, with reciprocity a variable of the network rather than a constitutive element. In effect, organizations were classified as networks simply because network analysis was applied to them. With the addition of technological networks and the Internet to the mix, the conflation of network analysis, network organizations, and several distinct conceptions of organizational forms can become very confusing indeed.

Network Organizations and Associative Clusters

The conclusion I draw from the preceding review of theory and literature is that network as a mode of organization and governance has two different meanings in social science, and that it is critical to keep them distinct.

Network can mean a loose but bounded and consciously constructed organization based mainly on leveraging the benefits of reciprocity, like an alliance of industrial researchers, an email discussion list on the Internet, or a free software development group. I will call this the *network organization*. *Network* can also be a name for an unbounded and decentered cluster of actors around repeated patterns of exchange or contact; I will call this an *associative cluster*.

29. Reinicke 1997 and 1999–2000; Benner, Reinicke, and Witte 2000.
30. See Kahler 2009 for a recent extension of this literature.
31. Hafner-Burton, Kahler, and Montgomery 2009.

There are two clear dividing lines between network organizations and associative clusters. Network organizations have a well-defined point of access and must explicitly decide on criteria for including and excluding participants. Associative clusters lack both features. Crucial to this analytical framework is the distinction between *consciously arranged* groupings and unconscious, de facto clustering patterns. Network organizations are bounded and consciously arranged; the actors who participate in them *design* the relationships among a bounded set of individuals or organizations to pursue a common objective. As such, network organizations are in fact *organizations*—they retain minimal elements of hierarchy, such as shared infrastructure, and sometimes budgets and employees, to support the operations of the network. The network form of organization is a *design choice*, a method of association that actors can use or refrain from using based on a conscious assessment of their objectives and constraints.

Associative clusters, on the other hand, denote de facto, relatively stable relational patterns among an unbounded set of actors. No one decides to create these larger communities; they just form. No single point of administration exists. No explicit policy determines who is and is not part of them. Far from being limited to bonds of trust and reciprocity, participants in these clusters may have different and even conflicting objectives but may nevertheless engage in sustained interaction, as in a policy network. Relationships of trust and reciprocity among actors are not transitive; thus associative clusters cannot be restricted to vetted members that all the others trust or approve of, as there is no organizational gateway. The relational patterns are consequences of their actions but are not intentional, and they are not formally bounded. There is no explicit, agreed-upon structure, like a contract or a constitution, which applies to all of its participants.

While associative clusters provide fertile ground for advocacy and mobilization, they do not have agency. If this kind of network is a *form of governance*, governance is a byproduct of many unilateral and bilateral decisions by its members to exchange or negotiate with other members. This is an invisible-hand-like process; the outcome is emergent and does not reflect the will of any of its individual members, and yet the aggregate results manage to reflect, in some sense, collective preferences, and to coordinate behavior in certain ways. Moreover, participants in such a cluster can gain by deliberating and learning from other participants and by formulating rules that order the sector in mutually beneficial ways. Policy networks thus help to identify the bargains and solutions around which institutional arrangements can equilibrate. There are also strict limits on what this kind of network governance can accomplish. As Scharpf points out, associative clusters cannot redistribute wealth.[32]

Table 3.1 attempts to categorize the literature into the two conceptions in a way that reveals critical similarities and differences.

To understand Internet governance, we need both concepts of networks as a form of organization, but we must not confuse them. If the line between network organizations and associative clusters is blurred, critical features of both phenomena are lost. Conflating a network organization with an associative cluster tends to obscure the design choices participants in network organizations make when constructing their relationships. Network organizations may be looser and less hierarchical than traditional organizations, but they do have structures and processes, which must be jointly negotiated and agreed by the parties involved. These design choices can have important political and economic implications.

If one examines real-world instances of global public policy networks, such as the Consultative Group on International Agricultural Research, the World Commission on Dams, or the Internet Governance Forum (IGF), one does not see completely unstructured, open networks but formally organized alliances or corporatist institutions. These entities enjoy funding from intergovernmental organizations and have charters describing their governance arrangements and decision-making procedures. The composition of their councils or commissions is shaped by ideas about appropriate representation levels for each stakeholder group. It is not enough to characterize these entities as "networks"—we must also be aware of the specific decisions about their authority, their organizational structure, or their procedures.

By the same token, if we equate associative clusters with bounded network organizations based on reciprocity and trust, we obscure the combination of competition, contention, negotiation and cooperation that characterize policy networks. It also draws attention away from the role that authoritative governance institutions play in serving as the magnet or convergence point for the clustering of actors.

Keck and Sikkink's concept of transnational advocacy networks (TANs) provides an example of how melding the two concepts of network organization can blunt analysis. They characterize TANs as Powell-type network organizations, implying that they are bounded, consciously arranged alliances based on relations of trust and reciprocity among familiar actors. But their own list of the typical constituents of a TAN corresponds more to an

32. Scharpf 1997, 146.

Table 3.1
Taxonomy of networks in social science

	Associative clusters (de facto networks)			Network organizations (arranged networks)	
	Policy networks	Issue networks	TANs	Powell	Benkler
Nodes	Corporate actors	Organizations or individuals	Organizations and individuals	Corporate actors or individuals	Individuals
Links	Interorganizational communication; exchange of "influence resources"	Discourse; dense information exchanges	Dense information exchanges	Exchange relations of any sort	Collaboration
Basis for link formation	Resource dependencies in a specific policy domain	Shared interest and expertise in defining and shaping a policy issue	Shared political principles and values	Trust and reciprocity	Resource and information sharing
Type of relations	Contentious cooperation	Contentious cooperation	Bonds of mutual trust, reciprocity	Bonds of mutual trust, reciprocity	Reciprocity, resource sharing
Bounded by . . .	Mutual recognition based on functional relevance and structural embeddedness	Subject matter discussed; mutual recognition	Unclear	Choice of organizers	Choice of organizers, or open
Stability	High	Low	??	High	Low

unbounded associative cluster than to a network organization. It includes "international NGOs, research and advocacy organizations at the national level, local social movements, foundations, the media, churches, trade unions, consumer organizations, intellectuals, parts of regional and international intergovernmental organizations, and parts of the executive or legislative branches of government," all linked by "dense information exchanges." Echoing Heclo, they write that the "network concept stresses fluid and open relationships among committed and knowledgeable actors working in specialized issue areas."[33] Indeed, earlier work by Sikkink labeled them "principled issue networks."[34]

TANs are really subsets of transnational policy networks. While it is true that advocacy groups cooperate and coalesce with organizations and individuals who share their principles and values, they also must network and contend with other groups in the broader policy network. Advocacy organizations engage in "dense exchanges of information" with the entire policy network, not just with each other. The informational networking embraces the media, private sector interests, and officials within governmental and intergovernmental agencies, not just actors who share the advocates' principles and values. Isolating TANs from transnational policy networks makes our understanding of their composition, organization, strategy, tactics, and influence less robust. TANs may provide the seedbed for more defined network organizations, such as coalitions or campaigns; in those cases it would be important to examine the specific organizational arrangements the network members establish.

Authority and Institutionalization in Networks

Based on the preceding discussion, it now is easier to see how the Internet triggers an explosion of new kinds of network organization and peer production processes; and also how the Internet enables a vast expansion of transnational issue networks or policy networks. How might this result in innovation and change in the governance of communication and information?

At this juncture it becomes useful to link discussions of networks more directly to theories of institutions and institutionalization.[35] When considering Internet governance we need to pay attention to the movement from

33. Keck and Sikkink 1998, 6.
34. Sikkink 1993.
35. Ostrom 2005; Knight 1992, Scharpf 1997; Libecap 1989; North 1990.

informal, de facto association to formal organization; from loose consensual or cooperative action to the adoption of binding, agreed procedures. It is precisely this movement from the partially institutionalized to the formally structured that is the most critical and revealing part of the global politics of Internet governance.

Institutionalization implies that the parties involved in regular interactions understand and accept certain norms, conventions, and explicitly formulated rules governing their interaction, and that these rules can be enforced. This results in what game theorists call equilibrium outcomes, or stable patterns of interaction that reproduce and reinforce the rules and the organizational roles as the precondition for action.[36] Mutual agreement on applicable rules and roles can generate collective benefits. Institutional theory suggests, however, that it is conflict or negotiation over the *distribution* of these benefits that moves loose associations of actors along the spectrum ranging from very informal, associative networks to more formal organization, and from there to the most hierarchical and binding forms of institutionalization.

The future shape of Internet governance will be worked out via negotiation of governance problems attendant upon the rise of transnational, networked forms of organization. As a heuristic we can identify four ways in which the network organizations and associative clusters formed around the Internet might lead to institutional change:

1. By formalizing and institutionalizing the network relations themselves
2. By states' attempts to impose hierarchical regulation upon networked forms
3. By states' utilization and adoption of networked forms
4. By changing the polity; namely, by realigning and expanding the associative clusters around governance institutions

Institutionalizing Network Relations

The new network forms of organization can be expected to generate their own distinctive kinds of internal contention and conflict. Some of these

36. Knight's (1992, 2) definition is as good as any: "Institutions are sets of rules that structure social interactions in particular ways. These rules (1) provide information about how people are expected to act in particular situations, (2) can be recognized by those who are members of the relevant group as the rules to which others conform in these situations, and (3) structure the strategic choices of actors in such a way as to produce equilibrium outcomes."

problems can be solved through networked governance; in other words, as a byproduct of the mutual adjustment decisions made by individual participants in the network. In other cases, they may lead to the creation of more formal, collectively binding rules and procedures within a network organization. Contention within a network can take place around a number of issues: how its boundaries are defined (i.e., who to admit or exclude); how the economic benefits it generates are distributed; over policies governing access to or control over bottleneck facilities on which the network's participants depend; over the regulation of conduct on the network. The stakes of these conflicts increase as network organizations grow. As networks grow they realize positive externalities, which makes it more costly and difficult for their members to abandon them and start a new one.

Wikipedia, so often used as an exemplar of voluntaristic peer production, provides a good example here. A nonprofit foundation administers and sustains this online encyclopedia's peer production process. Because of Wikipedia's success, its staff has grown to meet the need for an increasingly active governance role as controversies arise about changes in the encyclopedia's content or accuracy. Editors have been forced to devise an increasingly well-articulated set of procedures for locking down content and preventing its modification in response to disputes over inaccurate content or attempts to manipulate Wikipedia entries.[37] Chapter 2 noted how Wikipedia instituted procedures to "lock out" contributors who repeatedly vandalize entries. Similar pressures were visible in the Indymedia network in debates over whether to regulate or restrict open news wires.

It is also possible that the growth of Internet-based production networks can create chokepoints where policy or technical administrative authority or both are concentrated.[38] As sensitive points of interdependency, these bottlenecks can become the site of conflict over the distribution of power or benefits, and can lead to greater institutionalization. The domain name system root is the most obvious example. In some sense the root servers are just a loose network of computers distributing a zone file that the world voluntarily recognizes as authoritative. The loose and informal governance associated with the Internet's technical developers has been displaced by an increasingly institutionalized, politicized, and formalized international

37. See Solove (2007, 142) on the Siegenthaler case in Wikipedia: a Wikipedia article unfairly accused this former Kennedy aide of being involved in the assassination of the Kennedys.
38. Cowhey and Mueller 2009.

regime. The formalized regime has in turn attracted the attention of states. Chapter 11 will explain how the addressing-routing interface could become another such chokepoint in the future.

These organic, bottom-up institutionalization processes are strongly affected by the unique economics of networks. Networks require a critical mass of participants to generate benefits; they tend to exhibit winner-take-all forms of competition as actors converge on the same network to realize the benefits of a larger network. Once this convergence has taken place, inertia or lock-in can set in, giving established networks considerable power.

External Regulation of Networks

Internet-enabled networks may come into conflict with established institutions or organizations. While new networks of actors will grow and develop their own norms and procedures, their activities may clash with the interests of actors embedded in institutional arrangements that predate the networked economy. This can trigger attempts to make networks and networking processes objects of hierarchical regulation. The most salient example of this is the ongoing battle over peer-to-peer file sharing, which pits Internet users and their service providers against copyright holders. This problem is discussed in more detail in chapter 7. For now, it is enough to identify the inherent tension between the Internet-enabled capacity to pool, share, and transmit digital resources globally, and the ability of digital property owners to enforce boundaries, rooted in national law and intergovernmental treaties, that protect their exclusivity. Another example would be the attempt by traditional national security and law enforcement agencies to regulate and monitor networks of Internet-enabled actors to counter distributed denial of service (DDoS) attacks and terrorism. The network becomes an object of external regulation through, for example, data retention initiatives or laws and regulations that require network operators to configure and design their systems in ways that facilitate surveillance by the state.

States Can Network, Too

Traditional hierarchical organizations, including national governments, can create their own network organizations and avail themselves of the capabilities of networking to defend and advance their own interests. Networking among states, known in the literature as transgovernmental networks and introduced earlier in this chapter, constitutes a kind of transformation from within.

Empirical research suggests that states select TGNs over traditional intergovernmental agreements depending on the type of problem they are trying to solve.[39] TGNs have low startup costs, facilitate quick and efficient communication, are adaptable because of the relative ease with which new members (nodes) can be added, and are bonded in ways that are easily reversible. When a government's policy preferences differ substantially from other domestic groups (such as legislatures, interest groups, and the general public), the more likely the government is to favor networks. These very advantages, however, make networks inappropriate and ineffective for certain purposes. The consensual nature of networks means that reaching any collectively binding agreement can be slow and difficult. The ease of entry and exit also means a low level of commitment from network members. Network organizations are thus vulnerable to free riding as well as patchy monitoring and enforcement of how common goals are implemented. Also, the need for reciprocal trust among members can impose severe restrictions on the scope of the organization, which can undermine its legitimacy.

States, in other words, will use network organization strategically to advance their interests. However, the political scientists working in this area tend to look at network organizations as nothing more than a strategic choice by states with little structural significance. It is likely, however, that the utilization of that organizational form might alter the nature of the state itself over the long term: the substantial literature on e-government and networking among government departments suggests that it will.[40] Governments are beginning to adopt user-generated content mechanisms for their internal operations, and there is even a push for "open source intelligence." This question will resurface when we examine the role of states in ICANN and the IGF in later chapters.

The Coral Reef Effect

Along with the expanded capacity for network organizations comes an equally enhanced capacity for creating broader and more well-informed associative clusters, especially transnational policy networks. Often neglected in analysis of institutions is that stable patterns of interaction presume the existence of a more or less fixed community or polity. Usually this is presumed to be the national polity. But what happens when the boundaries of the polity shift and expand beyond the nation?

39. Eilstrup-Sangiovanni 2009.
40. Goldsmith and Eggers 2004.

Authoritative governance institutions and their peculiar structural biases and path-dependent equilibria are the basis for bringing political actors into interaction and exchange.[41] The symbiotic relationship between transnational politics and international institutions has been noted by Sidney Tarrow and Thomas Risse.[42] They compare international institutions to a coral reef; they provide a structure that attracts, in a cumulative or accretive fashion, actors who have an interest in their mission and can benefit from their actions. Such institutions provide the political opportunities, mobilizing structures, and resources that nourish both transnational policy networks and advocacy activities within them. Globalized information and communication technology would enhance the ability of political actors to cluster into new, transnational policy networks concerned with Internet governance. It follows from this that various international organizations, ranging from ICANN to the World Intellectual Property Organization (WIPO) to the IGF, would provide a reef for the sustenance of such a policy network—but only if they can generate the positive network externalities required to reach critical mass and generate self-sustaining growth.

In the long run, this clustering is at least as significant an indicator of institutional change as the use of network forms of organization by governments and private actors. Such a process reconfigures the relevant polity: it brings new stakeholders into policy discourse, and creates policy networks that span established national and institutional boundaries. In so doing, it can alter the demand structure for policies, and so have lasting impact on the global political economy of communication and information.

Summary and Overview

Can networks govern, or not? By now it should be evident that the network concept is useful in the analysis of international institutional change, but only if we avoid the temptation to collapse the idea of network into an all-embracing, undifferentiated theory of everything. The preceding discussion aims to establish clear distinctions between *the network* as an analytical

41. Empirical research that applies network analysis techniques to policy networks invariably identifies highly institutionalized structures (e.g., the European Commission or a Post, Telecommunication and Telegraph Ministry) as the central node in specific policy networks. Risse-Kappen 1995; Schneider and Werle 1991.
42. Tarrow 2001; Risse 2001.

technique and *the network* as a theory of organization. Once confined to organizational forms, we must also distinguish between the clustering of political actors in unbounded networks of influence around governance institutions, and networks as a bounded, consciously constructed type of organization. Networked relations may become institutionalized, or clash with preexisting institutions, to produce institutional change. Those distinctions are intended to provide the conceptual foundations for analyzing the pressures for international institutional change created by the demand for governance of the global Internet.

II Transnational Institutions

4 World Summit on the Information Society: The State-centric View

The rise of an Internet centered in the United States was a disruptive event in the system of international relations formed around communication and information policy. It is only natural that such a disturbance would provoke a reaction and adjustment. The United Nations' World Summit on the Information Society (WSIS) provided the institutional vehicle for the reaction. This chapter describes the politics of WSIS. It is portrayed as a clash between two models of global governance: one based on agreements among sovereign, territorial states; the other based on private contracting among transnational nonstate actors, but relying in some respects on the global hegemony of a single state. After analyzing how this conflict played out, the chapter assesses the impact of the WSIS process and explains why it can be considered an important turning point in the history of international communication.

The Liberal Internet

What made the Internet internationally disruptive? The story originates with profound changes in the political economy of telecommunications. Starting in the 1970s, the United States began to introduce competition into its telecommunication (or "telecom") industry. In the 1980s, the United States broke up the AT&T system, which it ruled a monopoly, and unbundled the public network into separate but interconnected elements to spur even more competition, innovation, and new entry. Other major developed economies followed suit, starting with Great Britain and Japan.[1]

---

1. The United Kingdom privatized British Telecom in 1981 (Brock 1994) and imitated the U.S. deregulation of value-added services with the issuance of the VANS General License in October 1982. See Smith 1985, 41–45.

Concerned with its trade deficit and international competitiveness, the United States pushed telecom liberalization to international markets.

One of the most important policies enabling liberalization generally, and the rise of the Internet specifically, was forged through the U.S. Federal Communications Commission's (FCC) *Computer Inquiries*.[2] Anticipating the convergence of computers and telecommunications, the FCC moved to separate "basic" telecommunication services from "enhanced" or "value-added" services that involved data processing and networked computers. The object of this separation was to create a free market in information services independent of the huge AT&T monopoly, which at the time dominated voice and other telecommunication markets. Basic telecommunications would continue to be regulated as a common carrier while value-added information services and data processing would be left unregulated and open.[3] This regulatory distinction diffused throughout the developed world in the 1980s, alongside the broader process of telecommunications liberalization.

The combination of a competitive telecommunication infrastructure with the separation and deregulation of value-added information services proved to be revolutionary in a way that was not anticipated by policy makers. *Together, those policies created the ideal platform for the unrestricted spread of the global Internet.* As a software-based protocol that moved packetized data among computers, the Internet was classified as an information service. Thus, market access was wide open and providers relatively unregulated. Thanks to trade negotiations, this classification was applied not only in the United States, but almost everywhere else in the developed economies.[4]

2. Regulatory and Policy Problems Presented by the Interdependence of Computer and Communication Services, *Notice of Inquiry*, 7 FCC2d 11, 8 Rad. Reg.2d (P & F) 1567 (1966); *Tentative Decision*, 28 FCC2d 291, 18 Rad. Reg.2d (P & F) 1713 (1970); *Final Decision*, 28 FCC2d 267, 21 Rad. Reg.2d (P & F) 1561 (1971).

3. The FCC defined as *telecommunications* a situation when the content of the message is transmitted over the network with no change in the content or form of the message. Data processing, on the other hand, was declared to involve "the use of the computer for operations which include, inter alia, the functions of storing, retrieving, sorting, merging and calculating data, according to programmed instructions." That distinction proved to be slippery, because as the network technology became more digitized the function of basic conveyance involved signaling and switching functions that relied on data processing.

4. One reason value-added information services escaped trade protectionism was that well into the mid-1990s they constituted a tiny portion (around 1 to 2 percent)

From 1993 to 1996, as the Internet was opened to the public and the Web browser made its use easy and popular, tens of thousands of commercial Internet service providers (ISPs) rushed into the market channel opened up by the deregulated information services regime. Not only could the ISPs enter markets relatively freely, but competition in telecom infrastructure was dramatically reducing the cost of the bandwidth and physical facilities needed to offer service. Competition was most advanced and thus prices lowest and services most developed in the United States, which meant that Internet connectivity came to be concentrated there. Interconnection of Internet service providers emerged without centralized regulation, through negotiated contractual agreements among private firms, and still managed to achieve universal global access. As contractual agreements replaced public regulation, governments lost an important form of control over communication services pricing, severely attenuating their power to redistribute wealth. And of course, because the Internet technologies were developed in the United States and because the core coordinating organizations were U.S. government contractors, a great deal of the expertise and administrative control was also centered in the United States. No wonder that, by 2000, complaints about a "U.S.-centric" Internet started to surface.

Origins of WSIS

UN summits, Hans Klein writes, are an institutional genre, that "involve thousands of policy makers working together over several years to develop consensual visions of principles and possible solutions to some of humankind's most challenging problems."[5] Global UN summits have been held on the environment, women, and health, among other issues. The high-visibility meetings are intended to generate the political will to motivate governments to negotiate politically binding declarations and commitments. As outgrowths of the United Nations system, world summits are exercises in global governance that reflect the peculiar strengths and weaknesses of institutional mechanisms that require consensual agreement

---

of the overall telecommunication services market. Thus, trade negotiators and regulators seeking to protect their companies from foreign and domestic competition concentrated on sheltering basic voice telephone services, where most of the money was at the time, and offered open market access in value-added information services as a seemingly cheap concession to the free trade demands of other countries.
5. Klein 2004, 3.

among sovereign states, each with widely divergent political and economic interests, cultures, and levels of development.

The push for a global summit on issues pertaining to the information society started modestly in 1998, with the adoption of a resolution on the last day of the International Telecommunication Union (ITU) Plenipotentiary Conference in Minneapolis. The resolution called for a "world summit on the information society" but was passed with no time for discussion of its nature or scope. The proposal was "enthusiastically received by a number of other UN agencies, notably UNESCO," where it was transmuted into a plan "probably much grander and more elaborate than participants in Minneapolis had envisaged."[6] In 2001, the UN General Assembly approved the proposal and designated the ITU as the lead agency for the new summit.[7] Feeding on concerns about a "global digital divide," the ITU envisioned a summit that would highlight the importance of the ITU and marshal corporate and state support for the finance and construction of telecommunication and information infrastructure in undeveloped and developing countries. The self-declared purpose of WSIS was "to formulate a common vision and understanding of the global information society," and to "harness the potential of knowledge and technology to promote the development goals of the Millennium Declaration."[8] WSIS was animated by the old model of a hierarchical, redistributionist government.

The actual summit process started in 2002, and concluded in November 2005. Competition over who would host the first summit led to its division into two phases so that both contending parties, the Swiss and the Tunisians, could play the host role. The first, "Geneva" phase of WSIS began in mid-2002 with a series of regional conferences and global Preparatory Committee (Prepcom) meetings. Prepcoms are where most of the real negotiating and drafting work took place to pave the way for agreement at the actual WSIS. The first phase culminated in a summit meeting in Geneva, Switzerland, December 10–13, 2003. More than 11,000 people attended it, including about 50 heads of state or vice presidents, and more than 100 ministers and vice ministers from 175 countries. The second, Tunis phase had its series of Prepcoms and regional meetings in 2004 and 2005. In mid-November 2005, more than 19,000 people

6. Souter 2007, 38.
7. WSIS has been called a "UN-style summit" rather than a UN summit per se, because it was organized by the ITU with support from other UN agencies rather than by the central United Nations staff itself. Souter 2007, 73.
8. UN General Assembly Resolution 56/183 (December 21, 2001).

attended the Tunis Summit and surrounding events, including about 50 heads of state or vice presidents and nearly 200 ministers from 174 governments.

As WSIS unfolded, its agenda morphed in two important ways. During the Geneva phase public interest advocacy groups—transnational in scope and emboldened by the burgeoning movements around globalization at the turn of the millennium—mobilized around it. The efforts of these groups attracted a growing number of nonstate actors into the process. These activists tried to broaden the scope of the discussions beyond the construction of telecommunications infrastructure. They promoted a broad range of equity and human rights claims related to communication-information policy. This will be discussed in greater detail in chapter 5.

The WSIS process took another unexpected turn when conflicts among states over Internet governance, and in particular the Internet Corporation for Assigned Names and Numbers (ICANN), came to dominate the summit agenda.[9] Several developing country governments, egged on by the ITU, challenged both the unilateral power held by the U.S. government over ICANN and the prevalence of nongovernmental policy-making mechanisms for the Internet. By the time of the Tunis summit, the World Summit on the Information Society had been transformed into the World Summit on Internet Governance.

WSIS was not a powerful process in most respects. The output of the Geneva phase was the Declaration of Principles and the Plan of Action;[10] the Tunis phase produced the Tunis Agenda for the Information Society and the Tunis Commitment.[11] The substance of those documents will be discussed later, but for the most part they are just words. The summit did not succeed in reallocating major sums of money. It did not pass binding treaties or conventions backed up by strong new organizations capable of enforcing them in a way that could reshape global communications. WSIS did not produce any binding pacts among Internet service providers that would fundamentally alter their ways of interacting. It did not eliminate

9. "When WSIS was first proposed, no-one expected Internet governance to be one of its priorities. In fact, there was almost no discussion of Internet governance in the first phase preparatory process until the Western Asia (Middle East) regional meeting—the last to be held—in February 2003." Souter 2007, 57.

10. Declaration of Principles: Building the Information Society: A Global Challenge in the New Millennium. UN Document: WSIS-03/GENEVA/DOC/4-E, December 13, 2003.

11. Tunis Agenda for the Information Society. UN Document: WSIS-05/TUNIS/DOC/6(Rev.1)-E, November 18, 2005.

ICANN or bring it under the control of the UN system. Nevertheless, one can claim that for the foreseeable future it will be impossible to talk meaningfully about the global governance of the Internet without referring to what happened during the WSIS.

Counter-revolution

WSIS inaugurated an explicit debate over the role of the nation-state in Internet governance. Governments, both democratic and undemocratic, felt the need to assert their belief that they should have authority over Internet-related public policy issues.[12] Although the "U.S.-centric" nature of the Internet and its liberation from the state provided the broader context, it was ICANN in particular that became the focal point of these concerns. The WSIS process gave certain developing countries and Europe an opportunity to openly challenge the legitimacy of the institutional innovation that was ICANN.

Why ICANN? During WSIS (and well beyond), it was common to hear its defenders (and others) complain that all the sound and fury related to ICANN was misdirected. Given the long list of Internet-related public policy issues, it may seem as if ICANN has a small and obscure role in the total picture. Why quibble about who edits the root zone file of the domain name system (DNS) when there are millions in Africa, Latin America and India with no access to the Internet at all? According to one famous commentator, Lawrence Lessig, ICANN is "just trying to serve technical functions in the narrowest possible way."[13]

An international development expert made a similar mistake in his assessment of WSIS: "Fifty years from now, it may well seem odd to those reflecting on it that a World Summit on the Information Society spent so much time discussing the domain name and root server systems and so little on major transformations in the relationships between people and their governments."[14]

These commentators missed an essential fact. *ICANN was one of the most prominent and important manifestations of the way the Internet was transforming the relationship between people and their governments.* ICANN's original institutional design marked a revolutionary departure from traditional

12. Tunis agenda, paragraph 35a, November 16, 2005.
13. Lawrence Lessig, "Seven questions: Battling for control of the Internet," *Foreign Policy Magazine*, November 2005, http://www.foreignpolicy.com/story/cms.php ?story_id=3306 (accessed January 14, 2010).
14. Souter 2007, 48.

approaches to global governance. It significantly reduced the power of national governments and existing intergovernmental organizations over communication and information policy. Four structural facts about ICANN explain why it became the lightning rod for negotiating the governance of the Internet at WSIS.

First, ICANN was set up to meet the need for *global* coordination of unique Internet names and addresses. A globally compatible Internet required globally coordinated mechanisms to manage name and address assignments. Whatever governance solution one preferred, it would have to be truly transnational if it was not to fragment the Internet.

Second, as the locus of global coordination ICANN was one of the few globally *centralized points of control over the Internet*. This control can be and sometimes is used to enforce policies in adjacent, nontechnical arenas of Internet policy.[15] In this respect Lessig was dead wrong about it serving "narrow technical functions." ICANN's monopoly over the root of the Internet's identifiers makes it a gatekeeper to parts of the Internet services market that can provide significant leverage over users. ICANN thus has the potential to make truly global and binding decisions about what is otherwise a highly distributed communications system not easily amenable to traditional forms of control.

Third, ICANN represented a *privatization* of significant aspects of the global governance function. Instead of plunging the Internet into the realm of geopolitics via an international treaty or intergovernmental organization, the Clinton administration chose to delegate policy-making authority to nonstate actors. As a U.S.-based private nonprofit corporation, ICANN relied on private contract law and a policy development process dominated by private business interests with some civil society input. Here was a multistakeholder model that went well beyond what anyone in the intergovernmental UN system was used to. Initially, the U.S. government proposed keeping governments out altogether—even, after a few years, itself. Although the United States later reneged on its pledge to withdraw, ICANN's articles of incorporation still prevent representatives of governments from sitting on its board of directors and (nominally) restrict governments to an advisory role. This was yet another sharp break from the norm of intergovernmental policy making.

Fourth, and perhaps most controversially, ICANN was supervised by and accountable to a single sovereign and the world's only remaining superpower, the United States. While ICANN's managers and its supporters in

15. Chapter 10 contains a more detailed discussion of the policy significance of ICANN and the regional Internet address registries.

business and the U.S. government often represented the organization to the public as a "bottom-up," nongovernmental entity, at the very top ICANN was in fact beholden—contractually and politically—to the U.S. government. ICANN was an expression of a *unilateral globalism*. As such, it can be characterized as a Hobbesian solution to the problem of global governance.[16] From a strictly Hobbesian standpoint, *any* sovereign that can ensure global order is preferable to none. But when situated in the specific historical environment of the Internet, which originated in the relatively liberal United States, a U.S.-based Leviathan can be seen by latter-day Hobbesians as relatively benign, or at least preferable to any known alternative.

U.S. political oversight of ICANN is conducted using three instruments. The first and most important is the so-called IANA contract. The contract is a zero-price, sole-source compact between ICANN and the U.S. government that authorizes ICANN to perform the technical functions of the Internet Assigned Numbers Authority (IANA).[17] These functions include allocating IP address blocks, editing the root zone file, and coordinating the assignment of unique protocol numbers.[18] Any changes in the root zone file IANA makes must be audited and approved by the U.S. Department of Commerce.[19] Without this contract, ICANN would have little, if any,

16. If one views relations among national governments as an anarchic "state of nature," multilateral governance institutions can only be expected to transfer the "war of all against all" into international institutions, producing conflict-prone, and probably incompetent, corrupt or unstable governance solutions and brutal competition over the global distribution of benefits. The only alternative (in the Hobbesian framework) is to create a global sovereign, an international version of the Leviathan.

17. For an excellent discussion of the nature of this contract in relation to U.S. administrative law, see Michael Froomkin, "Bring on the IANA competitors," *ICANN Watch*, February 3, 2003, http://www.icannwatch.org/article.pl?sid=03/02/03/2251 256&mode=thread.

18. See ICANN/U.S. Government Contract for Performance of the IANA Function, Section C.2 (Contractor Requirements), August 14, 2006, http://www.icann.org/ general/iana-contract-21mar01.htm. The IANA contract does not authorize the contractor to make or change the policies that guide the performance of the IANA functions; IANA must rely on ICANN processes to make and change policies (e.g., create a procedure for adding TLDs to the root).

19. Letter from Meredith Baker, acting assistant secretary for communications and information, to Peter Dengate-Thrush, chairman of the board of directors of ICANN, July 30, 2008.

hierarchical authority over the coordination of the Internet's identifier systems.

Second, there was a Memorandum of Understanding (now called a Joint Project Agreement, or JPA) between the U.S. Department of Commerce and ICANN.[20] The JPA provided a list of policy-making tasks that ICANN is supposed to perform. The specific priorities and milestones in those documents clearly reflected the interests of the U.S. government.

Third, there is a contract between the U.S. Commerce Department and VeriSign, Inc. VeriSign is the U.S. corporation that operates the master root server and owns the .com and .net top-level domains (TLDs), making it both a dominant supplier in the domain name industry and a critical part of the domain name system's infrastructure. The contract requires VeriSign to implement all the technical coordination decisions made via the ICANN process and to follow U.S. instructions regarding the root zone file.[21] These three contracts are held together by a fourth element: a sweeping U.S. assertion of policy authority over the Internet's name and address roots.[22]

So the new global institution set up in 1998 consisted of one national government with direct, formally unrestrained control over a private corporation that was delegated the authority to make policies affecting the core of the global Internet's identifier system. It was a truly global regime in which policy-making authority was delegated to transnational private actors under the supervision of the United States, and other governments were relegated to an advisory role in a "Governmental Advisory Committee" (GAC). Setting aside the question whether this is a good or a bad

20. Joint Project Agreements between the U.S. Department of Commerce and the Internet Corporation for Assigned Names and Numbers, September 26, 2006, http://www.icann.org/en/general/JPA-29sep06.pdf.

21. Cooperative Agreement between the Department of Commerce and VeriSign (Network Solutions), http://www.ntia.doc.gov/ntiahome/domainname/nsi.htm.

22. The U.S. Commerce Department has since October 1998 asserted what it calls "policy authority" over any and all modifications of the DNS root zone file. The claim first came in Amendment 11 of the cooperative agreement with Network Solutions, Inc., and requires VeriSign to "request written direction from an authorized USG official before making or rejecting any modifications, additions or deletions to the root zone file." During the creation of ICANN the United States repeatedly indicated that it would relinquish this authority and delegate it to ICANN. Later, it asserted a right to hold on to it forever. See the U.S. Principles on the Internet's Domain Name and Addressing System statement released by the U.S. government June 30, 2005, in the thick of the WSIS process, http://www.ntia.doc.gov/ntiahome/domainname/USDNSprinciples_06302005.htm.

governance model, in the fall of 2003 the catalyst of conflict at WSIS was simply how thoroughly it deviated from the multilateral agreements among sovereign nations, which many states took as the norm for global governance. ICANN could be, and has been, criticized from a cyber-libertarian perspective as a new form of centralized control over the Internet and a sharp departure from the earlier Internet's freer, self-governing, and technically neutral administration.[23] But from the standpoint of the nation-state regime, ICANN was still a radical departure. No one should be surprised that sovereigns outside the United States perceived it as a threat to their authority; no one should be surprised at the undisguised suspicion with which they greeted claims that ICANN was unimportant and purely technical. Other aspects of U.S. dominance of the Internet, such as concentrated technical expertise and its role as a hub for global connectivity, were too intangible or diffuse to be changed by policy or used as a target. It was therefore logical and predictable that ICANN became the target of a multilateral, intergovernmental process focused on Internet governance.

Who Has Policy Authority?

In November and December 2003, WSIS delegates went into the Geneva summit facing this conundrum. The government of Brazil took the lead in articulating the challenge of the critical countries. The critics argued that the Internet is a public resource that should be managed by national governments and, at an international level, by an intergovernmental body such as the International Telecommunication Union. Such critics were merely reasserting traditional models of governance process: through elections and legislation at the national level and the multilateral negotiation of agreements among sovereign peers at the international level.

The Geneva Declaration of Principles that emerged from the first phase announced that "The Internet has evolved into a global facility available to the public and its governance should constitute a core issue of the Information Society agenda." The document went on to articulate a set of broad principles regarding Internet governance, which became known popularly as "the Geneva principles": "The international management of the Internet should be multilateral, transparent and democratic, with the full involvement of governments, the private sector, civil society and international organizations."[24] These principles afforded formal

23. Mueller 2002.
24. Geneva Declaration of Principles, WSIS-03/GENEVA/DOC/0004, paragraph 48, http://www.itu.int/wsis/documents/doc_multi.asp?lang=en&id=1161|1160.

recognition to the principle of multistakeholder participation in Internet governance. Unlike the ICANN regime, however, the Geneva principles envisioned "full involvement" of national governments and posited "multilateral" governance as a norm, indirectly criticizing the unilateral regime put in place by the United States. The Geneva Declaration of Principles also made it clear that in multistakeholder arrangements, national governments held pride of place. Internet governance could, it asserted, be divided into "both technical and public policy issues," with governments claiming dominion over the latter: "Policy authority for Internet-related public policy issues is the sovereign right of States. They have rights and responsibilities for international Internet-related public policy issues."[25] By way of contrast, the Geneva declaration limited the private sector to an "important role" in the "technical and business development" of the Internet, while civil society was consigned to an "important role" on "Internet matters . . . at the community level." Thus the intergovernmental consensus of WSIS proposed a hierarchical relationship in which states, business, and civil society each had well-bounded "roles." Governments sit on top, setting the direction and steering the ship.[26] The term *political oversight* became the common label for this policy-setting role for governments.

The WSIS discussions of political oversight tended to conflate two aspects of Internet governance that were significantly different in scope. There was, first, the question of who should provide political oversight of ICANN; that is, the narrower problem of overseeing the private corporation charged with responsibility for the Internet's naming and addressing system. This kind of oversight, however, was often conflated with a much broader kind of authority: *who should define public policy for the entire Internet?* This would involve, presumably, oversight over all Internet service providers, content providers, and Internet users as well as ICANN. The latter framing, of course, substantially raised the stakes of the debate, encompassing a kind of global regulation. Many participants in this debate, however, realized that it would be difficult to exercise the broader kinds of control without also getting control of resource assignment and allocation.

25. Ibid, paragraph 49.
26. This approach did not grapple with the issue of what rights global civil society and business had to influence or participate in transnational policy making, nor did it show much awareness of the difficulty of defining a clear line between technical and policy decisions in the governance of the Internet.

This problem was too big and too new to be resolved at the first WSIS phase. The Geneva summit could only make progress on it by agreeing to create a working group to study and discuss the problem. The Geneva declaration asked "the Secretary-General of the United Nations to set up a working group on Internet governance, in an open and inclusive process that ensures a mechanism for the full and active participation of governments, the private sector and civil society from both developing and developed countries, involving relevant intergovernmental and international organizations and forums, to investigate and make proposals for action, as appropriate, on the governance of Internet by 2005." The working group's mandate was very clear: it was expected to "develop a working definition of Internet governance"; to "identify the public policy issues that are relevant to Internet governance"; and to "develop a common understanding of the respective roles and responsibilities" of the different stakeholder groups. It would then prepare a report covering these topics that would be presented to the Tunis phase of the WSIS for "consideration and appropriate action."[27]

The Working Group on Internet Governance (WGIG)

Study committees are not normally considered impressive responses to a problem; they often are used to sidestep or defuse controversies. The WGIG process and report was different, however. First, there really was a need to educate, exchange ideas, deliberate, and learn about the nature of Internet governance in the international community mobilized around WSIS. There were hard political conflicts at stake, but there were also misunderstandings and ignorance, due to the chasm that existed between the worlds of Internet aficionados and government diplomats, and between the politicians in the developing world and the politicians and high-tech industry leaders of the advanced economies. The need for dialogue was more than a platitude in this case. Second, the WGIG process turned into a model exercise in multistakeholder participation. The final composition of the group was evenly divided among governments, civil society, and business representatives with equal status in the group's deliberations. In making its selections, the UN Secretariat was able to utilize the self-organized WSIS civil society structures, issuing an open call for nominations to the WGIG. Finally, the report and recommendations would be timed to feed into the final phase of WSIS, so that if an acceptable consensus could be reached

27. Geneva Plan of Action WSIS-03/GENEVA/DOC/0005, paragraph 13 b, http://www.itu.int/wsis/documents/doc_multi.asp?lang=en&id=1161|1160.

there was the possibility that significant changes could be agreed upon by governments and others.

The UN named veteran Indian diplomat Nitin Desai, a former UN Undersecretary-General for economic and social affairs, and organizer of prior summits, as chair of the WGIG. Swiss diplomat Markus Kummer was made its executive coordinator. Forty WGIG members were appointed by the UN Secretary-General after nearly a year of consultations and nominations. The group, in which participants acted as individuals and not as "representatives" of any state or group, started developing its report in November 2004 and released it in July 2005.

The WGIG report produced a broad definition of *Internet governance*: "Internet governance is the development and application by Governments, the private sector and civil society, in their respective roles, of shared principles, norms, rules, decision-making procedures, and programmes that shape the evolution and use of the Internet." While anchored in the theory of international regimes from academic international relations literature,[28] the definition also reveals some of the political imperatives at work. In deference to the important role of private actors, it makes a point of noting that Internet governance is done not just by governments but also by other stakeholder groups. But the phrase "in their respective roles" signals a concession to the sovereigntists' insistence that governments alone are responsible for public policy. The report's concept broadened the definition of Internet governance beyond "ICANN issues" to include technical standard setting, interconnection of Internet service providers, telecommunications infrastructure, freedom of expression, and multilingual issues. Some of these (e.g., physical telecommunications infrastructure) are broader communication policy issues that cannot be affected much by what is done with the TCP/IP protocols. The attention now devoted to Internet governance, however, gave some actors an incentive to include their favorite issues under the umbrella of Internet governance. The overall effect was to make it possible to define practically any communication-information policy issue as Internet governance.

The WGIG report's recommendations for institutional change foretold the battles that would occur at the Tunis summit later that year, showing clearly where international consensus was possible and where it was not. The working group proposed creating a new "global multistakeholder forum"—an idea advanced by the civil society participants. The forum would provide a space for nonbinding "dialogue among all stakeholders"

28. Krasner 1983.

on Internet-related public policy issues. With respect to the creation of more authoritative institutions to establish "global public policy" for the Internet, the WGIG could agree on only one thing: "No single Government should have a pre-eminent role in relation to international Internet governance." The U.S. government had no representative in the group, facilitating agreement on this point; nevertheless, it is significant that all others in the group, including international business and European government representatives, agreed to this rather direct rejection of unilateral oversight.

Aside from that, the WGIG could not come up with a single agreed model for change. Instead, it proffered four sketchy proposals that focused mainly on defining the organizational arrangements for some kind of "political oversight" that could replace the special role of the U.S. government. Some of these proposals were more centralized and threatening to the freedom of the Internet, while others were minor adjustments to the status quo. But all of these proposals have been—and deserve to be—forgotten. As my colleagues and I have argued elsewhere, the WGIG (and WSIS generally) unwisely skipped foundational tasks required for the construction of an international regime. It attempted to propose specific organizational arrangements when there was no agreement on the basic principles and norms that such organizations should reflect and implement.[29] An even more basic fallacy than that underlay its proposals. The proposals were still based on the idea that effective governance arrangements for the Internet could be defined and imposed hierarchically, from the top down, through the agreement of a few governments.

The Political Debate over WSIS and IG

From the release of the WGIG report in mid-2005 until the opening of the Tunis meeting in November, a global debate over Internet governance gathered intensity. Widely reported in U.S. and foreign media, the debate focused on the political oversight issue that had led the WGIG to produce such indecisive results.

U.S. unilateralism fostered an increasingly divisive and nationalistic debate. It diverted dialogue away from the merits of a denationalized, multistakeholder global governance regime and focused it instead on geopolitical rivalries. An Internet "run" or "supervised" by the U.S. government sounded vaguely threatening to the rest of the world (especially after

29. Mueller, Mathiason, and Klein 2007.

the U.S. invasion of Iraq). And there was no denying that the current oversight arrangement gave the United States the de facto power to remove any country's top-level domain from the root zone file, effectively wiping it off the Internet, and gave the United States greater influence over ICANN policies. U.S. politics and law did in fact have a disproportionate influence on Internet governance.

But the prospect of foreign governments adamantly asserting their "sovereign authority" over the free-spirited world of the Internet alarmed many Americans and liberals in other parts of the world. This was true especially when the governments making such assertions included authoritarian states such as China, Saudi Arabia, Syria, and Iran. All had well-developed policies of restricting and censoring the Internet. The cleavage was widened by the demands of many of these same countries to restrict WSIS negotiations and deliberations to states, relegating other parties to secondary status. A poignant example of that occurred during a WSIS Prepcom when ICANN's CEO Paul Twomey was ejected from a committee meeting discussing ICANN itself, on the grounds that he was not part of a government delegation.

In this period, the principle of multistakeholder participation became one of the key legitimizing claims of the ICANN regime's defenders. As one of the more eloquent defenders of the ICANN regime from the private sector claimed, "ICANN's form of governance explicitly includes policy, technical, business and user interests under one roof. Each interest group has a formal role and voice in both policy making and governance. Each has a stake in the proceedings, and each is an important part of the system."[30] The emphasis on multiple stakeholders led to discussions of the proper "roles and responsibilities" of governments with respect to other "stakeholder groups" in the governance of the Internet. On these problems and on the issue of reliance on a private sector-led regime, the European Union basically supported the concept of "private sector leadership" that was often used to describe the ICANN regime.

Defenders of the ICANN status quo, however, were caught in a severe logical bind. If a nongovernmental model was the best and most appropriate one for the Internet, then what was the United States government doing with its hand on the tiller? In the context of WSIS, it was difficult to criticize U.S. oversight without aligning oneself with the sovereigntists.

30. Elliot Noss, "Perspective: A battle for the soul of the Internet," *CNET News*, June 8, 2005, http://news.cnet.com/A-battle-for-the-soul-of-the-Internet/2010-1071_3 -5737647.html.

On the other hand, if one conceded the need for some kind of governmental oversight, why should this oversight function be held exclusively by one national government given the globally distributed nature of the Internet and the strong effects that administration of domain names and IP addresses could have on Internet as a whole? Why shouldn't other states, especially those with the same democratic legitimacy, demand a negotiated agreement on the principles, terms, and conditions of such oversight? If bringing states into such a role would "politicize" the Internet, didn't the U.S. role also do so? There simply was no rationalization for the exceptional status afforded the United States that was both logically consistent and palatable to the rest of the world.

The June 2005 DNS "Principles" of the United States
The WGIG had concluded its work June 20, 2005, but did not publicly release its report until July 14. Two weeks before its public release, on June 30, 2005, the U.S. Commerce Department's National Telecommunications and Information Administration (NTIA) reanimated the debate over unilateral oversight by making its position explicit. It released a short, four-paragraph document entitled "US Statement of Principles on the Internet's Domain Name and Addressing System." The statement announced: "The United States Government intends to preserve the security and stability of the Internet's Domain Name and Addressing System." As a result of this commitment to "security and stability," the United States intended "to maintain its historic role in authorizing changes or modifications to the authoritative root zone file."[31] The statement recognized the sovereignty concerns of other countries with respect to the country code top-level domains (ccTLDs) and expressed a willingness to negotiate about that. It also expressed U.S. support for ICANN as "the appropriate technical manager of the Internet DNS," and stated that dialogue about Internet governance should continue in multiple forums, as "there is no one venue to appropriately address the subject in its entirety."

The release of the "US Principles" had a preemptive quality to it that exacerbated the growing conflict. Issued a few weeks before the WGIG report, the statement could have taken a different approach. It could have provided reassurances to the international community that the United States would not abuse its privileged position; the statement could have opened the door to exploring conditions for sharing the control and could

---

31. U.S. Principles on the Internet's Domain Name and Addressing System, see note 22.

have revived the idea of full privatization in order to preempt demands for internationalization. Instead, the Bush administration dug in its heels and flatly reasserted U.S. unilateral political oversight as a permanent feature of Internet governance. Whether intentionally or not, the timing and blunt language conveyed intransigence to the rest of the world, and may have played a role in pushing the European Union into a more confrontational stance a few months later.

The .xxx Veto

One of the most important arguments used to support U.S. control of the root was that the United States was the only country in the world that could be trusted with impartial supervision of ICANN. As a *Washington Post* editorial argued, "The striking feature of U.S. oversight of the Internet is that . . . abuses have not occurred."[32] The persuasiveness of that line of reasoning received a major jolt in the summer of 2005, when the Bush administration, bowing to domestic political pressure, actively intervened in ICANN.

For two years, ICANN had been reviewing applications to operate new top-level domains. One of the applicants, ICM Registry, proposed .xxx, a top-level domain that would be restricted to adult content. It would be a "red light district" on the Internet, based on the premise that clear identification of adult content would facilitate access by those who wanted it and enable avoidance or blocking of it by those who did not want it. As is true of anything associated with pornography, the proposal was controversial. Some child protection and antipornography advocates supported the idea; others saw it as legitimizing pornography on the Internet. Some free-expression advocates saw it as a laudable effort to deal with content regulation by voluntary, contractual means; others saw it as setting the table for mandatory classification and blocking of Web sites by states. Most porn content providers didn't like the idea, but some did.

After a long review process, ICANN made a decision that the .xxx proposal met all of its eligibility requirements and authorized its staff to enter into contract negotiations with ICM Registry. The decision hit the news media on June 2, 2005. Widespread publicity—*ICANN approves porn domain*—fueled a domestic political reaction. A number of social conservative groups in the United States, led by the Family Research Council, began to lobby the U.S. Commerce Department to use its authority over the root zone file to stop .xxx. FRC mounted an email campaign against approval

32. "The Internet at risk," editorial, *Washington Post*, November 21, 2005.

of the domain, urging its members to inundate the Commerce Department with messages in opposition.

Initially, NTIA officials reacted by emphasizing their lack of authority over the policy decisions of ICANN. They tried to divert the protests to the ICANN board. They even went out of their way to encourage news stories to delete any mention of NTIA approval authority over ICANN actions.[33] But the tone of the debate began to change as concern about the domestic political consequences grew. Eventually, the prophylactic relationship between the U.S. Commerce Department and ICANN began to erode. NTIA's Margaret Attwell circulated an email on June 21 stating, "I think there will be a call for [Commerce Department] Secretary Gutierrez to weigh in to urge ICANN not to approve it." Some time in early August 2005, the U.S. government abandoned its commitment to ICANN independence. The intervention came in the form of a letter from Michael Gallagher, the Commerce Department's assistant secretary for communications and information, to ICANN's Chairman of the Board Vint Cerf and CEO Paul Twomey.[34] The letter, dated August 11, 2005, expressed concern about the opposition to the .xxx domain and asked ICANN to delay a decision on it. The letter was also sent by email to Mohd Sharil Tarmizi, chairman of ICANN's Government Advisory Committee (GAC), and a dozen other GAC members.

At the behest of the U.S. Commerce Department, Tarmizi prepared his own letter to ICANN, saying that there was a "strong sense of discomfort" among governments about the .xxx proposal. The letter requested that "the Board should allow time for additional governmental and public policy concerns to be expressed before reaching a final decision on this TLD." Both ICANN and the Commerce Department pushed forward the Tarmizi letter as the basis for delaying a decision on .xxx in order to deflect attention away from the role of the U.S. government.[35] The trick worked:

33. Documents obtained through the Freedom of Information Act show that NTIA pressured news outlets to remove from their stories any references to the U.S. Commerce Department's approval authority over ICANN's additions to the root zone. The Commerce Department succeeded in getting CNN, Associated Press, and CNET reporters to delete references to the department in their stories about the .xxx case.
34. Michael Gallagher, assistant secretary of commerce, NTIA, to Paul Twomey, ICANN president, and Vint Cerf, chairman of the board, August 11, 2005.
35. On its Web site, ICANN dated the Commerce Department letter August 15, even though the record proves that they had received it as an email early on August 11. And ICANN announced the GAC chair's letter on its front page, while burying the Commerce Department letter in its "Correspondence" pages with no fanfare.

many news media reported that the GAC had requested the delay, when in fact it had been proposed and initiated by the U.S. government.

ICANN of course complied with the request for a delay. U.S. interference changed the position of ICANN CEO Twomey and key board members giving .xxx's opponents time to bring pressure to bear on ICANN so that eventually the application was killed. A Freedom of Information Act request by ICM Registry[36] laid bare a paper trail that exposed the domestic political pressure by the Religious Right that caused the U.S. government to alter its policy. Despite its WSIS-inspired claims that U.S. control of the DNS root was protecting the security and stability of the Internet from interference by power-hungry governments, in this case it was the U.S. government that took the lead role in subordinating ICANN to a domestic political agenda.

The U.S. use of the GAC to shield and legitimize its intervention, however, was significant. In the context of WSIS, pure unilateralism would have damaged ICANN's legitimacy too much. So the United States used a "multilateral" entity within the institutional framework of ICANN to exercise its influence. In some ways this was the most important result of the .xxx affair: in the course of its intervention, the United States adopted the conceptual framework of its own critics with respect to the role of governments. Needing a rationale to intervene, the U.S. Commerce Department now went along with the idea that governments should have special influence over public policy. Ironically, the United States found itself on the same side of the .xxx issue as the government of Brazil, which had gleefully seized upon the controversy as an example of how a private nonprofit California corporation was making global public policy.

This did not, however, deter many U.S.-based organizations from continuing to support U.S. unilateral control as the lesser of two evils: "If the triple-X decision was disturbing to you—and it was disturbing to us—try to imagine what 200 countries with 200 different ideologies will do when they have veto power over decisions," said David McGuire of the Washington, DC-based Center for Democracy and Technology. "If the problem is that U.S. is too involved, the answer is not to exponentially increase the number of governments involved in the Internet governance process."[37]

36. See Internet Governance Project, "Review of documents released under the Freedom of Information Act," May 19, 2006, http://www.Internetgovernance.org/pdf/xxx-foia.pdf.
37. Quoted in Kevin Poulsen, "Net dust storm blows into Tunis," *Wired News*, November 15, 2005.

The Break with the European Union

The U.S. position received another blow at the September 2005 Prepcoms for WSIS, when the European Union, under the presidency of the United Kingdom, publicly broke ranks with the United States and began calling for changes in the ICANN regime. The institutional design the Europeans contemplated was murky. But the general thrust was clear enough: it proposed fairly large steps toward internationalizing the U.S. government's ICANN oversight function and mandating governments to develop policy principles for governing Internet names and addresses. The EU proposed that governments should, on a multilateral basis, develop and apply "globally applicable public policy principles" related to ICANN's functions. What the EU variously called a "new cooperation model," or an internationalized "public-private partnership" would give governments the authority to set public policy—but only at "the level of principles" and "excluding any involvement in the day-to-day operations" of the Internet. The new model, the Europeans claimed, would "build on the existing structures of Internet governance" and not replace them. Specifically, it would provide for "international government involvement at the level of principles over . . . naming, numbering and addressing-related matters."[38] The EU proposal also emphasized "the importance of respecting the architectural principles of the Internet, including interoperability, openness and the end-to-end principle."

Bush administration officials were shocked and furious at the Europeans' open break with the United States. The sovereignty-oriented and authoritarian governments, on the other hand, saw the European proposal as a validation of their position and warmly embraced it, to the discomfort of the Europeans.

The Gutierrez-Rice Letter

The EU proposal finally had made clear to the United States government the degree to which it was politically isolated. In the run up to the Tunis

---

38. The proposed areas for policy intervention were enumerated as: "a) Provision for a global allocation system of IP number blocks, which is equitable and efficient; b) Procedures for changing the root zone file, specifically for the insertion of new top level domains in the root system and changes of ccTLD managers; c) Establishment of contingency plans to ensure the continuity of crucial DNS functions; d) Establishment of an arbitration and dispute resolution mechanism based on international law in case of disputes; e) Rules applicable to DNS system." Quoted in Mayer-Schönberger and Ziewitz 2007.

summit, it launched a major diplomatic effort to defend the *status quo*. The arguments it used are set out in a November 7, 2005, letter sent from the U.S. Secretary of Commerce Carlos Gutierrez and Secretary of State Condoleezza Rice to Foreign Minister Jack Straw of Great Britain, which held the presidency of the EU at the time.[39] The United States based its appeal, ironically, on keeping the Internet free of governments. "Support for the present structures for Internet governance is vital," U.S. officials claimed, because

the Internet will reach its full potential as a medium and facilitator for global economic expansion and development in an environment free from burdensome intergovernmental oversight and control. . . . We regret [that] the recent positions on Internet governance (i.e., the "new cooperation model") offered by the European Union, the Presidency of which is currently held by the United Kingdom, seems to propose just that—a new structure of intergovernmental control over the Internet.

The United States, which insisted on retaining direct control of the one centralized aspect of the Internet, stated in its letter that "the success of the Internet lies in its inherently decentralized nature, with the most significant growth taking place at the outer edges of the network through innovative new applications and services."

The position expressed by the U.S. government had strong domestic political support. Opposition to what was commonly tagged as a "UN takeover of the Internet" united a surprisingly broad range of the political spectrum in the United States—everyone from rightwing haters of the United Nations and "world government" to major industrial interests such as Google and Microsoft to the liberal editors of the *Washington Post* and *New York Times*. The UN could not be trusted with such authority because it was inefficient and bureaucratic; or because it was corrupt (the oil for food scandal was often cited); or because it would give authoritarian countries such as Iran, China, or Syria power over the Internet. Often, the debate on oversight was framed in the United States as a choice between an Internet free from government interference and an Internet burdened by oppressive, UN-based governmental controls. In that framing, the fact that governmental oversight of ICANN existed, but was unilateral and centered in the United States, tended to disappear from view. U.S. oversight was not

39. Kieren McCarthy, "Read the letter that won the Internet governance battle," *The Register*, December 2, 2005, http://www.theregister.co.uk/2005/12/02/rice_eu _letter/.

recognized as a form of governmental control, but was mentally processed as some kind of neutral bulwark against (other) governments. The domestic political incentives and foreign and domestic policy objectives of the U.S. state vanished from the interpretive framework.

Overlooked, too, was the growing role of ICANN's Governmental Advisory Committee, which had played a key role in reversing the outcome of an ICANN decision in the .xxx affair. Few defenders of the ICANN regime remarked on the degree to which the GAC reconstituted the politics of the United Nations in microcosm. Moreover, ICANN's decisions about the Internet's identifier systems usually had a truly global and binding effect, and did not permit jurisdictional variation, making it closer to the "world government" some of its defenders feared.

One measure of the degree to which global politics were polarized came from a joint resolution of the U.S. Congress, proposed and passed on the eve of the Tunis summit. The resolution expressed unqualified support for the June 30 DNS principles, as well as for freedom of expression. It concluded that "the authoritative root zone server should remain physically located in the United States and the Secretary of Commerce should maintain oversight of ICANN so that ICANN can continue to manage the day-to-day operation of the Internet's domain name and addressing system well, remain responsive to all Internet stakeholders worldwide, and otherwise fulfill its core technical mission."[40] That resolution passed by a *unanimous vote*, with 423 in favor, 0 against, and 10 not voting. Congressional staffers and participants in the ICANN process who were sometimes severe critics of ICANN closed ranks behind the U.S.-led regime, invoking the myth of its purely technical mandate.

The Tunis Agenda

In the end, the WSIS Internet governance debates pitted the United States against the rest of the world. But diplomats are under strong pressure to produce some results, and so Wednesday, November 16, after several days of tough but hurried negotiations, an agreed text was developed, known as "The Tunis Agenda for the Information Society." The Tunis Agenda, a product of intense negotiations over wording, had three main results:

1. *It praised the "existing arrangements for Internet governance."*

40. Expressing the sense of the U.S. Congress regarding oversight of the Internet Corporation for Assigned Names and Numbers. H. Con. Res. 268 [109th], November 16, 2005.

These "existing arrangements" were described as "the private sector taking the lead in day to day operations, and with innovation and value creation at the edges" (para. 61). The document ratified the U.S. claim that these arrangements had worked well; however, it did not endorse ICANN specifically and never mentions it by name. In that sense, the Tunis outcome simply accommodated a stubborn fact, rather than indicating positive acceptance of the ICANN regime. This outcome did, however, dash forever the dreams of some sovereigntists that ICANN's functions could be moved into or taken over by an intergovernmental forum such as the ITU. Indeed, control by the ITU, though often raised as a bogeyman by many apologists for ICANN and the U.S. position, was in fact taken off the table by the WGIG, which pointedly did not put that option into its report.[41] ICANN was therefore given a qualified delegation of public authority, but the details of how other governments relate to it are still being worked out (see chapter 10).

2. *It paved the way for long-term changes in ICANN.*

The official WSIS statement paved the way for long-term changes in the ICANN regime and in Internet governance generally. It did this, first, by incorporating challenges to specific aspects of the current ICANN regime in its text, and second, by insisting on the authority of governments to define "public policy" for the Internet. These aspects of the agreement set the stage for continuing evolutionary pressures on ICANN that will empower states.

Paragraph 63 rejected the need for countries to manage their ccTLDs via the U.S.-dominated ICANN regime. Paragraph 68 says that all governments, not just the United States, should have "an equal role and responsibility" for the DNS root and for Internet public policy oversight. Paragraphs 69 and 70 call for the development of "globally-applicable principles on public policy issues associated with the coordination and management of critical Internet resources," while paragraph 71 proposes a sketchy process for setting in motion this "enhanced cooperation." The European Union used the latter two paragraphs to claim victory. Its news release described the Tunis Agenda as "a worldwide political agreement

---

41. At the first Internet Governance Forum in 2006, outgoing ITU Director-General Utsumi made his famous and puzzling "hemlock" speech, in which he compared the world's rejection of ITU's recognition as the proper home for the ICANN functions to the refusal of the Greeks to accept the wisdom of Socrates, and offered to drink the hemlock.

providing for further internationalization of Internet governance, and enhanced intergovernmental cooperation to this end."[42]

Related and equally important, the WSIS document formalized the division of Internet governance into two parts: the domain of "technical management" or "day-to-day operation," which should be left to the private sector and civil society, and the domain of "public policy making," which is supposed to be ruled by governments. These aspects of the WSIS results paved the way for an assertion of greater power over policy making in ICANN by its GAC. If the U.S. position was animated by an attempt to defend "the soul of the Internet" from governments, it lost. If its position is conceived more realistically and accurately as an attempt to preserve a status quo in which one government—itself—held a privileged position, then it did win, but the resolution still sows the seeds for a long-term war of attrition in which those privileges may gradually be whittled away.

3. *It authorized the creation of an Internet Governance Forum.*

In what was correctly seen as the most tangible outcome of the summit process, WSIS mandated the creation of an Internet Governance Forum (IGF). The IGF was established as a nonbinding, multistakeholder forum for dialogue on Internet governance issues. The creation of the IGF was widely understood to be the kind of agreement that could get the WSIS out of its impasse; it allowed the critics to continue raising their issues in an official forum but, as a nonbinding discussion arena, could not do much harm to those interested in preserving the status quo. Thus the stalemate over ICANN and Internet governance was prolonged for another five years and given an institutionalized expression. The politics of the IGF and its significance for the future of Internet governance are explored in detail in chapter 6.

An Assessment

WSIS can be considered an important turning point for a number of reasons. One of the most significant, but least visible, was its impact on the way we think about the field of Internet governance. The WSIS process forced national governments, international organizations, and all other stakeholders to look at the issues of Internet policy and governance holisti-

42. European Union, press release, "EU brokers deal on progressive internationalization of Internet governance at Tunis World Summit," November 16, 2005, Document IP/05/1433, http://www.europa.eu/rapid/pressReleasesAction.do ?reference=IP/05/1433.

cally. The Internet and its governance were considered in a way that cut across multiple policy domains and multiple international institutions. This was new. Various international agencies had responded to policy problems raised by the Internet before WSIS. But they had done so mostly in isolation from each other, on a piecemeal basis—and their responses were usually shaped by the narrow set of interest groups clustered around a particular international organization.

The World Intellectual Property Organization (WIPO), for example, developed some Internet-related treaties around copyright issues starting in 1996, and took action around domain name and trademark issues in 1998 and 2000. But WIPO's initiatives were exclusively concerned with protecting the interests of incumbent copyright and trademark holders, whom it viewed as its constituency. WIPO had little capacity to take into account the different and sometimes competing norms and interests related to, say, the impact of intellectual property rules on privacy, development, or freedom of expression. Likewise, the ITU made an unsuccessful effort to get involved in the governance of Internet domain names in 1996, and later served as the venue for airing complaints about the costs of international Internet interconnection from 1999 to 2000. The ITU, however, was mainly moved by its core constituency of national telecommunication-operating companies, and by a desire to preserve or expand its eroding turf.

Many other examples could be cited, drawn from the alphabet soup of international agencies with an actual or potential interest in communications or the Internet.[43] The point is that before 2004, each policy issue associated with the Internet was still pigeonholed and dealt with in isolation by an existing international organization based on an earlier global segmentation of policy domains. The broader, more public and contentious global dialogue fostered by the WSIS process started to loosen up those discursive and institutional boundaries. The discussion was elevated to a more abstract level, involving principles, definitions, and general surveys of the territory. The holistic view was embodied most clearly by the Working Group on Internet Governance, but it was not the WGIG alone that produced this. The controversies around Internet governance led to a flood of policy papers, conferences, and consultation exercises focused on the topic. Prior to WSIS, *Internet governance* was a term strongly associated with the relatively narrow set of issues dealt with by ICANN.

43. For a more systematic mapping of how the rules and processes of various international agencies were related to Internet policy, see Mathiason et al. 2004.

Post-WSIS, it is now widely interpreted to include practically any transnational policy issue associated with the Internet, or even digital media generally.

By focusing so much attention on ICANN, WSIS also forced that organization and the policy network around it to engage more directly with governments, civil society, other international organizations, and global politics.

To sum up, the high politics of WSIS illustrate the ways the Internet has fostered institutional change in global governance of communication and information. The first ten years of the Internet's opening to the public and its commercialization constituted a profound disruption, a moment of disequilibrium in global communication-information policy, especially when combined with widespread liberalization of telecommunications. WSIS provided a vehicle for established, sovereignty-based international organizations and institutional frameworks to react to this disturbance. Although the situation is still not fully settled, it is clear that states failed to simply impose hierarchical regulation on ICANN specifically or the Internet generally. Key elements of the nonterritorial, multistakeholder ICANN regime have survived the challenge and their existence is no longer in peril. At the same time, governments have gained much greater authority over ICANN's activities by working themselves into the network. ICANN's GAC will begin to look more and more like a United Nations for the Internet, and governments' self-proclaimed right to "set public policy" for the Internet has been recognized by all the WSIS signatories, and actually exercised by the United States.

But while the Tunis Agenda contains many reassertions of sovereign nations' right to determine "public policy" for the Internet, the WSIS documents and outcomes concede significant ground to nonstate actors. The distributed architecture of the Internet and flexibility of information technology put into place severe checks and balances on the degree of control that can be exercised by both states and any single private actor. They can influence critical Internet resource policy only through the multistakeholder network converged around ICANN. In the end, the mere fact that the world's governments had to find a verbal construct defining some acceptable division of responsibility between state and nonstate actors with respect to the Internet's administration is an indication of the degree to which the problem of Internet governance really has challenged sovereign control of communications. Those who assert that the Internet poses no new problems in international relations or global governance would have a hard time explaining this outcome, or even the existence of this debate and the passion with which it was prosecuted.

5 Civil Society Mobilization

In addition to its encounter with ICANN, the WSIS process pushed against another frontier of global institutional change. It experimented with efforts to make international organizations more open and democratic by facilitating the participation of nonstate actors. This, too, had long-term effects, leaving in its wake a new transnational policy network on Internet governance and a new UN organization, the Internet Governance Forum.

These changes need to be placed in a broader context. Globalization has extended aspirations for democracy and participation from national to international institutions. Traditionally, international organizations were structured to represent governments, not people. There is no global enfranchisement of individuals, no election of a global parliament or chief executive. Leadership positions in international organizations are filled and decisions made by votes or negotiations among (unelected) representatives of national governments. Furthermore, in intergovernmental forums the policy positions taken by national governments tend to reflect a single, dominant political interest within a country rather than the full diversity of public viewpoints. For these reasons it is common to hear of a "democracy deficit" in international institutions.

Global civil society and *multistakeholder governance* are two commonly invoked responses to the problem of democratizing international institutions.[1] In its most general sense, global civil society refers to any nonstate actors, including both formal organizations and informally organized networks of organizations and individuals. John Keane defines civil society as a "vast, interconnected and multi-layered non-governmental space that comprises many hundreds of thousands of self-directing institutions and ways of life that generate global effects."[2] These views of civil society

1. Calabrese 2004; Keane 2003; Price 2003.
2. Keane 2003, 20.

strongly reinforce, and are reinforced by, concepts of cyberspace as a global space for human interaction where the territorial boundaries of states are often arbitrary or irrelevant constraints. In the context of contemporary economic globalization and growing demands for global governance, however, the concept takes on a more political cast: it is often seen as a "third force" (separable from governments and business) capable of developing and advocating some conception of the public interest across national borders.[3] These ideas are often institutionalized within the UN system, creating a formal role for civil society as if it were a distinct "estate."

The principle of multistakeholder governance provides the most common and popular rationale for including nongovernmental actors in international institutions. An admittedly ugly neologism, the term *multistakeholder* has etymological roots in the United Nations complex of organizations, where interested parties are often referred to as "stakeholders." Multistakeholderism means expanding opportunities for participation beyond governments to other stakeholders in society. A somewhat idealized definition of the "multistakeholder process" is "the coming together of different interest groups on an equal footing, to identify problems, define solutions and agree on roles and responsibilities for policy development, implementation, monitoring and evaluation."[4] Operationally, this means participation in intergovernmental policy deliberations by representatives of NGOs, businesses, and other interested parties alongside governments—sometimes as peers of governmental representatives, but more often in consultative or advisory roles. The United Nations system tends to classify stakeholders into three basic categories: governments, the private sector and civil society.[5] In WSIS (and in some other venues), the UN institutionalized this tripartite distinction, setting up separate accreditation and administrative apparatuses for each sector.

Bearing in mind this broader focus on the democratization of global governance, we now examine the World Summit on the Information Society from a bottom-up perspective. There are two distinct stories here. First, I will show how WSIS became a mobilizing structure for transnational

3. Florini 2000.
4. Banks 2005, 85.
5. The parallels between multistakeholderism and corporatism have been noted by Ottaway (2001). Instead of the older "business, government and labor" councils of the 1930s, which focused on economic interests, we now add civil society—or substitute it for labor.

civil society groups focused on issues in communication and information policy. It thus became the catalyst of what I will call a new *transnational policy network* around Internet governance. The new Internet Governance Forum produced by WSIS supplied an institutional venue with the potential to prolong and strengthen that network. As noted before, this aspect of the story corroborates theories about the symbiotic relationship between transnational politics and international institutions (the coral reef effect).

The second story is about the tensions and contradictions inherent in the institutionalization of civil society participation. Multistakeholder governance raises many institutional issues, and WSIS civil society learned this the hard way as it stumbled into them. The chapter explores how civil society actors in WSIS created their own organizational structures and collective decision-making processes. But along the way they encountered challenges to their legitimacy and were forced to walk a fine line between, on the one hand, the openness, diversity, and informality that are the hallmarks of civil society, and on the other hand, the need for formal mechanisms for representation and decision making to be effective in governance processes.

WSIS as Political Opportunity

Plans for a world summit put into play the full range of global public policies regarding the development and construction of an "information society." This created an unparalleled opportunity for advocacy groups to engage with international organizations and governments around communication-information policy. Such engagement could improve the involved organizations' opportunities for recruiting, influence, funding, and publicity. The administrators of WSIS had a strong incentive to encourage public participation as well. There were many large, widely publicized protests against international organizations during the late 1990s. The demonstrations put international organizations on the defensive and raised concerns about their legitimacy.

The Campaign for Communication Rights in the Information Society (the CRIS campaign) was a conscious effort to use the political opportunity afforded by WSIS to focus attention on an agenda of communication policy issues favored by leftist progressive groups. The CRIS campaign was launched in 2001 and played an important role during the first phase of WSIS in shaping the modalities of and galvanizing civil society participation.

CRIS was a network organization composed of several transnational activist groups formed in the 1980s. One such group was the MacBride Round Table, a collection of communication scholars, journalists, and policy makers who became involved in international communication issues at the time of the MacBride Commission and the controversies over the "New World Information and Communication Order" in the late 1970s.[6] Formed in 1989, many of its principal adherents were rooted in academic communication studies departments, and might be characterized as the political offshoot of the critical communication scholarship of the 1960s and 1970s. There was also the World Association of Community Radio Broadcasters (AMARC), founded in 1983; Vidéazimut, founded in 1989;[7] and the Association for Progressive Communications, which emerged from 1987 to 1990 as a network of environmental organizations that pioneered the use of information and communication technology for activist purposes. With common political values, continuous sharing of information and ideas, roots in the nonprofit sector, and loose, shifting organizational affiliations, this group corresponds well to the concept of a transnational advocacy network (TAN).

Within this TAN a small but dedicated set of activist-intellectuals— Cees Hamelink, Seán Ó Siochrú, Bruce Girard, George Gerbner, Robert McChesney, Alain Ambrosi, Kaarl Nordenstreng, Mark Raboy, Pradip Thomas, Richard Vincent, Dee Dee Halleck, and Michael Eisenmenger, to cite some of the most central—incubated ideas about democratizing communication even as the world's communication policies moved sharply in a direction they opposed—toward liberalization, freer markets, and competition. Various permutations of these individuals, the groups they founded, and the manifestos they issued appear in the mid-to-late 1990s: The Peoples Communication Charter (drafted by Hamelink in 1996);[8] the

6. The group describes the MacBride Round Table as "a communications rights advocacy group created in 1989 to stimulate discussion of issues embodied in the 1980 UNESCO MacBride Report. This report was critical of imbalances in world information flows. Sean MacBride headed the UNESCO commission in charge of the report." For a good account of the NWICO debates, see Carlsson 2003.

7. Vidéazimut was an international coalition for democratic communication with about seventy-five members located in about thirty-five countries in all continents, and was active until the late 1990s.

8. The People's Communication Charter was an initiative of the Centre for Communication & Human Rights (Amsterdam, the Netherlands), the Third World Network (Penang, Malaysia), the Cultural Environment Movement (United States), and the AMARC-World Association of Community Radio Broadcasters (Peru/ Canada). The charter is available at http://www.pccharter.net/charteren.html.

Platform for Cooperation on Democratization and Communication, London (led by Ó Siochrú in 1996); and the 1999 statement "A Global Movement for People's Voices in the 21st Century," issued by Voices 21, a loose transnational association of mostly the same academics and advocates.

The ambitious political vision of the advocacy network is evident in the minutes of the 1997 MacBride Round Table meeting. It reports optimistically that "the various components of an international movement on media and communications, that can challenge the current neo-liberal orthodoxy, seem to be emerging."[9] It viewed the absence of popular, "on-the-ground" support as responsible for the failure of the New World Information and Communication Order (NWICO) initiatives two decades earlier and speaks of "the creation of a global social movement" that might overcome those obstacles.

In the early planning stages of WSIS in December 2000, Mohammed Harbi, a special advisor to the secretary general of the ITU, told a community networking workshop attended by some of the Platform/Voices 21 activists that "the ITU was now trying to convince the UN General Assembly of the need for WSIS to be fully representative of the four partners on an equal footing,"[10] and that "ITU and he personally would be pushing for full civil society participation."[11] Harbi's outreach "sparked the imagination" of certain activists within the leftist-progressive TAN, alerting them to the potential of the proposed summit.[12] Sensing an opportunity, they revived the Platform for Cooperation on Democratization and Communication and began to monitor the progress of world summit plans. In November 2001 they launched the CRIS campaign during a meeting at the London offices of the World Association for Christian Communication (WACC). The purpose of the newly launched CRIS campaign would be "to ensure that communication rights are central to the information society and to the upcoming WSIS" (Raboy 2004).

9. The Boulder Statement of the MacBride Round Table on Communication 1997. http://archive.waccglobal.org/wacc/publications/media_development/archive/ 1998_1/the_boulder_statement_of_the_macbride_round_table_on_communication.
10. The "four partners" meant UN agencies, national governments, private business, and civil society.
11. Proceedings, Communication as a Human Right in the Information Society, A seminar organized by the Platform for Communication Rights and the Friedrich Ebert Stiftung, Geneva, November 19–20, 2001.
12. Raboy 2004, 95.

Harbi's promise seemed to be fulfilled shortly after, when the UN
General Assembly resolution authorizing WSIS encouraged "non-governmental organizations, civil society and the private sector to contribute to,
and actively participate in, the intergovernmental preparatory process of
the Summit and the Summit itself."[13] A Civil Society Division was created
as part of the WSIS Executive Secretariat, directed by Alain Clerc and Louise
Lassonde.

Only a few weeks after the launch of the CRIS campaign, the group held
a workshop in Geneva titled "Communication as a Human Right in the
Information Society: Issues for the World Summit on the Information
Society."[14] The event was, in effect, the first formal consultation between
the summit organizers and "civil society" as represented by the CRIS
network.[15] The WSIS Executive Secretariat was still in the early stages of
planning. Though it was committed rhetorically to a "tripartite Summit"
in which civil society, business, and governments would interact more or
less as peers, the UN administrators faced many questions about how to
execute that concept. How would civil society organizations be accredited?
Who would represent them in speeches and discussions? To what degree
would civil society representatives, or individual actors from civil society,
participate in decision making and in the drafting of the WSIS Declaration
and Plan of Action? Seizing the moment, CRIS activists put themselves
forward as intermediaries who could develop proposals for civil society
participation in the WSIS. Within two months they were hired as consultants by the WSIS Secretariat to do just that.[16] The CRIS organizers were
given a chance to enact their ideas about participatory governance.

13. UN General Assembly Resolution 56/183, December 21, 2001.
14. See "Communication rights in the information society: A platform initiative
for the WSIS," *Tracking Magazine* (March 2002), http://www.cmn.ie/cmnsitenew/
current/march2002/comm_rights_cris2.htm. The campaign's news release described
this initiative as "an opportunity for media NGOs and public service media to
develop positions and put them to the WSIS."
15. "The Geneva Workshop . . . was very successful . . . in generating serious interaction between ITU, UNESCO and civil society, and was the first occasion for a
debate on the WSIS and civil society. It set us up early as potentially having a lead
role in the process." Seán Ó Siochrú, "Comments on TNCA Project case study of the
CRIS campaign," correspondence with author, October 10, 2005.
16. Many of the materials produced for this consultation are no longer available on
the Web. One report that the author read but is no longer available: Seán Ó Siochrú
and Bruce Girard, "Report of Working Group on Civil Society Participation:
'Process.'" UNESCO WSIS Civil Society Consultation, Paris, April 22–23, 2002.

Underscoring the interdependence of international institutions and international politics and advocacy, the CRIS campaign's principal actors thus played an important role in proposing, defining, and operating the very structures through which civil society participated in WSIS. These structures then became an effective method for reaching larger numbers of people and gaining support for their ideas and their organizations. WSIS civil society became the CRIS campaign's basic mobilizing structure. This brought civil society actors directly into the process; it also encompassed some protest actions around the periphery of the WSIS process.[17]

In its approach to WSIS, the CRIS campaign positioned itself for a standard left–right political conflict; a second round of NWICO in which popular movements (instead of developing country states) challenged neoliberalism in communications and promoted participatory democracy and human values. The WSIS shift toward Internet governance in the second phase, however, created a very different kind of politics, which the campaigners had not anticipated and for which they were not well prepared. The Internet's development had thrived on liberalized, competitive telecommunication policies and open, denationalized flows of information. Although the new civil society advocates involved in Internet governance shared the leftists' interest in encouraging widespread public participation in global governance, they were far more favorable to markets and competition in communication industries and far more skeptical of states. The new politics of Internet governance was oriented around a critical stance toward the role of the nation-state in regulating communications, and took for granted a larger role for nonstate actors. Eventually, the shift toward Internet governance refocused WSIS civil society away from the CRIS campaign. But the campaign still played an important role in stimulating and structuring public participation in WSIS and in fostering an ethic of self-organization among the civil society actors.

The specific organizational structures that emerged from the interaction of civil society and the UN WSIS administrators will be analyzed in detail in the third section. The narrative turns next to an analysis of the civil society networks that converged on the WSIS process.

17. A series of actions publicized as "WSIS? We Seize" was carried out around the Geneva summit. This project was organized by Indymedia activists but had strong participation from a few CRIS affiliates.

A New Transnational Policy Network

As WSIS progressed, a growing number of civil society participants got involved. Table 5.1 shows the number of accredited civil society participants in the Geneva summit and the preparatory events leading up to it. If we count those who were regularly active, the WSIS civil society (WSIS-CS) network was fairly small (around 700 people) and could best be described as primarily composed of the "cosmopolitan, transnational activist elite that staffs International NGOs" (Tarrow 2001). Nevertheless, the WSIS events led to the convergence of a number of distinct issue networks that had been focused on separate aspects of communication-information policy. Where before these groups tended to focus on different institutional venues that were more or less isolated from each other, in WSIS they were brought together by a single event and required to work together as "civil society."

We can see in the WSIS process the convergence of a number of smaller issue networks into a broader network that, over the long term, is likely to become a more stable transnational policy network focused on Internet governance. There were five major issue networks that converged in WSIS. They can be identified as follows:

• *ICT for Development (ICT4D)* This network capitalizes on the UN system's interest in "development" by promoting information and communication technology (ICT) initiatives that claim to contribute to development. Because of the potential for links to industry and state-funded development projects, ICT4D is practically an industry unto itself; its members and organizations are well integrated into the processes and funding mechanisms of the United Nations system and the lines interconnecting government, civil society, and industry are often blurry. This issue network provided one the main sources of participation from developing

Table 5.1
Civil society participation in WSIS

WSIS event (Geneva phase)	Civil society participants
PrepCom 1	223
PrepCom 2	398
PrepCom 3	537
Geneva summit	3,418

Source: International Telecommunication Union.

countries. Exemplar organizations include the African Civil Society for the Information Society, IT for Change (India), Francophonie, the United Nations Development Project, Asia Pacific Development Information Project, various telecenters organizations, and Canadian development funding agencies.

• *Civil liberties/human rights* This international network of NGOs includes organizations that apply human rights principles specifically to communication-information technology, in areas such as censorship, privacy, gender, and racial equality. Exemplar organizations include European Digital Rights Initiative, the journalist organizations World Press Freedom Committee and Reporters Sans Frontiers, Article 19, the U.S.-based privacy organization EPIC, and feminist groups such as DAWN and IRIS. (More general and mainstream human rights advocacy organizations, such as Amnesty International, became involved later after the Internet Governance Forum was formed.)

• *ICANN/Internet governance* This issue network includes organizations and individuals who became involved in transnational advocacy through ICANN's constituencies and processes. People associated with this issue network came to dominate the WSIS civil society Internet governance caucus, which rose to prominence during the second phase of WSIS. The ICANN/Internet governance issue network included important private-sector stakeholders in the ICANN regime, such as Internet Society members, the Regional Internet Address Registries, academic researchers specializing in Internet governance, participants in ICANN from its Noncommercial Users Constituency (NCUC), ICANN's At Large Advisory Committee (ALAC), and the Internet Governance Project.

• *Access to Knowledge (A2K)* This issue network involves advocacy groups focused on resisting overly burdensome copyright and trademark policies, promoting free/open source software and other informational commons, and relaxing patent protection for drugs to help developing countries. While present in WSIS civil society, participants in this issue network focused more of their attention on advocacy within WIPO, but at WSIS links were forged that led later to more integration. Exemplar organizations include Knowledge Ecology International (KEI),[18] Free Software Foundation (FSF), European FSF, Latin American Free Software groups, and IP Justice.

• *Media activists* This issue network includes people and organizations that produce alternative media, operate community radio stations, or focus

18. At the time of WSIS, KEI was known as the Consumer Project on Technology (CPTech).

on the policies and regulations applied to the broadcast media. These networks were present in WSIS and in related venues (e.g., UNESCO). Exemplar organizations include AMARC, Indymedia, Free Press, and the World Association for Christian Communications.

It is useful to examine more closely the structure of the underlying relationships among civil society actors at WSIS. Network modes of analysis provide a means of both visualizing and quantifying the nature of the ties among actors. The network analysis presented here is based on surveys conducted during the WSIS process with civil society advocates. Each respondent was asked to provide a list of ten individuals that they correspond or meet with regarding their advocacy work most frequently and consistently over time. They were also asked to list the organizations they work with most closely, now or in the last five years. Finally, they were asked to list all the international meetings related to their advocacy attended in 2003, 2004, and 2005. In total, about one hundred WSIS civil society participants were approached, and complete mapping surveys from fifty-five of them were secured.[19] Six of the interviewees proved to be disconnected from the others, leaving a total of forty-nine nodes in a connected social network.[20]

One clear result from the data is that the WSIS process played a greater role than any other event in connecting transnational civil society actors involved in different communication-information policy issues. Respondents reported attending 415 separate events, occurring on almost every continent and involving a wide array of governmental, private sector, and civil society actors. The most central event was of course the WSIS Geneva summit, attended by forty of the fifty-five respondents.[21] The WSIS Prepcoms were the only other events that came anywhere near this level of commonality. By way of comparison, the World Social Forum at Porto Alegre was attended jointly by only seven of the fifty-five respondents.

19. Work by other researchers corroborates the representative status of our surveyed respondents. A frequency count of the emails exchanged on the WSIS Civil Society Plenary email listserv identifies a group of fifty-seven civil society actors who posted most frequently. Their list of the most active fifty-seven posters and our surveyed population of fifty-five overlap greatly, particularly the top twenty most active and most central participants; Zakaria and Cogburn 2006.
20. The network of forty-nine unique individuals was linked by 143 interpersonal relationships. The network density (matrix average) equaled 0.0608 (SD = 0.239). The average-path distance between reachable node pairs is 3.233, with a maximum of eight links.
21. The survey was conducted in 2004 and early 2005, before the Tunis summit.

In figure 5.1, these data are represented graphically as a two-mode affiliate network.[22] Nodes represent international meetings. Links are placed between these meetings whenever two individuals attended the same two events. Links are weighted depending on how many individuals attended an event pair. Event nodes are sized according to their betweenness score, which represents the extent to which an event linked other events in the overall network, by virtue of the people who attended it. In plain language, the network diagram highlights the extent to which any specific event facilitated interaction between actors and the development of common ideas across issue areas.[23] The larger the event's size as a node in the graph, and the more links to it, the greater its importance in forging a common network of actors. The dominance of the WSIS and its Prepcoms in linking actors transnationally across communication-information policy areas is so overwhelming that there are no real competitors.

Network analysis also reveals the tendency of actors to cluster within specific issue networks, and shows which people or organizations connect them all into a more cohesive global civil society network. More than 275 organizations were identified by the subjects, including loosely affiliated or time-limited working groups, formally structured domestic and international NGOs, and intergovernmental institutions. In figure 5.2, nodes represent organizations and links represent individuals who cited both organizations as ones they work with closely. The resulting network diagram illustrates the extent to which an activist organization serves as a hub for individual interaction, facilitating the development of common ideas across issues addressed by the set of organizations active around those issues. Links are darkened to indicate that three or more individuals cited the same pair of organizations. Organizations are sized according to their betweenness score, which represents the extent to which an organization links other organizations in the overall network.

By any measure of centrality, the Association for Progressive Communication (APC) was the organizational center of this particular advocacy

22. Borgatti and Everett 1997.
23. While it is possible that surveys of people who attended WSIS might overstate the centrality of the WSIS process, there are two responses to this. First, not all of our surveys were conducted at WSIS; we interviewed civil society activists at ICANN meetings, a WIPO meeting, and a few other venues as well. Second, if some other event or process was clearly more central than WSIS in connecting the civil society actors who showed up at WSIS, the responses would have reflected that. In fact, no event outside the WSIS sequence comes close; ICANN meetings comprise a distant second to the WSIS Prepcoms in common attendance.

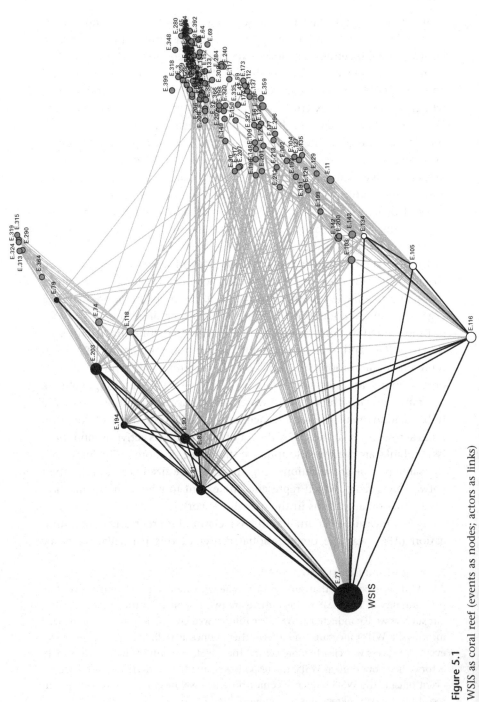

Figure 5.1

WSIS as coral reef (events as nodes; actors as links)

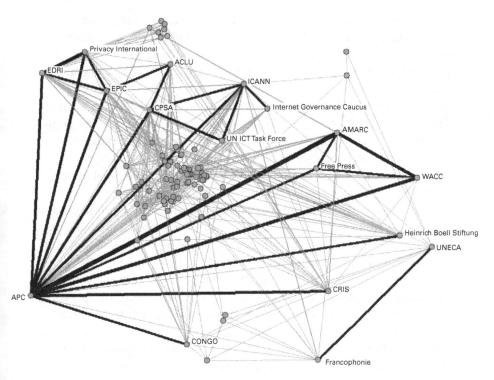

Figure 5.2
APC as hub of the civil society network (organizations as nodes; actors as links)

network. APC, one of the founders of the CRIS campaign, is a global NGO with a professional, full-time staff based in London and Johannesburg, South Africa, but its members are local and regional organizations focused on a variety of communication-information technology issues. APC rose to prominence in WSIS civil society because its organizational structure gave it the strongest capacity to span all of the issue areas previously identified. It has always had a focus on technology and its use to support activists. APC members and its global secretariat have been involved in ICANN-related issues, gender issues, domestic telecommunication policy, censorship issues, and ICT for development. One of its leaders, Karen Banks, emerged as the most central figure in the WSIS civil society interpersonal network (see figure 5.3).

The organizational network shown in figure 5.2 has a clear hub-and-spoke structure with APC at the hub. Some organizational spokes, such as the Congress of NGOs (CONGO), the CRIS campaign, or the Heinrich Boell Foundation, are not densely connected to other organizations; others, such as the civil liberties groups and the media activists, have strong horizontal ties among one another. The network structure shows clusters and cleavages based on issue areas, with human rights and civil liberties advocates clustered and well interlinked with Internet governance advocates, and a larger divide between those issue networks and the media activists associated with AMARC, Free Press, and WACC. Moreover, the ICT4D-oriented organizations UNECA (UN Economic Commission for Africa) and Francophonie are connected strongly to each other but somewhat isolated from the other issue networks.

The network diagram in figure 5.3 examines the interpersonal network of WSIS civil society. Nodes are individual people, and links between people are shown when an individual cited (or was cited by) other individuals as persons they work closely with in their advocacy around communication-information issues. In figure 5.3, the nodes are arranged and sized to reflect various measures of centrality. The position on the horizontal axis reflects eigenvector centrality, the position on the vertical axis represents betweenness, and the size of the node reflects the person's degree centrality.[24] The chart reveals that one actor, APC's Karen Banks (identified as #4), emerges as the hub of the WSIS civil society interpersonal network.[25] Banks had the highest scores in all three centrality measures. The data also show that WSIS civil society was Eurocentric. Seven of the ten most central actors were based in Europe, not surprising in that most of the meetings were held in Europe. Geography still matters in transnational politics, even when it is conducted about and through the Internet. The shading of the node symbol reflects the issue network the person is associated with. One can see that four of the ten most central actors are associated with the ICANN/Internet governance issue network. The number would be larger if Banks and a few of the civil liberties organizations, which also were involved in Internet governance, were counted.

In sum, WSIS brought together preexisting but fragmented advocacy networks around communication-information policy, and established stronger interpersonal and organizational relationships among transna-

24. The different centrality measures are defined as follows. Degree centrality is the number of ties a node has. Eigenvector centrality is a mathematical measure of the relative importance of a node in a network; Google's page rank algorithm is based on this method. Betweenness is a measure of the extent to which a node acts as an intermediary to other nodes; Borgatti and Foster 2003.
25. Survey respondents were promised confidentiality; in Banks's case, the respondent agreed to let her name and organizational affiliation be revealed.

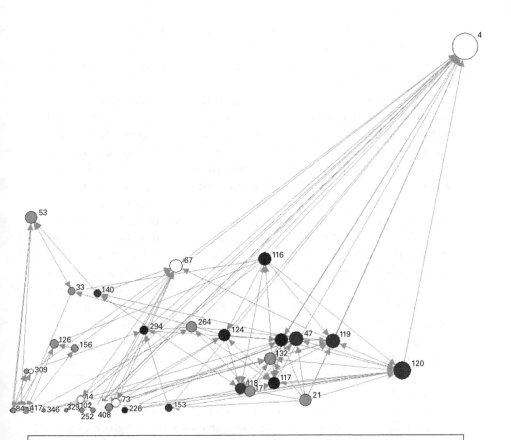

Node sizes reflect degree centrality. Position on the horizontal axis reflects eigenvector centrality. Position on the vertical axis reflects betweenness. Color coding of nodes: white = CRIS-affiliated actor; black = actors associated with human rights/ civil liberties organizations; dark gray = actors associated with ICANN/Internet governance; light gray = all other issue networks.

Figure 5.3
The interpersonal network of WSIS civil society (actors as nodes, links shown when one actor cited another as regular cooperator)

tional civil society actors in this policy domain. WSIS put a new transnational policy network on the map.

The Structures of Civil Society Participation

The previous section explored WSIS civil society from a relational standpoint, looking at networks of actors. This section examines the organizational structures and processes. A diagram of civil society participation as it evolved in the first phase of WSIS is shown in figure 5.4. To understand these structures, of course, one must also recount the stories of how they evolved.

At the first WSIS preparatory meeting in July 2002, thirty CRIS activists and about two hundred other accredited civil society participants arrived "with goodwill and optimism." But they soon were exposed to the hard realities of the intergovernmental system. For three days, government delegates held procedural debates on whether and to what extent business and civil society representatives would be allowed to speak.[26] For the rest of the WSIS process, the status of civil society and private sector participants was a point of tension and instability, and renegotiated at every turn. Wolfgang Kleinwachter described the situation as a revolving door to the negotiating room: observers were included, then excluded, then invited back in or fed information from the inside.[27] While WSIS civil society never achieved the peer status that its participants wanted, the summit never reverted to a purely intergovernmental affair, either. Though ultimately frustrated and disappointed by their less than equal status, CRIS helped form a Civil Society Plenary at the first Prepcom, and decided to continue to participate in the WSIS process "on the basis of skeptical engagement."

The UN's tripartite sectoral representational scheme created an imperative for coordinated, unified responses from civil society as a sector. This demanded a certain level of institutionalization. To the extent that civil society had any capacity to issue unified statements and designate speakers in WSIS, the transnational advocacy network led by the CRIS campaign and APC provided much of the ideas and organizational capacity.

WSIS civil society came to be organized around a large number of self-formed thematic and regional caucuses, whose existence was officially recognized by the Civil Society Plenary. There was, for example, a human rights caucus; a working group on patents, copyright, and trademark; a media caucus; a community media caucus; and an internet governance caucus. There were also regional caucuses for Africa, Latin America, and Asia.[28] Across this diverse array of groupings, there were two key organs of coordinated collective action: Content and Themes, a drafting group which

26. Raboy 2004.
27. Kleinwachter 2004.
28. As of January 2010 the caucuses were listed at http://www.wsis-cs.org/caucuses .html.

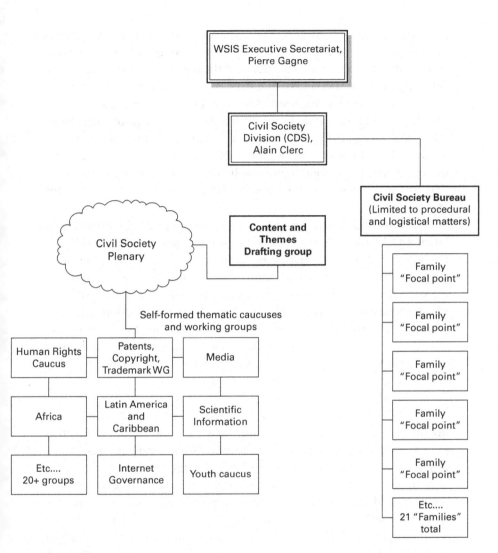

Figure 5.4
WSIS civil society organizational structure

produced statements recognized as the official civil society intervention into the process, and the Civil Society Plenary, a completely open physical and virtual assembly that nominally held the role of "ultimate civil society authority in the WSIS process."[29]

The civil society activists resisted attempts by UN administrators to chair the plenary, and ultimately it was chaired by a succession of participants informally appointed by the Civil Society Plenary—at first, Renata Bloem of the UN's Congress of NGOs, later APC's Karen Banks and other CRIS principals. The email communication lists of both organs were hosted by APC and administered by APC's Banks, also a key member of the Content and Themes group.

The Content and Themes group, coordinated by CRIS principals Sally Burch and William McIver, emerged as the real power behind WSIS-CS's public voice. It served a vital gatekeeping function, controlling the bandwidth for authoritative public communication between civil society and the official WSIS plenaries or working groups and the media. Serving in that leadership capacity, and blocked from direct participation with governments in formulating the official WSIS documents, the Content and Themes group facilitated the drafting of a "Civil Society Declaration"—an alternative statement of the norms and policies of the information society that paralleled the official Declaration of Principles of the governments.[30]

A third civil society organ was the Civil Society Bureau, which was intended to serve as the official interface with the Intergovernmental Bureau. It was proposed by the WSIS's official Civil Society Secretariat as a formal representative body composed of delegates sent from a taxonomy of civil society sectors called "families." The "family" groupings were rather arbitrary, and the procedures for selecting representatives from families were never well defined. The term *representative* was later replaced by the term *focal points*.[31] Standard procedures for creating new families or eliminating atrophied ones were never created. The Civil Society Bureau's

29. Seán Ó Siochrú, Wolfgang Kleinwachter, and Renata Bloem, "Overview of Civil Society Elements and how to get involved," December 9, 2003, WSIS Civil Society Meeting Point Web site, http://www.wsis-cs.org/cs-overview.html.
30. "Shaping Information Societies for Human Needs," Civil Society Declaration to the World Summit on the Information Society, December 8, 2003, http://www.itu .int/wsis/docs/geneva/civil-society-declaration.pdf.
31. For a listing of the WSIS "Families," see http://www.un-ngls.org/wsis--csb --families.htm.

intended status as a representative body was undermined as the number of "family" groups ballooned from ten to twenty-one, making the categories even more overlapping and arbitrary. Nevertheless, representatives on the Civil Society Bureau often received travel expenses to WSIS meetings.

There was thus a major disjunction between "bottom-up" civil society, with its organically evolved structures formed in response to the entrepreneurial efforts of the advocacy network led by CRIS, and "top-down" civil society, the structure created and recognized by the UN bureaucracy. The official Civil Society Division administrators hailed the Civil Society Bureau's creation as a "historic event."[32] Its reception by CRIS and its allies was decidedly less enthusiastic, perceived by them as potentially undermining the autonomy of civil society participation.[33] For that reason CRIS and its supporters pressed to restrict its authority to procedural and logistical matters, and succeeded largely in that goal. The Civil Society Bureau would reserve rooms for civil society meetings and be informed of the number and time of speaking slots. The development of substantive statements remained with Content and Themes, vetted by the Civil Society Plenary. Speaker lists occupied a contested middle ground. The Civil Society Bureau was thus almost completely disconnected from the thematic caucuses and the plenary, and over time the gulf widened.

The core network of advocacy groups—composed of the CRIS campaign organizers, APC, human rights groups, youth groups, feminist groups, engaged academics interested in Internet governance and telecommunication policy, and ICANN civil society and ICT4D groups—displayed remarkable energy, capacity, and staying power over the three-year period. In that respect, the opening to popular mobilization afforded by WSIS-CS worked amazingly well. The decentralized, open structures of civil society at the ground level permitted autonomous mobilization and participation, allowing even avowed enemies of CRIS like the World Press Freedom Committee

32. "The Civil Society Bureau is a decisive turning point in the history of the United Nations and of international negotiations. Indeed, it is the first time that civil society will have the means to effectively participate in the debate and will assume its responsibilities as a government interlocutor." Alain Clerc, quoted in the WSIS online newsletter, April 22, 2003, http://www.itu.int/wsis/newsletter/2003/apr/a2.html.

33. See http://www.wsis.ethz.ch/CRISverdict.pdf, where Ó Siochrú writes, "no-one is entirely happy with it—for this reason many argued that its activities must be as limited as possible." It might, they feared, be used to bypass the self-formed thematic/regional caucuses and plenary structure and substitute in its place a structure controlled by UN administrators.

(WPFC) to participate and sometimes constrain the campaign's ability to put forward its own ideology as the voice of civil society.[34]

But the problems of representation and institutionalization that crippled the Civil Society Bureau were endemic to all of WSIS civil society. Throughout most of the bottom-up structures, there were no formalized mechanisms for regularly electing or replacing representatives, coordinators, or chairs. Decision-making processes usually were improvised. At best, they were consensual; at worst, they were made informally by one or two people or by small cliques in a nontransparent manner. Often it was simply a matter of whoever got into a position first stayed there until that person agreed to leave, as there were no formalized procedures for replacing or removing anyone.

The model of decentralized, volunteer caucuses held together by email lists and consensual decision making in an open plenary could be considered a paradigmatic case of "network organization." But it provides a sobering test of the claims of some theorists that such mechanisms are powerful and efficient alternatives to traditional forms of organization. The WSIS civil society structure worked most smoothly only when participation was confined to a relatively small and ideologically compatible group of transnational advocacy groups. As soon as these structures were confronted with larger-scale participation and real ideological and political differences, they proved unwieldy or broke down.

A poignant example of this occurred on June 24, 2004, at the first PrepCom of the second phase of WSIS. This meeting was held in Hammamet, Tunisia, the country that would also host the second WSIS summit. The controversial choice of Tunisia as a host country for phase 2 was contested by many human rights groups because of the Tunisian government's overt suppression of political dissent. Provoked by civil society's mounting criticism of Tunisia, and in particular by WSIS civil society's decision to nominate a person from a banned Tunisian human rights organization for a speaking slot in the official plenary, a large number of new organizations from Tunisia and a few other African countries suddenly populated the Civil Society Plenary at the Hammamet meeting. They aggressively challenged the legitimacy of WSIS civil society's decision to select the Tunisian speaker; further, they demanded to be included in all WSIS civil society processes, including the Civil Society Bureau, Content & Themes group, and various caucuses and working groups. The Civil Society Plenary meeting degenerated to the point that APC's Karen Banks,

34. For records of the WPFC's opposition to and critiques of CRIS, see Koven 2003.

who was plenary chair at the time, was shouted down by the groups. This conflict, in the words of one civil society activist present, "revealed the fragility of what we had built."[35] Banks herself later criticized the way the intergovernmental process allowed repressive countries to exclude independent and critical civil society groups while permitting the inclusion of "a well-organized, pro-government civil society lobby from Tunisia that has continuously suppressed any references to human rights abuses by the Tunisian government and successfully exacerbated friction among civil society, particularly along North-South lines, by skillfully playing the race card."[36]

Thus, the CRIS-inspired plan for civil society participation in WSIS did not fully come to grips with the structural and political problems posed by the need to institutionalize participation by nonstate actors in international policy making. The CRIS proposals seemed to be animated, instead, by two simpler objectives: (1) a desire to mobilize the kind of transnational activist networks and NGOs with which it was familiar and compatible, and (2) a desire to ensure that those networks and NGOs would be heard in WSIS deliberations. Its plans thus emphasized opportunities for mobilization and structures for self-organization and self-expression. It skirted the problem (admittedly, a huge one) of creating mechanisms for legitimate representation, and had relatively weak mechanisms for timely collective decision making. By the end of the first phase of WSIS it had become evident that the longer-term institutional issues could not be avoided. The absence of representation and decision-making mechanisms continuously ground away at WSIS civil society's capacity and legitimacy. Midway into the second phase of WSIS, Ó Siochrú could claim, "We believe there is still a major legitimacy deficit in the whole of civil society structures."[37]

The Internet Governance Caucus

The eruption of the Internet governance problem in the midst of the WSIS process had a profound effect on WSIS civil society. In terms of substantive

35. Comment by Rik Panganiban 2005; personal recollection of author. For Panganiban's official report on the incident, see Congo Report on WSIS Phase II PrepCom-1, June 24–26, 2004, Hammamet, Tunisia, http://www.ngocongo.org/index.php?what=pag&id=255.
36. Banks 2005, 86.
37. "Report of the Networks & Coalition Family to the [Civil Society] Bureau," December 27, 2004, www.un-ngls.org/orf/wsis%20N&C%20family%20report2.doc.

policy advocacy, Internet governance became the primary point of convergence among many of the civil society groups and issue networks during the second phase of WSIS. Because it was a new issue that required knowledge of institutions and technological arrangements that were unique and unfamiliar to many of the traditional activists, it brought a new group of transnational actors drawn from ICANN civil society into the center of the WSIS civil society network. The organizational nexus of that convergence was the Internet Governance Caucus (IGC).

The caucus was formed relatively late in the Geneva phase of WSIS, at Prepcom 2 in late February 2003. A proposal to create it was submitted by Y. J. Park, a South Korean who had become involved in ICANN through ccTLD and multilingual domain name interests, and Wolfgang Kleinwachter, a German communication scholar who had been involved in ICANN's at-large membership. Park was interested in broadening and internationalizing awareness of ICANN controversies by bringing them into the WSIS process. An Internet Governance Caucus email list was set up March 31, hosted by Computer Professionals for Social Responsibility. Starting with only four initial participants, the caucus attracted more and more interest as the issue heated up.

But the definition of the caucus's identity was controversial, replaying in microcosm many of the global debates. Adam Peake, a prominent WSIS civil society participant who was also involved in ICANN, strongly objected to any intersection between WSIS and ICANN. He followed the position of the Internet Society, which had a longstanding strategy of trying to prevent public discussion and scrutiny of existing Internet governance arrangements in intergovernmental forums. This involved, first, a denial that ICANN engages in "governance" at all, and secondarily an assertion that "the status quo works" and should be left alone. In his initial emails to the new Internet Governance Caucus, Peake worried that "to explain ICANN's weaknesses (many), etc., would only serve to invite these governments and intergovernmental organizations to step in." The only proper response to WSIS, he felt, was to say: "WSIS, on this issue, go away."[38] There was also friction because, prior to the report of the Working Group on Internet Governance (WGIG), some involved intellectuals viewed Internet governance as a relatively narrow and not very important aspect of global governance of information and communication technologies. The two positions reinforced each other so that by September 2003 the

---

38. Adam Peake to governance list, Saturday, May 31, 2003, https://ssl.cpsr.org/pipermail/governance/2003-May/000014.html.

caucus moved to change its name to the ICT Global Governance Caucus. Ironically, on the eve of a historic global battle over Internet governance, civil society came very close to walking away from an easily identifiable forum for dealing with the issue. (The name change was reversed January 2004.)

From its earliest days, participants in the new caucus were immediately drawn into a debate on ICANN as a model for global governance. Few of the participants supported a reversion to control by intergovernmental institutions, yet few were entirely comfortable with the degree to which ordinary users could be heard in private sector-led self-regulatory institutions such as ICANN. Participants from ICANN, other WSIS civil society caucuses, and from outside the WSIS process began to gravitate to these discussions. After the Geneva summit it became obvious to all that Internet governance had emerged as the problem—and term—of the hour. Once it had become clear that the IGC would continue to exist and play an important role in a process increasingly focused on Internet governance, there was much more interest in who would lead it. Adam Peake and Jeanette Hofmann were informally designated co-coordinators of the Caucus, replacing the founders.

As it evolved and grew, the IGC never had the luxury of the assumed homogeneity of values characteristic of other approaches to global civil society. It included apologists for ICANN as well as some of its harshest critics; it included private sector actors who were interested stakeholders in important Internet governance institutions as well as public interest activists and advocacy groups from developing countries focused exclusively on distributional equity. It was, in short, a contentious space for deliberation and discussion of Internet policies and institutions, a place where taking a common position was difficult and often impossible. Within that space, however, positions did sometimes converge. Agreement on the need for multistakeholder participation and opposition to government-only deliberations could almost always be found. By the end of the Tunis summit in November 2005, the IGC email list had around three hundred subscribers and its email list traffic vastly exceeded the volume of any other civil society group.

The most important early test of the IGC's capacity came with the formation of the Working Group on Internet Governance. The need to populate the WGIG with representatives of civil society forced WSIS civil society to make a consequential decision. Everyone recognized that these positions would be ones of high visibility and prestige, and potentially influential; thus there was a lot of interest in—and competition for—slots. The IGC, whose leaders had already forged strong connections to WGIG Coordinator Markus Kummer, was eventually acknowledged by most of the other civil society entities as the proper entity to lead this selection process. Eventually a two-step method was settled on. Recommendations from the Civil Society Plenary and all the thematic and regional caucuses were sent to a five-person "nominating committee" created by the Internet Governance Caucus. This new committee put forward nine of the names to Kummer, the WGIG coordinator, as the official recommendations of civil society.[39] To the surprise of the IGC, all nine of those names were put on the WGIG. Of those nine, all but three were regulars in the ICANN process and active in the IGC.

The process of putting forward the names of civil society participants suffered from the under-institutionalized nature of the civil society structures, mentioned previously in connection with the plenary and the bureau. The caucus coordinators themselves had been vexed by the lack of any preexisting procedures for making a decision of that sort; they lacked any clear consensus on what those procedures should be and did not have the capacity or mandate to hold votes, yet wanted their decisions to be perceived as legitimate. Some of the caucuses had fights and split over the process. Nevertheless, the messy, ad hoc, and sometimes dangerously untimely processes eventually succeeded in placing a well-informed and effective group on the WGIG.

The Internet Governance Caucus managed to maintain a vigorous life beyond WSIS and has continued well into the fourth year of the IGF. In the middle of 2006, it created a formal charter and mission statement for itself; it also created an ongoing process for electing co-coordinators, and used that method to elect several rounds of coordinators. (Two of its former coordinators, Peake and Hofmann, were nominated by the IGC and selected by Kummer to serve on the IGF's Multistakeholder Advisory Group. See chapter 6). The caucus remains one of the livelier public forums for discussion of Internet governance among a relatively broad group of global actors.

This review of WSIS civil society reinforces some of the points made in chapter 4, while adding information about the unique politics of nonstate actors. Among civil society actors, as with state actors, the WSIS process

---

39. The people nominated were Carlos Afonso, Brazil, LAC Caucus; Peng Hwa Ang, Singapore; Karen Banks, APC; Vittorio Bertola, Italy; Avri Doria, United States; William Drake, United States; Raul Echeberria, Uruguay; Wolfgang Kleinwächter, Germany; Marlyn Tadros, Egypt.

fostered a holistic view of the problem of Internet governance, converging different issue networks that were focused on a fragmented set of institutional venues into a more integrated policy network. As a result of the WSIS process, the multistakeholder principle achieved a degree of legitimacy, acceptance, and elaboration in Internet governance that goes well beyond other sectors. The formation of the WGIG and the Internet Governance Forum perpetuated a policy discussion arena in which all stakeholders would have (more or less) equal status. The overall effect was not just an endorsement, but an *implementation* of the multistakeholder model of governance within the UN system. This display of openness by the UN system, in turn, strengthened the hand of civil society within ICANN, as ICANN bolstered its challenged legitimacy by emphasizing its inclusion of multiple stakeholders. Thus, the multistakeholder approach was legitimized and the structures of civil society participation took important steps toward institutionalization. And significantly, it was the institutions' attempt to deal with the Internet that pushed the World Summit's initially halting, equivocal steps toward multistakeholder governance into a firm embrace.

6 The Internet Governance Forum

At the World Summit on the Information Society in 2005, the United Nations responded to the institutional innovation of ICANN with an innovation of its own, the Internet Governance Forum (IGF). IGF has been described as if it were a pathbreaking innovation in global governance.[1] It has also been dismissed as a meaningless talk shop.[2] Whichever is right, the IGF constitutes a clear departure from sovereignty-based forms of international organization. In creating the forum all the WSIS signatories, including the most hard-core authoritarian governments, agreed to abandon a privileged and exclusive role for themselves and to participate in Internet policy discussions on roughly equal terms with civil society and business participants. The IGF thus has made the multistakeholder principle one of its key legitimating claims.

This chapter takes an extended look at the politics of the IGF. It examines how its institutional design and processes have been shaped by the networks of contentious political actors who have converged on it.

The Political Bargain behind the Forum

The IGF is described by the Tunis Agenda as a nonbinding, "lightweight" organization. It was made financially dependent on extrabudgetary contributions rather than funded through the regular, assessed budget of the UN. There is no guarantee it will exist beyond the five-year time period mandated by WSIS, although at this time it looks as if it will be renewed for another five years.

The mandate of the IGF is set out in paragraph 72 of the Tunis Agenda. The subsections of that paragraph empower the IGF to, among other things:

1. Malcolm 2008.
2. Zittrain 2008, 243.

• "Discuss public policy issues related to key elements of Internet governance";
• "Facilitate discourse between bodies dealing with different cross-cutting international public policies regarding the Internet and discuss issues that do not fall within the scope of any existing body";
• "Interface with appropriate inter-governmental organizations and other institutions on matters under their purview";
• "Facilitate the exchange of information and best practices";
• "Identify emerging issues, bring them to the attention of the relevant bodies and the general public, and, where appropriate, make recommendations."[3]

This arrangement is the product of a bargain that reconciled the political positions of four distinct parties involved in WSIS. First, there were state actors from the developing world who wanted dramatic, state-centric changes in global Internet governance arrangements. Second, there were state and private sector actors from the developed world who were sympathetic to an amelioration of U.S. unilateral control, but unwilling to let traditional intergovernmental institutions take control. Third, there were civil society actors who wanted to institutionalize their voice and participation in international communication policy. Last, there were U.S.-led state and private actors who wanted to keep other governments away from the Internet and deflect political pressure away from ICANN so as to preserve the essential features of the pre-WSIS status quo. All of these groups found that they could agree on the desirability of creating an Internet Governance Forum with the stated purpose of promoting "multi-stakeholder policy dialogue."

To the U.S. government-led group of stakeholders, a forum under the auspices of the UN was a grudging concession to intergovernmentalism and to other countries. By accepting it they intended to preempt what they saw as larger, less desirable changes demanded by actors questioning the legitimacy of U.S. oversight and the private sector institutions in control of critical Internet resources.[4] Creating the IGF was also a way of forum shifting to an arena where the power of the states arrayed against the United States and its private sector supporters would be diluted by the addition of civil society and private sector actors, who tend to

3. Quotes taken from paragraphs 72a, 72b, 72d, and 72g, respectively.
4. Nick Thorne, a diplomat at the Tunis summit, said the IGF was devised as "a fix to stop the bad guys controlling the Internet." Quoted in Richard Sarson, "ICANN makes a very British compromise over Net policing," *The Guardian*, May 29, 2008.

support keeping the Internet independent of traditional intergovernmental institutions. A discussion forum such as IGF allows the status quo interests to acknowledge the existence of problems and discuss them with the rest of the world without committing themselves to anything. At the same time, it does not prevent governments from engaging in intergovernmental negotiations or from forming more selective transgovernmental network organizations outside the IGF (and may even aid that process).

For the states that launched the attack on ICANN, the IGF keeps that issue and other, related ones alive. It binds the status quo-oriented actors, in particular other states and international organizations such as ICANN, to interacting with them on new turf. It also creates a public platform for mobilizing potential allies. Its home in the UN makes it a friendlier environment to them (just as the ICANN regime's anchorage in the U.S. government makes the private sector actors more comfortable). Still, their acceptance of the multistakeholder nature of the forum was a major concession to the pluralist, nongovernmental norms of the prevailing Internet regime. They are effectively forced to interact with the entire policy network around Internet governance and justify their views in an open environment.

For civil society constituents, an institutionalized venue for policy discourse in which they are formally equal in status to states and private sector businesses creates major benefits. (Indeed, civil society actors can probably claim credit for first floating the idea of a forum on Internet governance.[5]) The IGF is completely open to participation by advocacy groups and affords a rich site for connecting to policy makers and other interest groups with their messages. The promotion of nonbinding dialogue places a premium on expertise and new ideas, which is often civil society's strong suit. The annual meetings and consultations have had the effect of consolidating the transnational policy network formed around WSIS, giving civil society a focal point for their activities and sustaining the existence of the Internet Governance Caucus.

The divergent interests and ideas of its creators means that the IGF faces a tall order: it must engage those with vested interests *as well as* those who wish to challenge those interests; it must bring together those supportive of the status quo *as well as* those committed to change. To fulfill its

---

5. For example, the "observatory" idea first set out in the WSIS Civil Society Declaration and later, in the UN Working Group on Internet Governance.

mandate it cannot afford to be abandoned by *any* of the groups seriously engaged in the politics of Internet governance. And it must sustain this activity despite lacking any secure source of income or any hard authority over what governments, international organizations, and the suppliers of Internet services or Internet users can do.

The Sublimated Conflict

To understand the IGF, one must understand how its mandate, expressed in the Tunis Agenda, sublimated the conflicts of WSIS but did not resolve them. How one interprets and implements the mandate depends primarily on one's concept of the real purpose of the forum. On this issue, it is not too much of an oversimplification to see two distinct factions animated by different principles. Call them the IGF *hawks* and *doves*.

Forum Hawks

Forum hawks saw in the Tunis Agenda a mandate for a political transformation of global Internet governance. Most of them believed that the leverage of soft power might be able to shape adjacent institutions and policies. They conceived of the IGF as a central clearinghouse where the world's Internet users, suppliers, and public authorities could adopt an independent, reflective stance toward all of the relevant international arrangements. It would be a place for norm promotion and dissemination, a place where the effectiveness, methods, and policies of existing institutional arrangements relevant to Internet governance could be scrutinized and assessed independently. Policy initiatives could be developed and floated by emergent coalitions. Whenever possible and appropriate, hawks believed, the convergence of actors on the IGF should be leveraged to come to agreement on recommendations. State-actor forum hawks, exemplified by the government of Brazil, viewed the IGF as a preparatory and developmental process for an intergovernmental framework convention to realize the Tunis Agenda's call for "globally applicable public policy principles" for the Internet. Other state actors, notably Russia and China, probably wanted to see the IGF evolve into a more traditional intergovernmental arena, in which states can generate a hierarchical governance structure.

Civil society hawks, on the other hand, viewed the IGF as an ongoing, bottom-up process that should develop specific reports or policy recommendations and feed them into a plenary session where they would seek to achieve broad consensus.[6] Civil society hawks tended to support stronger institutionalization of bottom-up processes and more democratic procedures for selecting speakers and representatives. Like the state-based hawks, they wanted no limits on the agenda. And they wanted any intergovernmental negotiations over the future of the Internet to be brought into this multistakeholder environment and made transparent.

Forum Doves

Forum "doves" on the other hand emphasized those aspects of the mandate that were purely educational or informational. They were keen to prevent the IGF from becoming a starting point for disturbing the status quo. They were loath to allow it to criticize, assess, or scrutinize existing international organizations that touch upon Internet governance. They objected strongly to any attempt to get the IGF to adopt resolutions, official statements, or recommendations—and backed up those objections with threats of exit. Proponents of a weaker forum initially conceived of the IGF as an annual collection of presentations and discussions, and nothing more.

Western, developed country governments tend to be forum doves. So are most multinational business interests and the status quo Internet governance organizations such as the Internet Society, ICANN, the regional Internet address registries (RIRs), and major European ccTLD registries. They tended to view the IGF as a single annual event, and did not support the creation of an ongoing infrastructure of working groups and bottom-up policy development. Existing intergovernmental organizations also did not support the idea of building a policy development process into the IGF, tending to view it as encroachment on their turf. As the forum matured, however, a new class of forum dove emerged. Rather than seeing the IGF as a threat to be contained, they have begun to actively embrace the opportunities it affords to promote their own view of Internet self-governance. This has led to the proliferation of national or regional IGFs.

6. See Milton Mueller and John Mathiason, "Building an Internet Governance Forum," Internet Governance Project, Paper IGP06–001, February 3, 2006, http:// Internetgovernance.org/pdf/igp-forum.pdf. See also the Internet Governance Forum Input Statement of the Multistakeholder Modalities Working Group (MMWG), February 26, 2006, http://www.intgovforum.org/contributions/Internet%20Governance%20Forum%20Input%20Statement1.pdf.

Is the IGF a Decoy?

There is no clear model for the IGF. The OECD is sometimes mentioned because of its emphasis on policy research and its occasional ability to serve as the nexus for negotiating soft-law norms that can be globally applied.[7] But this analogy cannot be taken very far, because the OECD is an intergovernmental organization with a well-defined and limited membership. Even with its advisory committees for business and labor, and its recent overtures to civil society, the OECD is a traditional, hierarchical organization where governments make the decisions and the participation of other sectors is strictly segregated.[8]

The Internet Engineering Task Force (IETF) is another oft-cited model. The IETF is a private sector platform for technical experts who converge around the well-defined and narrower problem of developing technical standards. Like the IGF, the IETF must deal with the problems of open participation and strive for structured process without membership and voting. But the IETF cannot avoid making specific recommendations and agreeing on specific documents; its whole purpose is to "negotiate texts." Insofar as they are followed, these standards documents directly affect how the Internet works. Thus, insofar as the IETF is used as a model, it is a model that lends itself to the agenda of forum hawks. The difference, of course, is that IETF standards are not attempts to establish public policy. Although standardization has its political dimensions, there are qualitative differences between expert agreement on a technical standard and public policy agreements among contentious stakeholders. So the IETF is a model of limited applicability as well.

Perhaps the closest analog to IGF is the UN Forestry Forum. Deforestation is a longstanding transnational issue. Just as WSIS failed to create a legally binding agreement on Internet governance, so after many multilateral

7. Speaking at the first public consultation on the IGF, an OECD representative stated, "the OECD is in fact a multistakeholder group such as what the IGF will be as well. We enjoy the active and diverse participation of many groups in our work. . . . we see consensus on issues at the OECD that are nonbinding but in fact, bring with them moral pressure for countries to adopt them. In this sense, I think the functioning of the OECD may represent a model for the IGF." Transcript of the IGF public consultation, February 16, 2006, http://www.intgovforum.org/contributions/IGF-1-0216.txt.

8. The example of IGF has, however, put pressure on OECD (and other organizations, such as ITU) to open up more to multistakeholderism. At its 2008 Ministerial on the Future of the Internet, the OECD ICCP section agreed to institutionalize the participation of "civil society" via one of its advisory committees.

meetings over a period of ten years, states failed to create a legally binding agreement on forest management. Instead, in the year 2000 they created a multistakeholder discussion forum, the United Nations Forum on Forests (UNFF). Political scientist Radoslav Dimitrov views the creation of the UNFF as a fascinating paradox. In an area of policy where no international agreement seemed possible, "governments not only continue the talks but also create international institutions [that are] are purposefully stripped of policy-making capacity. . . . One would not expect proponents of multi-lateral action to seek utterly impotent institutions and [one would not expect] opponents of multilateral action to propose institutions in the first place!"[9]

Dimitrov explains this paradox by observing that states and other transnational actors adhere strongly to a "norm of environmental multilateralism"—the belief that governments should address global eco-logical issues in a collective, multilateral manner. So while divergent interests undermine global agreement on policy, the norm of multilateral-ism pressures governments to remain engaged in international discussions and show tangible results from them. According to Dimitrov, states squared this circle by creating a hollow institution. The UNFF maintains the *appearance* of multilateral engagement on forestry issues while serving as a substitute for any real action. Policy makers spend entire days reiter-ating their support for healthy forests, sustainable forest management practices, and environmental values while repeatedly failing to reach any substantive agreement on policies to advance those goals. Dimitrov's theory suggests that even if norms and agreements do emerge from the multistakeholder discussions in rhetoric or on paper, they will not be implemented because of the underlying conflicts that prevented govern-ments from agreeing in the first place. The conclusions he draws are strong, and negative: The UNFF is a "decoy deliberately designed to preempt governance," an "institutional excuse of governments for not having an international forest policy."[10] The end result is a "waste of financial resources, time, and institutional energy."[11] This is a harsh but appropriately strict standard against which to assess the IGF. Is the IGF nothing more than governments' "institutional excuse" for not having a global Internet policy?

9. Dimitrov 2005, 2.
10. Ibid., 20.
11. Ibid., 19.

The IGF So Far: Politics Shaping Institutions

That question is best answered empirically, by examining the evolution of the IGF in its first four years. The political equilibrium evident in the choices made by the organizers of the forum illuminates the way in which the IGF institutionalizes a global politics of Internet governance. After four years of experience with the IGF, we know that the seemingly simple act of bringing people from government, business, and civil society together for nonbinding dialogue about policy can be intensely political. And we know that these politics are "real" because the parties invest significant resources in them.[12]

Three kinds of politics can be discerned in the IGF. There is, first, a politics of *agenda setting*. The contentious parties bargain and compete over what problems should be elevated to public attention; over the balance or mix of views that are expressed; over who will be allowed to speak in plenary sessions and workshops. Second, there is a politics of *representation*, in which stakeholder groups push to maximize their presence on the forum's "Multistakeholder Advisory Group" (MAG). The MAG, which serves as a program-planning committee and as an interface between the IGF Secretariat and its community of engaged participants led inexorably to ongoing contention over who would be on it. Third, underlying the shadowboxing over agendas and representation are deeper divisions over the actors' *principles* regarding the nature of global Internet governance and the role of the IGF in it. This refers to the divide between forum hawks and doves, and reflects the unresolved tensions in the political bargain that created the IGF.

The Politics of Representation
The IGF's charter, the Tunis Agenda, does not explicitly call for the creation of an advisory group, saying merely that the forum should be run in an "open and inclusive" manner. But in the earliest stages of its formation the UN and other parties suggested the creation of a multistakeholder

12. In particular, established Internet governance bodies such as ICANN and the regional Internet address registries (RIRs) have all taken a keen interest in maintaining a presence in the IGF and in defending their interests against possible threats that might emerge around it. International organizations such as OECD and ITU also are developing a partially competitive, partially complementary relationship to it.

body, variously referred to as an "advisory group," "program committee" or "steering committee," to help it develop the agenda and content of its meetings.[13]

The prospect of an advisory group immediately raised three structural issues: How big should it be? How should its members be appointed? How should the "seats" in this group be distributed among the political groups involved? Civil society actors pushed for a more heavily institutionalized solution emphasizing self-governance. They wanted a small, multistakeholder committee to assist the Secretariat, and they wanted each sector to select its own representatives using the remnants of WSIS structures as an "electorate." They proposed giving each sector (governments, business, civil society) one third of the seats. Some civil society entities also proposed that such a body would eventually elect the coordinator and chair of the IGF.[14] Business stakeholders also supported a smaller and evenly balanced group. They were less comfortable with the vision of participatory democracy, however, preferring to give the Secretariat the discretion to make selections based on external nominations.

National governments in the G77 countries and China took a different view. Like the civil society hawks they pushed for a more heavily institutionalized solution, but one that followed a traditional intergovernmental pattern. The IGF in their view should be supervised by three distinct UN bureaus: one for governments, one for business, and one for civil society. Civil society actors, business interests, and developed country governments all strongly opposed this proposal.

After a long consultation process that fed nominations to the Secretariat, the UN Secretary General appointed a unified MAG consisting of forty members and seven "special advisors"—about the same size as the WGIG. In an outcome that disappointed many of the civil society advocates promoting democratic norms, it became increasingly clear that there would be no bottom-up selection of representatives but rather a model of *nomination* to the Secretariat, which would then have almost complete discretion to make up a list of recommendations to be approved by the

13. "Secretary-General Establishes Advisory Group to Assist Him in Convening Internet Governance Forum," UN Press Release, SG/A/1006, PI/1717 (May 17, 2006), http://www.un.org/News/Press/docs//2006/sga1006.doc.htm.
14. Milton Mueller and John Mathiason, "Building an Internet Governance Forum," Internet Governance Project, Paper IGP06–001, February 3, 2006, http://Internet-governance.org/pdf/igp-forum.pdf.

UN Secretary-General. The process by which the Secretariat selected its favored nominees was entirely opaque.[15]

The Secretariat's actual selections raised eyebrows as much as the process. In the initial MAG selection, half of the positions were set aside for governments. Another surprising but revealing result was that, of the twenty nongovernmental positions, all but a handful were directly associated with ICANN regime insiders. Three were sitting ICANN board members; one was an ICANN staff member; two more were former ICANN board members situated in private business; two were major ccTLD operators; and two others were drawn from RIRs. There was an IETF representative often utilized by ICANN as a consultant, the Internet Society's public policy advocate,[16] and the former U.S. Commerce Department official who had been in charge of ICANN oversight during WSIS, and had since become a lobbyist for the Entertainment Software Association. Intensive behind-the-scenes lobbying by the supporters of the Internet Society and ICANN contributed to this result. It did not hurt that ICANN had pledged to provide U.S. $200,000 to support the IGF.

A later agreement to rotate positions on the MAG intensified debates over representation. The debate was most vivid among civil society actors, both because they had gotten the short end of the stick the first time around, and because the boundaries separating civil society from other sectors were often the most difficult to discern. An Internet Governance Caucus statement prepared for the February 2008 consultation complained about the limited representation of civil society and called for more balanced distribution.[17] But that statement only emerged after civil society networks spent countless hours debating the degree to which people associated with or employed by private-sector Internet governance entities (which tended to refer to themselves as the "Internet technical community") could be classified as, or nominated as representatives of, civil society.[18] People employed by or closely associated with this so-called

15. As one civil society activist complained, "In no sense could the Secretariat's selection of candidates for the Advisory Group, in a closed process pursuant to criteria that were never published, be described as consensual or democratic." Malcolm 2008.
16. ISOC is the corporate parent of the IETF, the owner of the .org registry and a backer of ICANN.
17. "Civil society has been under represented in the multi-stakeholder advisory groups appointed in 2006 and 2007, this anomaly should be corrected in this round of rotation." Civil Society Internet Governance Caucus's Inputs for the Open IGF Consultations, Geneva, February, 26, 2008, http://www.igcaucus.org/node/9.
18. See archives of governance list, http://lists.cpsr.org/lists/info/governance.

Internet technical community insisted that they were part of nongovernmental voluntary associations, and that ICANN and the RIRs were nonprofit organizations and thus part of civil society. Their opponents,
however, saw these people and their arguments as stalking horses for organizations with a vested interest in maintaining the status quo and in
insulating themselves against independent criticism that might emerge
from the IGF.[19] These discussions revealed the problems inherent in using
the "sector-stakeholder" concept as the basis for political representation.

The Politics of Agenda Setting

Similar alignments emerged around debates over the IGF's substantive
agenda. Initially, forum doves pushed to avoid controversial issues and
limit discussion to less threatening topics such as "development" and
"capacity building." Advocates of a stronger forum wanted an open, expansive agenda and hoped to embrace contentious topics in order to make
progress on them.

Contention around the IGF agenda was driven especially by the degree
to which actors wanted the forum to engage with the unresolved issues of
WSIS; specifically, management of "critical Internet resources" (i.e., ICANN
issues) and the Tunis Agenda's call for "enhanced cooperation" (code
words for efforts to ameliorate or reform U.S. unilateralism in Internet
governance). Also, forum hawks in civil society pushed for agenda items
that put the IGF in the role of assessing the conformity of other international institutions to the Geneva Principles of WSIS, while forum doves
wanted to confine it to topics that did not "duplicate" or "overlap" with
other institutions, most especially ICANN and WIPO.

The agenda of the first IGF annual meeting in Athens was very dovish
in nature. With an overriding focus on "Internet Governance and
Development," plenary sessions were organized around four generic
themes: openness, access, security, and diversity. Although *openness* as
a theme encompassed the issues of censorship and free expression, and
security likewise raised the contentious privacy-security tradeoff, none

19. These suspicions were fueled by the ISOC-led technical community's earlier
history. ISOC members had insisted, first, that there was no such thing as "Internet
governance," only "technical coordination"; when that myth was exploded they
reverted to the view that there was no need for an Internet governance forum; when
the IGF was established and began to be taken seriously they lobbied heavily to
populate the MAG and insisted that the IGF should confine its attention to promoting physical access in developing countries and conveyance of best practices, and
avoid policy issues associated with critical Internet resources.

of the themes easily encompassed the debates over control of critical Internet resources, enhanced cooperation, or global intellectual property protection.

However, the IGF also created a space for participant-proposed and organized workshops. Although they occupied a less prominent place in the agenda, the topics, format, and speakers at IGF workshops were under the control of the participants who proposed them, and thus could reflect controversial themes. At the first IGF session, a very liberal approach to approving workshop proposals was taken. The IGF Secretariat insisted only on multistakeholder participation and did not reject any of them based on the type of policy issue addressed.[20]

After the Athens meeting, pressure from developing country governments and civil society forced the Secretariat and the other stakeholders to abandon their attempt to keep critical Internet resource-related issues off the IGF agenda. Forum hawks in civil society and government united to advocate inclusion of a dedicated agenda item on governance of "Critical Internet Resources" at all future IGF meetings. Critical Internet resources duly became one of the IGF's officially recognized themes at Rio de Janeiro, the location of the second annual IGF meeting.[21] The plenary session on that topic attracted the largest attendance and stimulated some of the most interesting exchanges of the Rio meeting. These exchanges refuted fears that public discussion of the topic in the context of UN-sponsored meetings would be destructive. If anything, the issues had been defused, given that no clear alternatives to the current regime surfaced as consensus points.

Enhanced cooperation, another issue linking the IGF to WSIS and the Tunis Agenda, also tested the limits of the forum's agenda-setting

20. For example, the Internet Governance Project and Third World Network pioneered discussion of critical Internet resources by hosting a workshop on Domain Name System Security Extensions (DNSSEC) and its impact on the management of the root zone file. IGP workshop report, "New Technical and Policy Challenges in DNS Root Zone Management," Athens, Greece, http://internetgovernance.org/pdf/DNS_Workshop_Report-edit1.pdf.
21. The composition of the panel on critical Internet resources was so hotly contested (and the MAG so badly organized) that some of the speakers did not know whether they would be on it or not until about ten days before the event. In an amusing example of the Internet establishment's continuing efforts to preempt discussion, many of their spokespersons then attempted to define as "critical Internet resources" virtually anything that could possibly affect Internet access in a country, such as electric power supply.

politics.[22] In early consultations on the IGF's agenda, the European Union insisted that "enhanced cooperation" should *not* be discussed within the forum, and implied that it should be confined to a separate, purely intergovernmental process. This position received support from Australia and the tacit assent of the United States, but led to strong objections from forum hawks in civil society and from other governments.

As the IGF's agenda progressed over the next two years, forum hawks repeatedly pressed for an explanation of what had happened to the enhanced cooperation process called for in the Tunis Agenda. All they got, in the end, was an explanation from Nitin Desai, the chair of the IGF, that "for six months, I personally met with people to find out whether there could be some basis, some common ground which could be found for a process, leaving it very flexible and elastic as to what this process could be. . . . And the fact is that there isn't that common ground as yet."[23] This suggests that there was no change in the EU-U.S. division over internationalization of U.S. oversight of the Internet's name and address roots, and that those two great powers did not want the issue to be taken up by the IGF. Still, the third IGF meeting in 2008 in Hyderabad, India, had a plenary session devoted to the topic. What enhanced cooperation has come to mean in practice is the idea of making special outreach efforts and creating new interfaces between states and the Internet technical community.

From Athens to Rio to Hyderabad there was significant growth in the number of workshop proposals put forward by stakeholder groups. At the same time, it became evident in the IGF's second year that the blander plenary sessions put together by the MAG and the Secretariat attracted fewer attendees than the workshops in aggregate. The IGF participants began to learn that the many workshops were more focused and relevant than the program content served up by the politicized gatekeepers in the MAG. The forum also instituted a new class of workshops, known as Open Forums, where incumbent international institutions would explain their activities. While the agenda of these workshops were largely under the control of the incumbent institutions, they did accommodate the Tunis

22. The Iranian government spokesperson said that enhanced cooperation is "in the Tunis document to enable governments on an equal footing to carry out their roles and responsibilities in international public policy issues pertaining to the Internet." Transcript of 2007 Preparatory meeting, Geneva, May 23, http://intgovforum.org/May_contributions/IGF-23May07Consultation.txt.
23. "Internet Governance Forum Consultations Wednesday 23 May 2007 10:00 a.m.," http://www.intgovforum.org/May_contributions/IGF-23May07Consultation.txt.

Agenda's calls for integration with other international organizations (table 6.1).

The thawing politics of agenda setting has contributed to the emergence of a more moderate class of forum dove, exemplified by Great Britain's Nominet UK, the domain name registry that operates the successful .uk country code top-level domain. From Rio onward these more relaxed doves and similar status quo interests, including ICANN itself, have put more emphasis on using the IGF as a way to promote their views of policy issues and governance structures. Nominet has even gone so far as to support and sponsor a national-level Internet Governance Forum in Great Britain that acts as a preparatory meeting to the global meeting. Similar national and regional IGF preparatory processes now exist in Europe, Africa, and Latin America.[24] And in 2009, U.S. business interests initiated efforts to create an American IGF.

The Politics of Principles (Outcomes)

The emphasis in the first IGF meeting was on facilitating equal-status interactions among representatives of governments, business, and civil society. While this worked well, it also meant avoiding any joint conclusions or declarations; the Secretariat merely passively recorded, summarized and published what was said and done.

With the preparations for the second IGF meeting came a push for stronger outcomes, led by forum hawks among developing states and civil

Table 6.1
Attendance and participation at IGF

	Athens	Rio de Janeiro	Hyderabad
Attendance	500	1,360	1,280
Workshops proposed	40	55	104
Workshops accepted	37	36	64
Open forums	0	8	6
Best practice forums	0	23	12
Dynamic coalitions		11	4

24. Uganda holds a National Internet Governance Forum Consultative Workshop; UNECA sponsors a regional effort for Africa. The Brazilian Internet Governance Steering Committee (CGI.br), a state-sponsored multistakeholder effort in effect since 2003, provides similar support in Latin America. The Caribbean Internet Governance Forum is another multistakeholder effort.

society. The government of Brazil, in particular, began to stress the need for some kind of agreed statement as a product of the forum. There is evidence that Brazil attempted to use its position as host of the Rio de Janeiro meeting to reshape the IGF into a more hawkish mold.[25] In consultations it pushed for more formal outcomes, and some private sector interests worried that it planned to produce a "Rio statement on Internet Governance." At a Geneva preparatory meeting Russia, too, called for the adoption of "a concluding document which would show international agreement on Internet issues and show how far the international community understands Internet issues."[26]

Civil society focused less on concluding documents and more on the issue of recommendations. Some advocacy groups noted the precedent of the WGIG, whose report had made recommendations generally acknowledged to be constructive. Civil society advocates also advocated a process to formalize the criteria for recognizing Dynamic Coalitions, which were supposed to be multistakeholder coalitions organized around specific policy positions or perspectives. They also pushed to link the IGF's agenda directly to bottom-up processes, giving forum participants a more direct agenda-setting power. Recognition of the need for stronger outcomes was reflected by Chairman Desai's summary of post-Athens stocktaking consultation: "You can't carry on for five years just doing education and awareness . . . something has to emerge out of this process of dialogue. This is not a negotiating process. It definitely is not an executive process. . . . But it must have a structure, a format and an outcome, if you like, which is capable of influencing things which can lead to real results at the ground level."[27] But there was also strong resistance to this tack from forum doves. As the push for stronger outcomes gathered momentum in 2007, Chris Disspain of the Australian country code registry sent a private message (that was quickly leaked) to Markus Kummer, Desai, and the MAG. The email noted with alarm the apparent agreement on "final recommendations arising from the IGF," equating such recommendations with "a negotiated document." Disspain claimed that this was "unacceptable to the majority of nongovernment [i.e., private business sector] people here"

25. Brazil appointed a "co-chair" alongside Nitin Desai, and stuffed the MAG with a large number of "special advisors."
26. Transcript of "Internet Governance Forum Consultations Wednesday 23 May 2007," http://www.intgovforum.org/May_contributions/IGF-23May07Consultation .txt.
27. Nitin Desai, transcript of the February 13, 2007, IFG Consultations, Geneva, Switzerland, http://intgovforum.org/Feb_igf_meeting/13_February_Consult_2007.txt.

and threatened "there is a grave danger that financial support and general involvement of nongovernment participants will be withdrawn."[28] This was an explicit threat of exit, and it proved effective. The IGF Secretariat dropped the subject of outcomes, and Brazil's recommendations for more formal outcomes were not followed up.

In the years following this turning point, the exit threat of the ICANN regime defenders was matched by similar threats from state-actor forum hawks. At an ICANN meeting in March 2008, a speech by the ITU's secretary-general dismissed the IGF as "a waste of time." At the Hyderabad IGF meeting, a representative of China threatened to vote against the continuation of the IGF in the UN General Assembly unless it more directly addressed and took action on the unsolved WSIS issues.[29] Later, China announced that it would vote against continuation of the IGF.[30]

The IGF as "Network"

The intent and design of the IGF conform closely to the model of a "global public policy network." It can be seen as a relatively nonhierarchical way of mobilizing resources and knowledge that are dispersed across public and private actors, and as a way of facilitating the consensus and legitimacy needed to develop and implement policy in other arenas. The IGF institutionalizes our recognition that authority over Internet governance is highly distributed and therefore can benefit from nonbinding forms of association among relevant actors—associations that facilitate information sharing, creative deliberation, and cooperation—if not actual governance.

Implementation of this concept, however, requires a mixture of formal organization and open networking. Where formal organization exists, so

28. Cited in Malcolm 2008, 387–388.
29. "China threatens to leave IGF," *Internet Governance Project* blog, December 5, 2008, http://blog.Internetgovernance.org/blog/_archives/2008/12/5/4008174.html.
30. "So we repeat that the delegation of China does not agree with extending the mission of the IGF beyond the five years. We feel that after the five years are up, we would need to look at the results that have been achieved. And we need, then, to launch into an intergovernmental discussion." Transcript of the May 13 Open Consultations of the Internet Governance Forum, http://www.intgovforum.org/cms/index.php/component/content/article/71-transcripts-/410-transcript-of-the-13-may-open-consultations-.

do the traditional constraints of "institutionalized joint decision making."[31] The need to agree upon a common agenda, to select a few panelists to be given privileged speaking slots, or the elevation of a few individuals to the status of members of an advisory group generates very traditional forms of political and distributional conflict. Program planning and MAG representation require binding joint decisions, and it is evident from the discussion in this chapter that these areas have animated the most intense IGF politics. And yet these are not a politics of Internet governance per se; they are a politics of the IGF itself. These conflicts over the agenda and representation, however, are rooted in deeper differences over how the Internet should be governed and what the role of the different stakeholder groups should be in it.

Nevertheless, the IGF is the organizational capstone of a transnational policy network. As such, it is still highly susceptible to the dynamics of network formation, growth, and collapse. Its design and its activities must succeed in holding the parties together and bringing new ones in. But the ties and commitments involved are relatively weak. While entry into the process is easy and relatively cost free, so is exit.

The success or failure of the IGF, therefore, hinges on a logic of network effects. Following the well-known network analysis principle that "popularity is attractive,"[32] a successful IGF will trigger a positive feedback process in which contentious parties progressively become interdependent parts of a self-sustaining and productive global policy network with IGF at its center. Its meetings need to generate associative clusters that facilitate fruitful interactions among the dispersed and heterogeneous actors who have authority or influence over small parts of the Internet. If it succeeds at this, the IGF will then attract more participants by virtue of its prior success. This in turn will reinforce further engagement and participation, as important stakeholders in Internet governance come to feel that they cannot afford *not* to be present in its meetings and discussions. This will make the IGF a magnet for further advocacy and for policy entrepreneurs. A key assumption of this vision of growth, however, is that the agreements, bargains, bottom-up norm setting, and policy development that occur through the forum will influence organizations and institutions with

31. Scharpf 1993 discusses decisions that require unanimous agreement or some kind of majority vote, which he calls "institutionalized joint decision systems" (143). He emphasizes the "cumbersome, difficult to manage and easy to block" nature of joint-decision systems in the network context.
32. Dorogovtsev and Mendes 2003, chapter 2.

harder forms of power over global communications and change their conduct. That means it must attract serious participation from network operators and content/application providers as well as from national governments, international organizations, and advocacy groups.

The IGF has not yet made this breakthrough. The biggest problem is that it has failed to attract to its policy network actors with operational control over parts of the Internet. Major industry players tend to act as observers; ICANN and other major institutional actors tend to enter the IGF as promoters or passive defenders of their predetermined organizational interests rather than as negotiators seeking new, complementary relationships. There is no evidence that key players in the industry view the forum as an indispensable platform for affiliating with other actors and for influencing their decisions. Meanwhile, hard-core prosovereignty nation-states like China are becoming openly dissatisfied with the IGF and are turning back to the more traditional, intergovernmental forum of the ITU.

The IGF must make sure that its policy network does not reach a tipping point where a major group of actors chooses to exit, provoking an accelerating cascade of exits by other actors. It is not hard to imagine scenarios in which the IGF loses the allegiance and participation of key actors. The forum could come to be perceived as nothing more than a platform for civil society advocacy groups, and lose the participation of governments or businesses or both. Vested interests in existing international Internet governance regimes, such as ICANN, could become too powerful and exercise a preemptive influence over its activities, triggering exit from some governments and civil society. An equivalent danger is that the IGF will become dominated by governments and UN-style intergovernmental politics. As China's viable threat of exit demonstrates, the IGF already teeters on the brink of an imbalance that might lead to the exit of certain states.

The IGF's persistently unsatisfactory approach to programming its plenary sessions is related to the fact that the problem of *outcomes* or *principles* is stuck in a stalemate. A key faction in the forum (the Internet Society/ICANN network) uses it in a way that corresponds exactly to Dimitrov's critique of the UN Forestry Forum: it serves a preemptive function and as an "institutional excuse for not having a global [Internet] policy." The tension between IGF's status as a nonbinding discussion arena and its need to have some impact on global governance is fundamental to its makeup. The reason the plenary sessions are so desultory is that the IGF still does not know how to bridge that gap. At best, general plenary sessions could be the means of forging agreements via deliberation and common discussion, and of airing fundamental disagreements in a way that would lead to some movement on how to overcome them. As of now, the sessions are little more than presentations that conform to a lowest-common-denominator logic that can gain consensus in the MAG.

Experience with the IGF also clarifies some important distinctions between networked governance and multistakeholderism. Insofar as it is open, networked governance is not limited to any particular stakeholder group or sector. In that sense, networked governance produces multistakeholder participation. But the reverse is not true. The mere act of putting representatives of government, business, and civil society in the same room to engage in nonbinding dialogue does not necessarily contribute anything valuable to global Internet governance. At best, networked governance perceives differences among stakeholders not as rigid categories that demand proportional positions in a formal representational scheme, but as complementary resources—unique pieces in a puzzle that, if assembled, can solve a problem. If the IGF can only offer a formalized multistakeholderism, it will either fail outright or gradually fade into irrelevance and obscurity.

The most tangible outcome of the IGF so far is the reproduction of its institutional assumptions at the national and regional levels. The proliferation of regional or national Internet governance forums has the potential to broaden the coral reef, but until and unless the global forum's participants succeed in triggering creative transactions and associations that solve problems other venues can't, reproducing the IGF experiment on smaller scales won't accomplish much.

III   Drivers of Internet Governance

7   IP versus IP

As Internet protocol began to spread virally over telecommunication networks in the early 1990s, a T-shirt sported by Vint Cerf, one of the inventors of the protocol, proudly proclaimed "IP on everything!" A few years later, Cerf's T-shirt motto became "Everything on IP!" as he celebrated the coming together of all modes of communication—voice, data, video—on the Internet platform.[1]

To Cerf, IP meant *Internet protocol*. But to most lawyers IP has a different connotation. It is an acronym for *intellectual property*: a contested umbrella term[2] that encompasses the law of copyrights, trademarks, and patents. Until about 1994, the two IPs occupied completely separate worlds. Since then, the conjunction and clash of the two has become one of the main drivers of the global politics of Internet governance. There is an ongoing struggle between the Internet's ability to facilitate open networking and information sharing on a borderless basis and the attempts of the owners of trademarked names and digitized content to build legal and technical fences around their assets. Property rights require boundaries; inherent in the nature of property is the ability of the owner to exclude others from benefits so that they can make profitable exchanges. In the modern world, states are the primary enforcers of said boundaries and they, too, are founded on boundaries, an exclusivity over the power to legislate and

1. The T-shirts were worn at conferences of the Internet Engineering Task Force (IETF). A picture of Cerf wearing one can still be found on the Internet at http://www.pcmag.com/encyclopedia_term/0,2542,t=IP+on+Everything&i=45362,00.asp.
2. In particular, Richard Stallman of the Free Software Foundation has mounted a crusade against the term intellectual property. According to Stallman, patent, copyright, and trademark law "originated separately, evolved differently, cover different activities, have different rules, and raise different public policy issues." In Stallman's article "Did you say 'intellectual property'? It's a seductive mirage," *Third World Network*, 2004, http://www.twnside.org.sg/title2/twr171g.htm.

police. Thus, the IP vs. IP conflict also provides a key arena in which
national politics and power structures intersect with the global politics of
Internet governance.

There is a vast literature on the legal, cultural, and political aspects of
copyright protection in the digital age,[3] and a sizable scholarly and professional literature on trademarks and the Internet.[4] Likewise, nonproprietary
or "free" software has inspired an avalanche of scholarly analysis and
popular writing.[5] Oddly, however, those problems are rarely if ever grouped
together and understood holistically as an aspect of Internet governance.
It's as if we were so focused on fish that we've lost sight of the ocean. The
report of the UN Working Group on Internet Governance was symptom-
atic. It listed intellectual property rights ninth in a list of thirteen "public
policy issues that are relevant to Internet governance." The relationship
between Internet governance and intellectual property was classified with
trade as a public policy issue that is "relevant to the Internet" but that has
"an impact much wider than the Internet and for which existing organizations are responsible."[6]

While not exactly incorrect, the WGIG's treatment of the issue massively understated both the centrality of intellectual property to the governance of the Internet, and the importance of the Internet to the future
of intellectual property. If anything, the IP vs. IP struggles exceed the
ICANN controversies in their shaping impact on Internet governance. The
WGIG report also failed to appreciate the degree to which the problem of
intellectual property on the Internet has eroded neat sectoral categories of
responsibility for different policy domains among existing international
organizations. It brings together concerns about trade, human rights, and
Internet security as well as copyright and trademark. In fact, those aware
of the behind-the-scenes politics know that the reference to "existing
organizations" in the WGIG report came from status quo-oriented intellectual property interests and states. They wanted to ensure that responsibility for global intellectual property governance remained safely within
entities such as WIPO (World Intellectual Property Organization) and the
WTO (World Trade Organization), where they felt that things were pretty

3. Boyle 1996 and 1997; Litman 2001; Vaidhyanathan 2001; Landes and Posner
2003; Lessig 2001 and 2005; Elkin-Koren 2005. See also the extensive oeuvre of
Pamela Samuelson at http://people.ischool.berkeley.edu/~pam/papers.html.
4. Burk 1995; Froomkin 2002 and 2004; Litman 2000.
5. In addition to those already cited there is Stallman 2002; Williams 2002; Crowston
and Howison 2005; Elliott and Scacchi 2008; Weber 2004; and many others.
6. WGIG 2005, paragraphs 23 and 13(c), respectively.

much under control. Classifying intellectual property policy as part of a broader domain of "Internet governance" might have encouraged multi-stakeholder institutions such as the IGF to take a fresh look at the tradeoffs between intellectual property protection and other values, such as freedom of expression, privacy, development, and competition policy, which might undermine the political equilibrium. To this day, intellectual property issues have been successfully kept off the IGF's agenda.

But there is no way around it: most of the recent political and policy battles over intellectual property rights are about *the Internet*. Copyright? The Internet is a gigantic, globally distributed, always-on copying machine. It offers perfect reproduction of digital materials for an incremental cost of practically zero. It is also the most powerful mechanism in history for locating and retrieving information that you might want to copy, no matter how remote or obscure, and for facilitating the sharing of it with limitless others. Accordingly, the institutional solutions to copyright problems in the digital age increasingly involve regulating the suppliers and users of public Internet services. Trademark? The names, brands, links, taxonomies, registers, and indexes that really matter in the contemporary age are those that function on the Internet. This is true of names that may or may not be protected by existing laws, such as country names, place names, or personal names. What matters now is not whether there is some abstract legal or economic rationale for protecting them, but how much economic impact their protection might have given the prominence of the Internet. And thus many if not most of the institutional solutions to trademark issues involve regulating the identifiers people can claim and use on the Internet. To govern copyright and trademark in the digital world is to govern the Internet.

The issue of patents, of course, does go well beyond the Internet in scope, as it encompasses (as yet) undigitizable *things*: pharmaceuticals, genetically engineered life forms, machinery. But the problem of software patents is central to Internet governance, too. For many years, the organizations that govern Internet standards, primarily the IETF and World Wide Web Consortium, have tried to steer clear of proprietary software and avoid technical standards based on patented technologies. The movement for free/open source software, something we consider later, has some of its deepest roots in the communities of software developers who built the Internet. The argument is that patent boundaries threaten the openness of the Internet.

This chapter brings to the foreground the problem of intellectual property protection as a formative influence on Internet governance. It begins with some underappreciated historical background about the relationship between global liberalization policies in telecommunications and the simultaneous attempt to globalize the collection of royalties for intellectual property. It then explores the intersection and clash between the two IPs from the mid-1990s to the present. Contention around intellectual property emerges as one of the key drivers of the global politics of Internet governance. The narrative calls attention to two features of this contention in particular. One is the growing attempt by copyright owners to push the responsibility for policing intellectual property rights onto Internet service providers. The other is the emergence of a transnational social movement promoting "access to knowledge" as a countervailing force to the globally coordinated lobbying of multinational copyright, trademark, and patent holders.

Trade, TRIPS, and Telecommunications

Two parallel processes that began in the United States in the 1980s set the stage for the meeting of the two IPs. One was the liberalization of the telecommunications industry, which paved the way for the spread of a distributed and free Internet; the other was a concerted effort to globalize the protection of intellectual property rights. Although both came to center on trade policy, before 1993 the dramatic changes in telecommunications and intellectual property protection were trains running on separate tracks. Each was a separate and distinct process, driven by different institutional and interest group dynamics.

Telecommunications Liberalization
As noted at the beginning of chapter 4, the United States began to liberalize its telecommunications industry in the 1970s. In the 1980s it broke up the AT&T system and unbundled the public network into separate but interconnected elements to spur competition, innovation, and new entry. As the United States sought to spread telecom liberalization to international markets, it perceived the International Telecommunication Union (ITU) as an obstacle to that goal. The ITU, the world's oldest international organization, was at the time dominated by national telephone monopolies in Europe and by protectionist developing countries. In its quest to create a new liberalized global order in the sector, the United States shifted the rule-making power for telecommunications away from the ITU toward a new institution, the World Trade Organization.[7] It used the concept of

7. Drake and Nicolaidis 1992; Drake 2000; Cowhey 1990; Cowhey, Aronson, and Richards 2009.

"trade in services" as the rationale for opening international telecommunication markets to competition. In 1997 it achieved agreement on a sweeping free trade in basic telecommunication services pact.[8] This occurred only a few months after a trade agreement on information technology equipment.[9]

Telecommunications was globalized by a combination of domestic industry liberalization and free trade agreements for equipment and services. But as noted before, it was the growth of the Internet after 1995 that really benefited from and consolidated the gains of global liberalization. The widely diffused model of fostering competition in value-added information services allowed almost anyone to enter the market for Internet service without burdensome permissions.[10] There is a strong correlation between the degree to which countries have liberalized their telecommunication sector, the growth of the sector, widespread diffusion of telecommunications, and the level of Internet penetration.

The TRIPS Regime

During roughly the same period, the United States also linked intellectual property protection to the trade regime. A 1962 amendment to the U.S. trade law, known as Section 301, gave the president the power to unilaterally retaliate against countries that had "unreasonable" limits on imports from the United States. In 1984, intellectual property interests succeeded in getting the U.S. government to add "inadequate protection for intellectual property" to the list of "unreasonable practices" that could trigger action under Section 301. The IP interests favored the use of trade sanctions

8. Concluded in February 1997, the WTO Agreement on Basic Telecommunications Services (BTA) is an annex to the Fourth Protocol of the General Agreement on Trade and Services (GATS). It was implemented on February 5, 1998.

9. The Declaration on Trade in Information Technology Products (ITA) was concluded by twenty-nine participants at the Singapore Ministerial Conference in December 1996. The ITA provides for participants to completely eliminate duties on IT products covered by the agreement. Developing country participants have been granted extended periods for some products. The number of participants has grown to seventy, representing about 97 percent of world trade in information technology products.

10. Lemley and Lessig (2000) contend that it was a technical design principle—the end-to-end argument—that accounted for the innovation and growth of the Internet. This is partially true, but tends to understate the importance of simple open entry as an economic policy. Countries that had Internet protocols but insisted on monopolistic Internet service provider market structures were not so successful.

because the international treaties specifically devoted to intellectual property had weak enforcement mechanisms.[11] The use of trade sanctions by the United States as the teeth for IP enforcement was strengthened considerably in 1988, when a new Omnibus Foreign Trade and Competitiveness Act moved the power to unilaterally impose trade sanctions from the president to the U.S. Trade Representative's office and created statutory mandates for investigating and sanctioning countries deemed to be violating U.S. intellectual property law. Note that the United States was projecting globally its own standards of IP, and insisted on imposing sanctions even if the acts involved did not violate local law or any negotiated treaties with the countries involved.

The 1994 international treaty on Trade-Related Aspects of Intellectual Property (TRIPS) extended the use of trade sanctions as the leverage for global IP protection from the United States to a multilateral, nearly universal institution: the World Trade Organization. The TRIPS agreement was the culmination of a concerted effort by drug companies, the software industry, and motion picture producers.[12] It established minimum standards for many forms of intellectual property protection and strengthened global enforcement against countries or actors who deviated from those standards. Aggrieved IPR owners or their governments could invoke the WTO's authoritative dispute resolution process to enforce their rights.

There are important parallels and important differences between the globalization of intellectual property protection under TRIPS/Special 301 and the U.S. unilateral globalism that liberalized telecommunications. Both represented an important act of forum shifting by the U.S. government. TRIPS shifted responsibility away from WIPO (which was, like the ITU, a specialized Geneva-based intergovernmental organization) as the international enforcement mechanism for IP matters and relied instead on the trade regime. Both phenomena exemplify a key structural feature of the global political economy of information in the digital age, where the need for a global order is overcome initially through the leadership and market dominance of a single, hegemonic superstate, and only partially through multilateral negotiations among states. Indeed, leftist critics are always happy to link the two processes together as aspects of their own construct, "neoliberalism."

But in reality, both the policy objectives and the effects of market liberalism in telecommunications were directly opposed to those supporting

11. Sell 1998.
12. Drahos 2003.

the globalization of IP protection. Moving international telecommunication policy away from the ITU and into a trade-in-services paradigm
administered by the WTO undermined monopoly power and broke open
markets to new entry and competition. Open telecom markets and open
network architecture paved the way for a decentralized, competitive global
Internet. The linkage of intellectual property to trade, in contrast, was
designed to do just the opposite: to strengthen and globalize state-granted
exclusivities over movies, music, drugs, software, and other kinds of IP.
More than one trade economist viewed the linkage between trade and IP
as an abuse of the WTO and its mission. Free trade advocate Jagdish
Bhagwati, for example, called TRIPS "an astonishing capture of the WTO"
and complained, "the corporate lobbies in pharmaceuticals and software
had distorted and deformed an important multilateral institution, turning
it away from its trade mission and transforming it into a royalty collection
agency."[13] As trade policy in telecommunications was undermining the
monopoly rents associated with decades of closed telecommunication
markets, the subordination of trade to "royalty collection" for IP was doing
just the opposite.

There were, in other words, already inherent tensions between IP and
IP. These quickly became evident when the two intersected in the 1990s.

IP Meets IP

The meeting of the two worlds can be dated fairly precisely. It occurred in
1994, the year Web browsers made the Internet popular; the year the
Clinton administration initiated an effort to reform copyright law as part
of an effort to create a new National Information Infrastructure (NII);[14] the
year the first trademark–domain name litigation occurred in the United
States.[15] These events signaled the beginning of an era in which the fate
of intellectual property and digital networks became totally interdepen-

13. Bhagwati 2004, 183.
14. U.S. Patent Commissioner Bruce Lehman convened a working group in 1993,
which was heavily weighted toward the motion picture industry and other copy-
right-holding interests. Lehman had been a lawyer for Hollywood entertainment
interests. His working group issued its Green Paper in July 1994.
15. *KnowledgeNet Inc. v. David Boone, Network Solutions, Inc., and Digital Express
Group*, U.S. District Court for the Northern District of Illinois, Eastern Division No.
94 C 7 1 95. Another early case involved the registration of kaplan.com by com-
petitor Princeton Review. See "'Address poacher' loses Internet ruling," *San Jose
Mercury News*, October 6, 1994, 1E.

dent. Despite paroxysms of legal and institutional change since then, the relationship remains unstable. Copyright and trademark industry associations are still unhappy with the degree of protection they get; many Internet users and advocates of liberty and privacy are still worried about the intellectual property interests' efforts to engineer controls into the network and its governance institutions.

Digital Copyright and Trademark

The tension is fundamental to digital media. Digital networks collapse the distinction between transmitting, copying, and using information.[16] When you ship a book from one place to another, there is still only one book and you don't have it anymore. When you transmit a digitized text over the Internet, you don't lose it, and the sending and receiving computers and every server and router along the way are creating a perfect reproduction of the copyrighted material in their random access memory, and possibly also in their caches and hard drives. "The riddle is this," says law professor James Boyle: "if our property can be infinitely reproduced and instantaneously distributed all over the planet without cost, without our knowledge, without its even leaving our possession, how can we protect it?"[17]

Digitization destabilized earlier legal and policy bargains over copyright. For users, it vastly expanded opportunities for sharing and using copyrighted information, a potential that has been realized with the "rip and burn" culture and peer-to-peer file sharing of the past decade. For copyright owners, in contrast, digitization created an opportunity to modify or even overthrow traditional concepts of fair use and the first sale doctrine. Every act of accessing a book, song, or movie from a network or physical media like CDs or DVDs might require new permissions from the copyright holder.[18] One could define *fixation in a medium* so expansively that holding a digital object in a computer's temporary memory as part of the act of

16. Vaidhyanathan 2004, 53.
17. Boyle 1997a.
18. As Jessica Litman (2001, 28) put it, "Until now, copyright has regulated multiplication and distribution of works, but it hasn't regulated consumption. If you buy a book, or even borrow a book, you're free to read it as many times as you like. You can loan it to someone else. You can sell it or give it away or even rent it out. You can't make copies of it but you can use it and use it and use it again. But, if every time a work appears in the Random Access Memory of your computer, you are making an actionable copy, then we have for the first time given copyright owners extensive control over the consumption of their works."

Internet browsing would constitute the creation of a legally actionable copy. This extreme view, dubbed "copyright maximalism" by its detractors, would have meant that the very functioning of the network would require Internet service providers to get permission for transmitting copyrighted material over the network. It also suggested that online service providers could be made strictly liable for any copyright violations committed by their subscribers.[19] In fact, strict liability for ISPs became a central feature in the Clinton administration's NII policy and its proposals for international treaties at WIPO.

The Internet also destabilized the policy bargains over trademark protection. With its thoroughly globalized name space, the Internet domain name system fundamentally altered the structure of trademark registration and recognition. Trademarks are based on reputation and consumers' association of names with products and services. But the Internet washed away the spatial and contextual limits that characterized the use of names as source identifiers. Where before the boundaries of geography and industry had made concurrent use of the same names possible without undermining exclusivity, the global connectivity of digital networks collapsed these distinctions and created new forms of contention among users and uses.

The October (1998) Revolution
October 1998 was a watershed in the interaction of the Internet and intellectual property. That was when a first-generation approach to resolving the tensions between them was put into place. The United States passed the Digital Millennium Copyright Act (DMCA). In the same month and year the U.S. Commerce Department provisionally recognized the newly incorporated ICANN, and in conjunction with a WIPO proceeding, made intellectual property protection one of the top priorities for the global management of the Internet's domain name system. Although these changes occurred in one country, the United States, their impact was global. The mechanisms they established either eroded territorial jurisdiction indirectly, transcended it completely, or established models that were followed by other key jurisdictions (sometimes on their own, sometimes under U.S. pressure). One must understand the nature of the bargain that was struck then, and the reasons for its subsequent instability, to understand where we are headed now and the growing pressure at the nation-state level to build surveillance and enforcement mechanisms into the network.

19. Casey 2000.

The new regime gave intellectual property interests some extraordinary benefits. But it did not give the copyright maximalists their strict
liability regime. Instead, the DMCA responded to the demands of the
copyright holders while making important concessions to the Internet
service provider industry and the nascent copyright resistance. The main
features of the DMCA were: decades-long extensions in the time period
for copyright protection; prohibitions on the circumvention of technological measures for securing intellectual property; and an exemption of
ISPs from much of the liability for the actions of their users under
certain conditions. The exemption, however, was contingent upon an
obligation (dubbed *notice and takedown*) to yank infringing materials off
the Internet when notified of their existence. Congress, public interest
groups, and the communications industry rejected strict liability, fearing
that it would raise the cost of access for consumers, or possibly even
destroy the Internet service industry. They also feared that the implied
obligation to monitor transmissions for infringement would hinder
users' freedom of expression and privacy. Notice and takedown was a
halfway house between provider liability and Internet freedom. From the
user perspective, however, notice and takedown can be and has been
abused to suppress speech.[20]

In Europe, a similar bargain was struck. In 2000 the European
Commission promulgated a harmonized set of rules to limit the liability
of ISPs for illegal activities by their customers.[21] Articles 12 and 15 of the
2000 E-Commerce Directive ruled that mere conduits, caching services,
and hosting services are not liable for the information stored or transmitted on the Internet, provided they do not initiate the transmission, exercise
any control over the content of the information, and in the case of caches
and hosts, that they remove or disable access to the information upon

20. Urban and Quilter 2006. In the Netherlands, a local activist posted ancient
public domain materials on multiple Dutch hosting sites and then sent letters com-
plaining that they were copyright infringements to local ISPs. In almost all cases,
ISPs removed the materials no questions asked; some even supplied the name of the
account holder. Only local access provider XS4All respected the rights of its customers enough to question the request and see through it.

21. The EU E-Commerce Directive was partly due to the influence of the WIPO
treaties and partly in response to a German case when a managing director of an
ISP was sentenced to prison for pornography unknowingly held on its servers.
Although the German decision was reversed on appeal, it drew attention to the need
for clear guidelines on the liability of ISPs, especially when they do not have knowledge of the infringing material. Van Eecke and Ooms 2007.

obtaining knowledge of illegal activity.[22] Internet intermediaries can be requested to terminate or prevent specific infringements (e.g., monitoring specific user accounts for a limited time). But the E-Commerce Directive prohibits the imposition of general monitoring requirements on ISPs or the imposition of a general obligation to actively seek the facts or circumstances indicating illegal activity.

The new ICANN–WIPO regime emerged in tandem with these developments in copyright law. Early on, there were efforts to impose strict liability on domain name registries, by making them monitor and evaluate trademark-infringing registrations at the point of registration. But the courts rejected imposing this burden on domain name registries. Instead, the ICANN regime was used to create a globally applicable private arbitration process that allowed trademark owners to quickly and inexpensively challenge and recover domain names registrations outside the court system. The ICANN regime's Uniform Domain Name Dispute Resolution Policy (UDRP) forces every domain name registry and registrar, and thus indirectly every domain name registrant, to bind themselves to this procedure. Although ICANN's direct authority is limited to the so-called generic top-level domains (.com, .net, .org, .info, .mobi, and so on) the UDRP procedure has been imitated by most major country code domain registries.[23]

Just as important as the UDRP is the way ICANN's contracts governing new top-level domain registries have evolved. The addition of new gTLDs was slowed to a trickle, and each new one was forced to institute policies, known as "sunrise periods," which gave incumbent trademark owners a right of first refusal to register second-level domain names corresponding to their trademarks.

The Whois service was another important feature that the ICANN–WIPO regime instituted in response to the intellectual property interests.

22. Directive 2000/31/EC of the European Parliament and the Council of June 8, 2000. The notice and takedown regime of the E-Commerce Directive, however, is not as well-defined as the U.S. procedure, and affords ISPs much less legal certainty.
23. The U.S.-based trademark interests, not content with ICANN's global UDRP process, succeeded in passing the Anticybersquatting Consumer Protection Act (ACPA) in 2000. ACPA allows trademark holders to assert *in rem* jurisdiction; that is, they can file an action against the domain name itself, regardless of where its registrant resides and what laws that person lives under. The registrants of the domain might be located in South Korea, Afghanistan, or India, but if the *registry* is located in the United States the American courts can assert jurisdiction anywhere.

The Whois service allows any Internet user to type a domain name into a Web interface and be immediately returned the name and contact details of whoever has registered the domain. Because of the open and often anonymous nature of the Internet, Whois came to be seen by the trademark and copyright interests as the equivalent of an Internet identification card, a way of identifying and tracking down Internet users for service of legal process.[24]

A common feature of both of these pillars of the 1998 regime was that the Internet created allegations of infringement in such volume that normal legal process seemed too slow and too expensive, leading to delegation to private operators. Tens of thousands of cybersquatting registrations and millions of postings and movements of files (mixed in, of course, with even larger numbers of legitimate registrations and publications that might nevertheless be challenged) occurred monthly. In both cases lawmakers responded by moving dispute resolution out of the courts of national governments, with their expensive due process requirements, and into the hands of private actors—though the process was guided by public or quasi-public rules. And in both cases the scales of justice were tipped noticeably to favor copyright and trademark holders, who were given fairly open-ended rights to challenge and suspend uses based mainly on their own allegations, with few sanctions against misuse of the new capability.

This new regime could be characterized as national in origin, but it was transnational in effect, either through extraterritorial assertions of authority or through imitation. ICANN of course was a new global institution. While the DMCA was a (U.S.) national law, its anticircumvention provisions led to some sensational assertions of extraterritorial jurisdiction. In July 2001, a twenty-seven-year-old Russian computer programmer named Dmitry Sklyarov came to the United States to speak at DEFCON, a hacker conference in Las Vegas, Nevada. His talk focused on the security weaknesses of Adobe eBooks. Prompted by the software company Adobe Systems, Inc., the FBI arrested Sklyarov as soon as he finished the talk. The Russian citizen was violating the DMCA, the FBI claimed, and because his demonstration program was available over the Internet to all countries he was subject to jurisdiction in U.S. courts. Likewise, the European counterpart to DMCA was a transnational form of legislation. In keeping with the precedent of TRIPS and Special 301, the United States also sought to globally extend the copyright and trademark protection regime through trade

24. Mueller and Chango 2008.

leverage. It incorporated DMCA-like provisions and Whois requirements into regional and bilateral free trade agreements.[25]

IP vs. IP as Driver of Internet Governance

One would think, given the strong and often preemptive nature of the 1998 Internet governance regime, that the problem of intellectual property on the Internet would have been settled for a time. But after 1998 the conflict did not go away; it intensified. We are currently in a period of extreme polarization, in which state and corporate advocates of intellectual property protection propose ever harsher and more systemic interventions into the ecology of information-communication technology, while a countermovement forms and business arrangements adjust. A brief recounting of the continued manifestations of the Internet/intellectual property tension shows that many were unanticipated by the 1998 regime, some are reassertions of older problems, and some are reactions to the consequences of the DMCA itself.

Trademark Maximalism and New Rights to Names
When ICANN finally developed a procedure for regular addition of new top-level domains in 2008,[26] it triggered another extended battle over trademark rights and domain names. Once it decided to move ahead with creating new top-level domains, it bent over backward to accommodate trademark interests, offering them a chance to propose major changes in policy without going through the consensus policy process. A so-called "Implementation Review Team" was created, composed almost entirely of trademark lawyers, and allowed to develop a wish list of policy proposals.[27]

25. "The U.S.-Singapore Free Trade Agreement: The Intellectual Property Provisions," Report of the Industry Functional Advisory Committee on Intellectual Property Rights for Trade Policy Matters (IFAC-3), February 28, 2003; "The US-Peru Trade Promotion Agreement (TPA): The intellectual property provisions," Report of the U.S. government's Industry Trade Advisory Committee on Intellectual Property Rights (ITAC-15). See also Roffe 2004.
26. ICANN discussion draft, "New gTLD Programme: Draft Applicant Guidebook," November 2008.
27. See "IRT Final Report on Trademark Protection Issues," ICANN Web site, http://www.icann.org/en/topics/new-gtlds/irt-final-report-trademark-protection-29may09-en.pdf.

The outcome was a set of radical innovations in globalized trademark protection, innovations that fully exploited ICANN's status as a gatekeeper to the global name space. Ten years earlier, the Uniform Domain Name Dispute Resolution Policy (UDRP) had been created because litigation through national courts was considered too slow and expensive. This time, trademark interests complained that the UDRP was too slow and expensive and demanded sweeping new measures. Ten years earlier, registry-based policing of domain name registrations was rejected as an excessive demand; this time, it was taken seriously and implemented.

Under the Implementation Review Team proposal, ICANN would create a trademark "clearing house" that would, for a "reasonable fee," allow all trademark owners in the world to download all of their marks, in any linguistic script. All domain name registries would be required to consult this database prior to making a registration. If anyone tried to register a domain name corresponding to one of these registered names, the registry would be required to notify the trademark owner and warn prospective registrants of any match with trademarked names. Before registration could proceed, the consumer would have to make "certain representations and warranties and acknowledgements." Thus the burden of trademark protection shifted to the infrastructure operators in a system of preemptive regulation. The innovations did not stop there; the trademark interests within ICANN demanded what WIPO and the intergovernmental treaty process was never able to deliver, namely a "Globally Protected Marks List." This is a policy for elevating certain trademarks to a higher standard of protection and literally blocking them from being used, in any context, regardless of free expression rights.[28] The proposals also would provide a "uniform rapid suspension system," allowing Web sites at abusive domains to be frozen and taken down in a process that is even faster and less procedural (although more limited in effect) than the UDRP. The trademark owners also demanded that all registries operating new TLDs maintain a "thick" Whois service (i.e., one that contains more information about the registrant) and for ICANN to revive the idea of a centralized Whois system that would enable globalized searching from one source. Not all of these

28. An applicant can register a second-level domain name corresponding to a globally protected mark if it participates in a dispute resolution process and demonstrates that its use of the applied-for domain name would not violate the trademark rights of the globally protected mark owner. In other words, the burden of proof is completely reversed: one must prove one's innocence of trademark violation in advance of using the name, rather than the trademark owner being required to prove infringement.

ideas made it through the ICANN process, but it is clear that when it comes to trademark protection the institutional regime moves in only one way: toward stronger excusivities.

In its new TLD process ICANN also created new international law by giving governments de facto property rights over all "geographical names" as well as "certain other types of sub-national place names." It is impossible to find any basis for this reservation in known international law, yet governments got veto power over geographical names because they insisted on it.

The p2p "Plague"

The most important post-1998 expression of the antagonism between IP and IP has centered on peer-to-peer file sharing (p2p). Peer-to-peer networks, as chapter 3 explained, are instances of the kind of scaled-up network organization the Internet makes possible. They coordinate the sharing and joint use of informational resources on a vast scale, with no territorial limits and trivial incremental costs. The p2p phenomenon began with music files, spread to news clips and other shorter video files, and finally began to encroach on the distribution of entire motion pictures. The proliferation of file sharing services pushed the IP interests into an ever more systematic—and transnational—quest for new forms of Internet governance.

Legislators in the United States and the European Union were unaware of the possibility of organized p2p file sharing when the DMCA and the E-Commerce Directive were drafted. But in 1999, an eighteen-year-old computer science student developed Napster, a file sharing and indexing software that could be downloaded for free. The idea was quickly taken up by dozens of others. The IP interests initially responded to p2p with a set of enforcement tools based on traditional nation-based copyright infringement litigation. The targets of lawsuits were the developers and operators of p2p services. They were accused of contributory and vicarious copyright infringement, a well-established form of third-party liability. The litigation was led by the Recording Industry Association of America (RIAA) in the United States and by the International Federation of the Phonographic Industry (IFPI) and record industry associations in other countries. Superficially, these efforts succeeded. Napster was convicted of contributory and vicarious copyright infringement in early 2001. Its reliance on a centralized indexing system for tracking files and managing connections between peers convinced the court that the service had the ability to prevent users from illegally sharing copyrighted files. Similar conclusions were drawn in other jurisdictions. MMO, a Japanese service similar to Napster, and Soribada, the "Korean Napster," were shut down by injunction in 2002 and lost their final legal appeals in 2005. A Taiwanese p2p that was sued by copyright interests in 2003 resulted in a criminal conviction in 2005.

But in the wake of these defeats new p2p services sprang up (Grokster, Gnutella, KaZaA, BitTorrent, Lime Wire) with the same file-sharing capabilities but no centralized file-indexing or tracking capabilities. Like Napster, however, they attempted to capitalize on the mass "audiences" attracted by file sharing to sell advertising or even subscriptions. In addition to altering their technical architecture, the post-Napster services avoided U.S. jurisdiction as an organizational hook for liability. As *Wired Magazine* wrote in reference to KaZaA in 2003, "The servers are in Denmark. The software is in Estonia. The domain is registered Down Under, the corporation on a tiny island in the South Pacific. The users—60 million of them—are everywhere around the world."[29]

The new, more distributed p2p tools did succeed in undercutting the contributory infringement argument in a jurisdiction or two. A Dutch court, for example, ruled that KaZaA could not be held responsible for the infringing activities of some of its users.[30] Appeals courts issued varying opinions. But in most cases these more distributed commercial services were eventually found guilty of some form of copyright infringement. The new theory was known as "inducement," and was articulated in the 2005 *MGM v. Grokster* decision of the U.S. Supreme Court. The court shifted the analysis of liability away from the technical architecture of the p2p network toward the overall conduct of the service's owners or promoters, such as its marketing, its interactions with end users, its efforts to curtail illegal file sharing, and how the service generates revenue.[31] Likewise, the attempt by p2p suppliers to exploit the territorial limits of jurisdiction failed in most cases. Courts and law enforcement agencies, especially in the United States, took an increasingly expansive view of jurisdiction.[32] In 2004 IFPI

29. Todd Woody, "The race to kill Kazaa," *Wired* 11, no. 2 (February 2003): 104, http://www.wired.com/wired/archive/11.02/kazaa.html.
30. Jan Libbenga, "Dutch Supreme Court rules Kazaa legal (but using it might not be)," *The Register*, December 19, 2003, http://www.theregister.co.uk/2003/12/19/dutch_supreme_court_rules_kazaa/.
31. *Metro-Goldwyn-Mayer Studios Inc. v. Grokster Ltd.*, 125 S.Ct. 2764 (2005).
32. In cases involving Grokster, KaZaA, PureTunes, and Imesh, U.S. courts consistently asserted jurisdiction over entities based outside the country, ruling that engaging in "interactive electronic transactions" provided the sort of "continuous"

claimed to have secured the takedown of 69,000 copyright-infringing Web sites, 477 unauthorized p2p services, and 1.6 billion infringing files across 102 countries.

But the evisceration of the commercial prospects of decentralized and advertiser-supported services did not seem to put a dent in the scale of file sharing. File sharing continued with new forms of p2p, such as Gnutella and BitTorrent—software protocols that do not depend on any single organization to manage their operation. Thus the recording industry shifted to a new tactic: it mounted efforts to identify and prosecute individual file sharers on a mass scale. The U.S. recording industry started bringing civil copyright infringement lawsuits against alleged illegal file sharers in 2002. They identified file sharers by participating in the downloading services and collecting the IP address of suspected infringers.[33] By the end of 2005, over 15,597 lawsuits were filed with 3,590 settlements averaging several thousand U.S. dollars each. Between 2004 and 2005 the British Phonographic Industry (BPI) undertook concerted action against file sharers in the UK. The IFPI launched a further two thousand cases in 2006 against individuals in ten countries. Aside from bringing a new harshness to the battle, the litigation against individuals raised profound implications for privacy rights on the Internet. Copyright interests insisted that ISPs reveal to them, on demand, the identification information behind the IP addresses they had identified as sources of file sharing. In the United States, RIAA filed a new type of subpoena, issued by the clerk of a court rather than a judge or magistrate, demanding that ISPs turn over the names of customers whom the RIAA accused of possessing illegal copies of copyrighted music files. U.S. Internet service provider Verizon resisted this pressure and eventually won a lawsuit, as a U.S. Appeals Court held that the RIAA subpoenas did not comply with the requirements of the Digital Millennium Copyright Act.[34] In Europe, the BPI in 2006 resorted to asking ISPs to terminate the Internet access of the alleged file sharers it had identified. In the UK regulators have issued a consultation asking whether ISPs

---

and "systematic" contacts with their territory as sufficient to support jurisdiction. A legal scholar concludes, "peer-to peer networks will find it difficult to evade legal action for copyright infringement by secreting themselves in foreign jurisdictions." Rimmer 2005, 186.

33. See Piatek, Kohno, and Krishnamurthy 2008.

34. United States Court of Appeals for the District of Columbia Circuit, argued September 16, 2003, decided December 19, 2003, No. 03–7015. *RECORDING INDUSTRY ASSOCIATION OF AMERICA, INC., APPELLEE v. VERIZON INTERNET SERVICES, INC., APPELLANT,* http://epic.org/privacy/copyright/verizon/dc-cir-op.pdf.

should be required to make this information easily available to intellectual property holders.[35]

In this escalation process, there were also some attempts to impose outright bans on p2p technologies, reminiscent of the attempt by motion picture interests to ban the home video recorder. In France, a proposed law would have imposed broad liability on software developers and publishers if their products were used illegally by third-party peer-to-peer activities. Such companies would have been forced to pay daily fines for copyright infringements by unknown users of their software. Courts could have ordered software companies to "fix" their products to stop infringement. In the United States the 2004 "Inducing Infringement of Copyrights Act" also attempted to impose liability on the producer of the technology, based on the theory that creating a technological capability for infringement might be construed as contributing to it. "It's simple and it's deadly," said Philip Corwin, at that time a lobbyist for Sharman Networks, which distributed the KaZaA client. "If you make a product that has dual uses, infringing and not infringing, and you know there's infringement, you're liable."[36] These more extreme forms of legislation, while useful indicators of the agenda of IP interests, generated strong resistance from technology companies and public interest groups and failed to pass.

Still, most of the IP interests' litigation strategies succeeded on their own, narrow legal terms. Services were shut down; individuals were fined. But each nevertheless failed in that file sharing was not significantly deterred. In 2008, IFPI's annual report on digital music conceded that "in total, 17.6 per cent of Internet users in Europe regularly file-shared in 2007—a figure that is roughly the same as in 2003."[37]

The offensive against peer-to-peer file sharing can be seen as an assault on networked organization itself. The lawsuits against individual Internet users signaled the inherent antagonism between a technology-enabled capacity to pool, share, and transmit resources with minimal organizational hierarchy, and the ability of digital property owners to erect and enforce fences that protect their exclusivity. This has led to a new and

35. UK Department for Business Enterprise and Regulatory Reform (BERR) Consultation on Legislative Options to Address Illicit Peer-to-Peer (p2p) File-Sharing, July 2008.
36. Declan McCullough, "Antipiracy bill targets technology," CNET News, June 17, 2004, http://news.cnet.com/Antipiracy-bill-targets-technology/2100-1028_3-5238140.html.
37. IFPI Digital Music Report 2008: Revolution, Innovation, Responsibility, page 28, http://www.ifpi.org/content/library/dmr2008.pdf.

critical phase in the IP interests' quest for effective Internet governance: a systematic attempt to make intermediaries—and especially Internet access providers—more responsible for policing copyright.

Convergence of Broadcasting and Internet

Internet broadcasting has opened up another new front. In 1999 a Canadian entrepreneur operating under the name iCraveTV took U.S. broadcast television signals and streamed them over the Internet, claiming that Canadian law made it possible for cable operators to retransmit over-the-air signals without permissions or payments. The service was quickly torpedoed by copyright lawsuits, but the incident provoked broadcasters into seeking a new international treaty that would give them property rights over their transmissions. The proposed WIPO Broadcast Treaty led to eight years of negotiations that eventually foundered. The sticking point was a tussle over the proper limits of content exclusivity in digital media.[38] Critics of the proposed agreement, such as the Electronic Frontier Foundation, asserted that "a TV channel broadcasting your Creative Commons-licensed movie could legally demand that no one record or redistribute it—and sue anyone who does. And TV companies could use their new rights to go after TiVo or MythTV for daring to let you skip advertisements or record programs in DRM-free formats." This issue is still unresolved. The fate of technologies like Slingbox, which allow paid cable TV subscribers to "space shift" content from one computer to another by transmitting it over the Internet, exemplifies what is at stake.

Since 2006, nearly every major network television show and many of the biggest cable programs in the United States have become available on the Internet.[39] Anticipating a digital world, broadcasters in the United States fought for technical regulations, known as the *broadcast flag*, that would have forced all future digital television (DTV) tuners to include Digital Rights Management (DRM) technologies designed to protect

---

38. A good summary of the status of the WIPO broadcasting treaty as of late 2008 can be found at Nate Anderson, "WIPO Broadcast Treaty Still Alive (But Less Terrifying)," Ars Technica Web site, November 10, 2008, http://arstechnica.com/old/content/2008/11/wipo-broadcast-treaty-alive-but-less-terrifying.ars.

39. A report in the *Wall Street Journal* cites an October 2008 survey of 500 viewers that claims that more than half of the people who saw the *Saturday Night Live* television program skits featuring comedian Tina Fey as vice presidential candidate Sarah Palin watched the skits over the Internet. Nick Wingfield, "Turn on, tune out, click here: TV viewers cut cable's cord; Here's what they're watching online instead," *Wall Street Journal*, October 3, 2008.

broadcast content from unauthorized copying. Those regulations made it through the FCC but were struck down in May 2005 by an appeals court. The broadcast flag seemed dead until May 2008, when users attempting to record NBC TV shows using Microsoft's Vista Media Center were unable to do so. Microsoft later admitted that its Media Center software was made to be compliant to the broadcast flag rules. Agreements between computer software providers and content providers would thus be able to create the same regulatory effect as federal legislation. However, Internet users can more or less easily abandon Microsoft's media player for other alternatives.

At the time of this writing, we can only speculate on the full, long-term impact of the Internet on broadcasting, and especially the territorial exclusivity of signal distribution. As video migrates to the Web, it reenacts the clash between the bordered world of intellectual property and the borderless world of Internet protocol. Content owners are accustomed to using contracts to create territorial exclusivity in the distribution of their works. This increases their ability to price discriminate and protects the right of distributors to minimize competition from other distributors or from disintermediation by the supplier. But these practices were based on terrestrial distribution infrastructures like broadcasting or cable TV systems and do not mesh well with the expectations of Internet users and the distributional structure of the global Web.

One of the most comprehensive and well-financed attempts to bring video to the web is Hulu.com. Founded in March 2007 by NBC Universal and News Corp, Hulu is a place to watch popular American TV shows and movies. But Hulu suffers from one irritating flaw: it must block users' ability to view the shows if they are accessing the site from outside the United States. It enforces these boundaries by checking to see whether the IP address of the person accessing the site was allocated to an Internet service provider in the United States or not. Web surfers in Europe attempting to watch an episode of *Family Guy* see only a back screen with the following words: "Unfortunately, this video is not currently available in your country or region. We apologize for the inconvenience." Hulu explains that "our intention is to make Hulu's growing content lineup available worldwide. This requires clearing the rights for each show or film in each specific geography and will take time."

The BBC's iPlayer for television programs, another comprehensive attempt to transfer broadcast content to the Internet, is also geolocked. In this case the territorial imperative is driven by governmental rather than commercial considerations; the intent is to restrict service to citizens of Great Britain who pay the license fees that support the programming, while reserving the right to make others pay.

In the globally integrated world of the Internet, these barriers attract derisive verbal attacks and technical circumvention measures. They put the services that conform to them at a competitive disadvantage to illegal file sharing practices or semilegal user-generated sites like YouTube, which may carry some of the same material. The use of IP addresses as a bounding mechanism can be fooled in various ways, but as others have noted the use of Internet identifier resources to link users and uses to geographies and policies has far-reaching implications for Internet governance.[40] It is quite unclear how this will play out. Whatever happens, however, will require substantial institutional changes to reconfigure the relationship between national media regulation, private licensing of content, and globalized markets for digital material.

The Network as Policer

The regulatory trend that constantly emerges from the IP v. IP tension is a shift of the responsibility for monitoring and policing Internet conduct onto strategically positioned private sector intermediaries. It is not only territorial boundaries that pose a problem, it is also the massive scale and scope of the interactions enabled by the Internet. If it is too difficult and costly for the state to police the billions of interactions among a billion-plus individuals connected by the Net, then one can vest those who provide the platforms and capabilities for digital communications with the responsibility for infringing actions by their users. Or one can rely on state-sanctioned "codes of conduct" among cartels of suppliers. This method focuses, as Boyle (1997b) put it, "on building the [regulatory] regime into the architecture of transactions in the first place—both technically and economically —rather than policing the transactions after the fact." Delegating responsibility to the private sector can be a strategy for overcoming the limitations of territorial jurisdiction, as it was with ICANN, but it can also be a way of scaling up and making more efficient the policing function by harnessing the incentives and resources of private actors who are closer to the actual operations. The intermediaries could be online service providers, financial and credit networks, universities, or any other

40. Goldsmith and Wu 2006.

organizational bottleneck.[41] From the standpoint of Internet governance, however, the most important intermediary is the large-scale commercial Internet access provider, the critical gateway to Internet connectivity.

Campaign for ISP Responsibility

Some time in 2006, copyright industry associations began a campaign for "ISP responsibility." The content industry began to stress "cooperation" with ISPs, and their mutual interest in eliminating abuses of p2p. The head of the Motion Picture Association of America, for example, made many public statements in 2006 and 2007 advocating the use of filtering or deep packet inspection technologies by ISPs to detect copyright infringement.[42] Playing on one of the ISPs' weakest points of resistance, they emphasized the degree to which p2p file sharing consumed large amounts of bandwidth, imposing cost burdens on an industry not known for its fat profit margins. Comcast, a cable modem supplier of Internet access (one that, as a cable TV system, is also integrated into content production and distribution), was later discovered to have been technically disrupting peer-to-peer-protocols on its network without informing its customers. Thanks to an organized Net Neutrality movement, this practice backfired. The U.S. regulator sanctioned the company and it was required to submit "protocol-agnostic" plans for bandwidth management.

The British House of Lords issued a report in 2007 with stern insistence on greater liability and responsibility for ISPs.[43] This was followed up by a 2008 consultation by the UK Department of Business Enterprise and

41. Boyle (1997a) has asserted that this involves a short-circuiting of due process and the traditional rights associated with the state-citizen relationship. This can be true; but just as often it vests the private sector actors with procedural and bureaucratic constraints derived from public sector norms. Consider the increasingly bureaucratic procedures, accountability mechanisms, and notice and comment processes built into ICANN's supposedly privatized policy-making processes. Or consider the notice and takedown, and counter-notice procedures to which ISPs are subject under the DMCA. The delegation of governmental functions is just as likely to saddle private actors with governmental qualities as it is to provide governments with an escape from those qualities. The real shift here is in the distribution of costs regarding the seeking of a remedy.

42. Nate Anderson, "MPAA Head Wants Deeper Relationship (Read: Content Filtering) with ISPs," Ars Technica Web site, September 19, 2007, http://arstechnica.com/news.ars/post/20070919-mpaa-head-wants-deeper-relationship-read-content-filtering-with-isps.html?rel.

43. UK House of Lords, Science and Technology Committee, *Personal Internet Security*. Volume I: Report. 5th Report of Session 2006–2007. Published August 10, 2007.

Regulatory Reform containing a wide variety of new efforts to enlist ISPs in copyright enforcement.[44] The consultation raised such alternatives as requiring ISPs to hand over personal data relating to a given Internet protocol address to copyright holder on request, without any need for court action; forcing ISPs to take direct action themselves against claimed file-swappers; and forcing ISPs to allow installation of filters to block infringing material.

In 2007 a memorandum of understanding between the Sarkozy government, ISPs, and French copyright holders proposed to cut off repeat p2p infringers from the Internet. The French "three strikes" proposal, as it became known, would have committed French ISPs to the development of extensive monitoring capabilities such as deep packet inspection (DPI) technology that could identify the transmission of copyrighted content on their networks. Under the French presidency in 2008, some EU-level attempts to translate some of the harsh French measures into EU law were made, although without much success.

Deep Packet Inspection

Calls for regulating copyright via ISPs often invoke DPI technology. DPI is specialized hardware with powerful and fast information-processing capabilities. Once DPI is embedded in a network its operator can analyze what is inside the individual packets that constitute Internet traffic and take action on them according to defined policies. Its development up this point seems to have been driven by network intrusion detection, meaning security-oriented applications. DPI has profound implications for the freedom, privacy, and security of Internet users. Before this, ISPs were more or less passive movers of Internet datagrams, reading only the header information needed to deliver the packet to its destination. DPI opens up the packet and applies algorithms or pattern matching to its contents, and makes decisions in real time based on that analysis. As an integrated technology of control, DPI can be used to catch viruses and other malware in transit, to manage bandwidth and, possibly, to identify and regulate the type of files end users are sharing with each other.

A court ruling in Belgium in 2008 for a brief period gave the IP interests exactly what they were asking for. In a lawsuit brought by the music industry, an ISP was ordered to prevent illegal downloads by using DPI technologies to automatically detect illegal content and prevent its transmission. The judge dismissed objections that these obligations constituted

44. BERR, see note 35.

a general obligation to monitor the network, which would contravene both Belgian and EU law, invoking ambiguities in the law regarding the use of technical surveillance instruments. The decision was reversed on appeal. The appeals court decision did not reject DPI on privacy or civil liberties grounds, however, holding mainly that it simply did not work as advertised and that its advocates had overstated its capabilities. This narrow basis of the ruling means that the issue is not really settled yet. Even though it was not court mandated, it provides a clear glimpse into the future direction of Internet governance if the intellectual property interests have their way.

A Transnational Resistance Movement: A2K

A key part of the story of IP v. IP is a new social movement that challenges the prevailing narrative of intellectual property. This movement, like its targets, is transnational in scope. It has converged around an innovative institutional arrangement—namely, a private, contractually constructed commons. With its origin in the movement for free/open source software, the adherents of this social movement resist intrusive and oppressive forms of copyright protection and digital rights management, and tolerate or support peer-to-peer file sharing. They oppose software patents. They promote freedom of expression and open access to government information, unlicensed radio spectrum, and (more ambiguously) network neutrality and opposition to media consolidation. The movement has forged links to developing country governments and civil society actors that would limit or override patent rights in drugs and food production in the name of public health and biodiversity.

The movement goes by various labels. Some term it the *commons* movement.[45] Others refer to *free culture* or the *cultural environment movement*.[46] The label that now seems to be acquiring hegemony is *Access to Knowledge*. Often known by the acronym A2K, it has become a master frame linking many formerly disparate elements of communication and information politics, business, policy, and law. As an intellectual and political movement, A2K is based on a reappraisal of the nature of property rights over information and networks—a reappraisal that might be called *radical* in the original sense of the word, meaning *arising from or going to a root or source*. Yet, as I will explain in a later chapter, the thinking behind the A2K movement does not quite go deep enough.

45. Kranich 2004.
46. Lessig 2005; Boyle 1997a.

A2K has its own distinctive ideology and organizational method, as we shall see, but the movement has three distinct roots. The first was the free/ open source software movement (F/OSS). The second was the copyright resistance that galvanized in the United States around opposition to the DMCA in the mid-1990s. The third was a challenge to the TRIPS regime around drug patents, which engaged developing country governments as well as civil society. Each emerged more or less independently, but they began to converge into a self-conscious movement after 2002.

Four critical features of the A2K movement warrant the attention I give to it here: (1) its reach for an all-encompassing ideology of a revolutionary character; (2) its transnational outlook; (3) its development of institutional innovations in law and in networked governance; and (4) its increasing political engagement with the institutions of global Internet governance, mainly WIPO but also ICANN and IGF.

Ideology

On the ideological front, the A2K movement actively strives to develop a coherent, all-encompassing ideology relevant to communication-information policy. This ideology is grounded in its own distinctive political economy, developed by legal scholars such as Lessig and Benkler. In books such as *Free Culture*, *The Future of Ideas*, and the *Wealth of Networks*, they analyze the dynamics of the digital economy and develop normative policies for it.[47] Yale Law School's Jack Balkin, whose Information Society Project considers itself one of the leaders of A2K, links his support for freedom of expression to "something much larger," which he calls *knowledge and information policy* and which others, including myself, have encapsulated as *communication-information policy*.[48] By that he means that the A2K frame provides a coherent basis for approaching not just intellectual

47. Including quasi-historicist, dialectical claims about the market economy bearing within it the seeds of its own negation: "If there is one lesson we can learn from globalization and the ever-increasing reach of the market, it is that the logic of the market exerts enormous pressure on existing social structures. If we are indeed seeing the emergence of a substantial component of non-market production at the very core of our economic engine—the production and exchange of information, and through it of information-based goods, tools, services, and capabilities—then this change suggests a genuine limit on the extent of the market. Such a limit, growing from within the very market that it limits, in its most advanced loci, would represent a genuine shift in direction for what appeared to be the ever-increasing global reach of the market economy and society in the past half century." Benkler 2006, 18–19.
48. Mueller, Kuerbis, and Page 2004.

property issues, but also a wide range of other policy domains pertaining
to information infrastructure, culture, government, and education: "Access
to Knowledge demands that we structure telecommunications law, intellectual property law, and government provisioning and procurement policies to promote the goals of knowledge and information policy and the
achievement of a global democratic culture."[49] As an ideological force, A2K
strives to be "revolutionary"—meaning not that it advocates violent
overthrow of the government, but that it promotes fundamental institutional changes and juxtaposes those changes against an old order that
should be overthrown or cast away. "It seems *passé* today to speak of "the
Internet revolution," says Benkler. "But it should not be. The change
brought about by the networked information environment is deep. It is
structural. It goes to the very foundations of how liberal markets and liberal
democracies have coevolved for almost two centuries."[50]

The intellectual side of the A2K movement, as one may have gathered,
is centered in a new generation of law professors based in elite American
law schools. Just as the Chicago School economists of the 1960s and 1970s
developed a new political economy around the economic analysis of law,
leading to the market liberalism of the 1980s and 1990s, so the legal scholars focused on the normative, economic, and political implications of
informational property rights comprised the intellectual cadre of A2K. The
movement has catapulted Lawrence Lessig into rock star status; he commands tens of thousands of dollars for appearances at which he gives the
same speech he might have given five years ago. It has done something
similar to the Free Software Foundation's Richard Stallman. More substantively, it has used the global environmental movement as a model.[51]

Transnational in Scope
The A2K movement is also self-consciously transnational in outlook. It
asserts the universality of its own ideological appeal. "Access to Knowledge
is global; it is not limited to the confines of a single nation state."[52] While
respectful of diversity and heterogeneity, its concept of "democratic
culture" transcends the jurisdiction of any nation or the bounds of any
specific culture. Its tenets have shown an ability to mobilize activists in

49. Address delivered at the Second Access to Knowledge Conference (A2K2), Yale
University, April 27, 2007. Text available at http://balkin.blogspot.com/2007/04/
two-ideas-for-access-to-knowledge.html.
50. Benkler 2006, 1.
51. Boyle 1997a.
52. Balkin, see note 49.

Latin America, Europe, and East Asia. It has also generated coalitions with developing country governments and major multinational corporations. Despite this globalist outlook, however, the A2K movement has not developed an institutional critique of the nation-state, nor has it thought much about the institutional alternatives for exercising global governance. This is one of its main intellectual and political limitations.

Institutional Innovation

The movement for free software has produced its own institutional innovations, ones that can virally replicate through private ordering. These are contracts that use copyright law to protect resources from private appropriation instead of preserving and protecting exclusivity. As such, they constitute an ingenious inversion of normal copyright law. The free software movement pioneered these new legal institutions in the early 1980s, by developing the GNU General Public License. The free software movement also pioneered and was the first to self-consciously discuss and promote the new forms of collaborative, nonhierarchical production of the sort celebrated by Eric Raymond and later Yochai Benkler. The idea of using contract law to protect and expand the public domain rather than as a tool of private appropriation was then imitated by Lessig and the movement against copyright maximalism, as the Creative Commons license.

Engagement with Global Institutions

To some extent, the A2K movement avoids or circumvents traditional public policy making forums—which it perceives, not unjustifiably, as captured by special interests—and relies instead on institutional innovations such as the new collaborative networks and nonproprietary licenses already mentioned. But more recently A2K has tended to combine this kind of activism with participation in more traditional policy battles in national and international institutions. Since about the year 2000, the movement has become more engaged politically (as advocates and pressure groups) with global public institutions of communication-information policy. At the transnational level, most of its energy is directed at WIPO. But its adherents can also be found in ICANN, the WTO, and the IGF.

A variant of the A2K movement has even entered electoral politics. Building on the publicity generated by governmental prosecution of Sweden's Pirate Bay, a haven for p2p file-sharing activity, a "Pirate Party" was formed in 2006. It advocated strong privacy rights and the elimination of patents, criticized "unbalanced" copyright protection, and promoted the decriminalization of file sharing. The conviction of the Pirate Bay founders in April 2009 led to a tripling of the Pirate Party's membership. It now has over forty-eight thousand registered members in Sweden, making it the third largest political party there. In the 2009 elections to the European Parliament, the Swedish Pirate Party captured 7 percent of the votes, ensuring it of at least one and possibly two of the eighteen available seats for Sweden. Pirate parties now have been established in thirty-three countries.

Conclusion

Because of the high economic stakes and its centrality to the problem of freedom vs. control, the problem of intellectual property protection on the Internet is producing a transnational politics around Internet governance. The ongoing conflict of IP vs. IP embraces not only ICANN but also intergovernmental institutions such as WIPO and the WTO. At the same time, it engages institutions with strong roots in traditional nation-states, such as the European Union as well as national institutions with global effects, such as the DMCA. It is also evident in the coordinated efforts of intellectual property interests and their opponents to view national legislation as precedents or models that might spread globally. At present, the main battleground of IP v. IP is the regulation of Internet service providers.

There is a growing congruence between the mechanisms and procedures being proposed to control IP on the Internet with the mechanisms used to control other forms of conduct. The semilegal economy of peer-to-peer file sharing, for example, routinely gets linked, however spuriously, to child pornography and terrorism.[53] We also see a convergence between the systematic surveillance practices proposed by would-be enforcers of IP protection and those utilized or proposed by the national security state. Copyright and trademark violations become examples of the need to regulate and control human action on the Internet. So IP vs. IP is as much

53. The late Jack Valenti provides a typically lurid, near-comical example of an attempt to exploit this alleged connection: "downloading KaZaA, Gnutella, Morpheus, Grokster, etc., can lay bare your most private financial and personal information to identity thieves. It can bring into your home and expose your children to pornography of the most vile and depraved character imaginable. Most insidious of all, the pornography finds its way to your children disguised as wholesome material: your son or daughter may search for "Harry Potter" or "Britney Spears," and be confronted with files that contain bestiality." Statement of Jack Valenti before the U.S. Senate Committee on Governmental Affairs, 108th Cong., "Privacy and Piracy: The Paradox of Illegal File Sharing on Peer-to-Peer Networks and the Impact of Technology on the Entertainment Industry" (September 2003), 93–94.

about freedom of expression and privacy—in other words, about individual rights and the proper scope for unrestricted human action—as it is about the technicalities of establishing property rights over names and digital materials. There is the distinct possibility of a "regulatory alliance" between content regulators, intellectual property interests, and security advocates, which attempts to reassert and strengthen hierarchical, nation-state based control over the Internet. This tendency is opposed by the new social movement around access to knowledge, as well as more traditional forms of market liberalism and civil libertarians.

8 Security Governance on the Internet

From a news story "Desperate Botnet Battlers Call for an Internet Driver's License": "Internet-crime fighters from security companies, law enforcement agencies, banks and e-commerce sites huddled at a secretive conference last week to confer on new tactics in the war on cybercrime. . . . A few audience members argued seriously that computer users should have to take a test to get an Internet license, maintain botnet insurance and have their machines inspected for information-super highway worthiness."[1]

The Internet's "Security Problem"

Security has become a generic watchword that signals the downside of the Internet's openness and freedom. Security more often than not is associated with efforts to reassert hierarchy and control. If anything can reanimate the desire for the nation-state, for traditional government, surely it is the demand for security.

In Internet governance, the term *security* now encompasses a host of problems, perhaps too many to fit properly under one word. It includes the fight against spam, viruses, and phishing. It applies to the more sinister threat of malware-infested computers organized into remote-controlled botnets that can be used to deliver spam or to execute denial of service attacks.[2] It covers both unauthorized intrusion into private networks by outsiders and efforts by organizations to prevent insiders from stealing data, identities, and money. It refers to bugs in protocols and operating

1. Ryan Singel, "Desperate botnet battlers call for an Internet driver's license," *Wired.com*, June 4, 2007, http://www.wired.com/politics/security/news/2007/06/bot_strategy.
2. Franklin et al. 2007; Turner 2008; van Eeten and Bauer 2008.

systems on computers, mobile phones, and other devices that create opportunities for exploitation by clever programmers. It is also commonly used in connection with privacy rights and data protection. Somehow, all of these phenomena have come under the umbrella of Internet security discourse. But that is not all.

The most challenging and expansive uses of the term come when Internet security is alleged to intersect with the military or political security of the state. The cyberattacks on Estonia and Georgia constituted real-world examples of this intersection. The Internet can indeed be used as a weapon, although its destructive force pales in comparison to missiles and tanks. Dire warnings about threats to "critical infrastructure" that might arise from cyberattacks are proliferating, often based on the flimsiest evidence.[3] The drumbeat of fear provides a textbook example of what political scientists have called *securitization*. Securitization refers to speech acts that characterize some problem as an existential threat in a calculated attempt to justify extraordinary measures, such as the suspension of civil liberties or preemptive strikes.[4] The Internet is being securitized.[5] Reflecting the political mileage that securitization brings, even copyright protection and the control of illegal content are now redefined, by some, as security issues.

Worse yet, there is a growing tendency to link the Internet's security problems to the very properties that made it innovative and revolutionary in the first place. Jonathan Zittrain has contended that general-purpose computers and open networks foster not just innovation and freedom but also abuse and organized cybercrime. He worries that the Internet's very success might push digital systems back to the model of locked-down devices and tethered, centrally controlled information appliances.[6]

Without question, security and securitization are becoming preeminent drivers of Internet governance. But where Zittrain and others understand both the problem and the solutions in terms of protocol designs, operating systems, and standards, this chapter argues that the real battle is being waged around institutions and organizational forms. If we look at how security is actually produced, we discover that most of the actual work is

3. Morozov (2009) picks apart an April 2009 *Wall Street Journal* article claiming that the U.S. electrical grid had been "penetrated by foreign spies," noting that it quoted no attributable sources, named no utility companies, and mentioned only one actual cyberattack in Australia nine years ago that was conducted by an insider rather than an external hacker.
4. Waever 1997.
5. Deibert and Rohozinski 2009a.
6. Zittrain 2008, see especially chapter 5.

done not by national states promulgating and enforcing public law, but by private actors in emergent forms of peer production, network organizations, and markets.[7] Among states, the problem of cybersecurity intensifies the need for international cooperation and harmonization as much as it fosters national responses. The reality of security governance, then, is one of structural change and adaptation at the national and international levels to the problem of distributed, transnational control.

This chapter begins by identifying what is different about law enforcement in cyberspace. It then looks at two instances of security governance through peer production: spam and phishing. From there, it moves to an examination of the changing role of the state in cyberspace. It concludes with a focus on the problem of identity.

Why Is Cybercrime Different?

If cybercrime is just another form of crime, why isn't traditional law enforcement—which is what states specialize in and have institutionalized for more than a century—sufficient to counter it? The answer is that there are qualitative differences between cybercrime and physical crime.[8] Not surprisingly, the differences parallel our analysis in chapter 1 of three critical features of the Internet: increased scale, transnational scope, and distributed control. We have already seen, in the last chapter, how these factors made enforcement of trademark and copyright in cyberspace different from pre-Internet intellectual property enforcement.

When a crime occurs in the physical world, it involves bodies interacting in physical space. Victim and offender must be in close proximity when the offense takes place. These aspects of offline crime both limit its scale and narrow the range in which police must search for evidence and suspects. The direct, physical linkage between criminal and victim and crime

---

7. Lewis 2008; UK House of Lords, Science and Technology Committee, Personal Internet Security. Volume I: Report. 5th Report of Session 2006–0007 (August 10, 2007).

8. The discussion of the differences between cybercrime and real-world crime draws on Brenner 2005. However, Brenner believes that the ability to identify probable patterns of crime is a key factor in real-world crime response, but not in cybercrime. "Over time," she says, "it becomes possible to identify the general contours and incidence of the real-world crimes." I think the same is true of cybercrime, which is far from random in its contours and incidence. We already know a lot about such patterns and our knowledge is growing daily. We are also developing automated tools that feed into that knowledge.

scene imposes limits on what criminals can do and imposes physical and temporal constraints on the planning and execution of the crime. A robber can only hit one convenience store at a time. Technology can enhance the destructive or threat capability of meat-space crime, but even automated weapons are localized in effect.[9] The law enforcement institutions and procedures of territorial government, the police, and the courts are the institutional response to these localized, scale-limited crimes.

Cybercrime alters the parameters of this equation. It involves not one human victimizing another but machines interacting in virtual space. Proximity is unnecessary. The scale of criminal activity can be greatly multiplied, because the information exchanges that enact the crime can be automated and replicated (increased scale) and cheaply distributed throughout the network (increased scope). Botnets and mass distribution of spam industrialize cybercrimes. Many of the physical constraints on planning and execution are overcome by a globally interconnected network in which billions of users rely on common, standardized protocols, operating systems, and applications. The evidence trail is fleeting and evanescent, and distributed over multiple jurisdictions. The costs associated with cooperation across multiple jurisdictions, on the other hand, are high. Moreover, for law enforcement agencies cybercrime is a net addition to, not a substitute for, other forms of crime. The overall result is that police resources are both overloaded and disoriented.

At the moment, the gap between traditional law enforcement and the capabilities of cybercrime is filled by other methods. Organizations protect themselves. A huge market for security services and technologies has developed. And new forms of networked organization and governance have emerged (discussion follows). But this may be only a temporary phenomenon, a reflection of an institutional disequilibrium. The critical point here is that the mismatch between cybercrime and ordinary law enforcement creates pressure for institutional change at the transnational level. If the nation-state cannot deliver the requisite capacity for order, something else will.

Some have suggested that there could be a technical fix to the Internet's security problems. But the problem of Internet security is inherent in the widespread distribution of computing power and network access across the

9. To be sure, weapons technology, and especially WMD can increase the scale of offline crimes, but precisely for that reason we have devised legal and institutional responses that restrict such technologies to public bodies that presumably can be trusted to use them responsibly, such as states.

population. By its very nature, contemporary information technology is malleable and multifunctional; it can be creatively configured and reconfigured and scripted to execute anyone's instructions. Given these inexpensive, powerful, globally interconnected information technology tools, it is inevitable that users can and will exploit those capabilities for evil as well as good purposes. The Internet security problem, in short, is an extension of human problems to cyberspace. No one believes that the problem of crime in offline society can be "solved" by some kind of comprehensive, top-down redesign of the way we live, work, and move about. Why should it be different with the virtual space created by the Internet?

Meaningful responses to cybersecurity problems, therefore, will occur at the *institutional* level. They will involve not just new technological capabilities but also efforts to shape actors' economic incentives (e.g., through the assignment of liability), changes in organizational routines and procedures, new laws and regulations, and at a higher level, new relationships among states and between state actors and private actors. Only when we turn away decisively from the chimera of a technological fix can we pay full attention to the reality of security governance.

Peer Production of Security

Security governance in cyberspace takes place mainly through informal, trust-based relationships among the Internet operational community members. These can be characterized as network forms of organization or as a kind of peer production or both. States are players in these arrangements, but are rarely in a position to exert hierarchical power.

Interpersonal and organizational networks among Internet service providers (ISPs), computer security incident response teams (CSIRTs or CERTs), domain name registrars, hosting companies, email-based expert discussion forums, the information technology departments of major user organizations and government agencies, and a burgeoning market for private security services bear the brunt of the burden of protecting networks. These communities are not coterminous with national boundaries and their transnational nature can be viewed as responses to the limitations and obstacles of territorial law enforcement. The procedures used are heavily reliant on the Internet itself and on computationally enabled analytical tools to monitor incidents, identify problems, communicate among the parties, and formulate and implement responses.

Manifestations of this form of governance include spam blacklists, antiphishing organizations, messaging antiabuse groups, a variety of private and government-sponsored CERTs, and entities such the North American Network Operators Group (NANOG). The common denominator of these efforts is that they are predicated on the need for rapid action informed by specialized technical expertise; the need for close cooperation across multiple organizational and jurisdictional boundaries; and direct operational control of some form of access to the Internet (e.g., servers, bandwidth, domain names). States and law enforcement agencies are involved, of course. There are even some newly formed transgovernmental networks, such as the London Action Plan (to be discussed), which bring law enforcement agencies into loosely affiliated cooperative relationships. Laws are passed at the national level; there is at least one relevant international convention. But most of the day-to-day work of identifying, preventing, and responding to threats seems to be done by a transnational network that relies on cooperative frameworks and norms that were developed independently of states.[10] It is a mode of interaction that, as Fritz Scharpf suggests in his discussion of "unilateral action in anarchic fields," allows actors to "communicate and conclude agreements" but which also leaves them "free to break such agreements if it suits their interests."[11]

The discussion that follows reviews two characteristic examples of security governance on the Internet. The first section examines briefly some techniques in the fight against spam. The second discusses the Anti-Phishing Working Group. The material is illustrative, not comprehensive. It is not intended to present peer production and networked governance as the optimal solution to the problem of Internet security. Legitimate questions about the overall effectiveness of current methods are often raised and many proposals for improvement are worth considering. The discussion also recognizes that there is a gradation between the peer production of Internet security and what some might call vigilantism and others might call anarchy. It shows very clearly that the flexibility and the lack of formality of these methods sacrifices what many would see as due process. The point is that these are the methods that *have in fact evolved*

10. A Dutch research agency report describes the interrelationships among business, government, and technical and academic stakeholders as "a network model"; Bruce et al. 2005. The report claims: "Because the Internet has no natural political boundaries, national boundaries are not effective to partition cyber security policy responsibilities. And even though security is a basic public sector concern, and typically regulated at the government level, the bulk of the capability for dealing with cyber security risk is not in the hands of governments but lies with the private or semi-private sector entities that actually manage and operate the ICT infrastructure" (iii).
11. Scharpf 1997, 98.

as the tools of choice in the existing environment. It is the attempt to capture the benefits and avoid the problems of these methods that sustain efforts to transform institutions and move beyond the territorial nation-state.

Spam

In the case of spam, the disjunction is unusually clear between legislation/ formal law enforcement at the national level and the actual governance procedure used. Spam emerged as a serious problem in the late 1990s. By the mid-2000s there were tough national laws against it in most developed countries.[12] An EC Directive passed in 2003, for example, outlawed spamming unless consent had previously been obtained from the recipient. But this directive was translated into legislation and enforced at the national level. Most of the spam received in the EU—over 90 percent—originates outside the EU, with about half from the United States, and a quarter from the far Eastern countries.[13] The United States, likewise, passed the CAN-SPAM Act in 2003. While not as strong as the EU law (it relied on opt-out principles) it still made illegal some of the most prevalent types of unsolicited bulk email. And the laws have been enforced. In both the United States and the United Kingdom there have been dozens of successful prosecutions and/or convictions of spammers under these laws.[14]

There is no decline in the volume or virulence of spam since these laws were passed. Estimates from one expert group claim that as of the second half of 2007, 85 percent of incoming mail is "abusive," and that number has not changed substantially since 2004.[15] Another specialist group esti-

12. See Schryen 2007.
13. Wall 2004, 319. On December 11, 2003, the UK introduced compulsory opt-in legislation in the form of the Privacy and Electronic Communications (EC Directive) Regulations 2003 (SI/2003/2426), which brought into effect Article 13 of EU Directive 2002/58/EC7 on privacy and electronic communications passed in July of the previous year. Prior to December 2003, the UK had adopted a self-regulatory model in which spammers were supposed to provide those on their mail lists the facility to opt out.
14. A good compilation of spam convictions, indictments, and civil litigation centered in the United States can be found at Spamlinks.net: http://spamlinks.net/ legal-action.htm#isp. It also contains links to cases in the UK, Netherlands, Denmark, Australia, France, and South Korea.
15. Messaging Anti-Abuse Working Group (MAAWG), Email Metrics Program: The Network Operators' Perspective. Report #7—Third and Fourth Quarters 2007 (issued April 2008). The sample size for the MAAWG's study was over 100 million mailboxes.

mates that by June 2008, 96.5 percent of email received by businesses was spam.

Insofar as Internet users are shielded against spam, protection comes from a combination of peer-produced lists of spam sources, and market-based filtering services and software. One of the most highly developed forms of security peer production is the spam blacklist, also known as the DNS blacklist (DNSBL). These are lists of IP addresses that someone believes to be the source of spam, or that are associated with Internet service providers or hosts who tolerate or harbor spam. These lists are published on the Internet in a format that can be easily queried by computers on the Internet so that they can be propagated to email administrators at ISPs and private businesses. Email administrators can then configure their email server software to reject or flag messages that have been sent from an address listed on one or more of the blacklists.

Spam blacklists have their origin in the work of Internet technical elders who became antispam activists in the mid-1990s. Paul Vixie's Realtime Blackhole List (RBL), created in 1997, is widely credited with being the first. Others developed their own lists with different policies, such as ORBS (open relay behavior modification system). The Spam Prevention Early Warning System (SPEWS) became notorious for its deliberate use of "collateral damage" to escalate complaints about spam to higher levels. The point is that *anyone* can maintain and publish a blacklist, and different lists use their own, self-determined policies for placing IP addresses onto their lists. Some lists are user-generated (i.e., based on reports from users who have received spam)—and as such conform closely to the organizational model of peer production. Others are based on honeypots (email accounts deliberately set up to attract and identify spammers); still others are judgment calls based on information exchanged on discussion lists of antispam activists.[16] Each list maintainer also sets his or her own policies regarding how long alleged sources of spam stay on the blacklist and how they might be removed.[17]

Spam blacklists are used by ISPs and major corporate networks seeking to protect their users. Some are commercial services; most are maintained

16. The main public spam discussion forums include news.admin.net-abuse.email (also known as nanae) and SPAM-L.
17. There is no exhaustive and complete list of DNSBLs. Cole 2007 writes: "Many DNSBL's exist. Many are quite extreme about listings, and as a result are not used by any mail server that exists to actually deliver mail. Many others are rather conservative and list only actual spam sources, as best the maintainers can determine, and so have broad use."

and propagated on a voluntary basis. Despite the seemingly large amount of junk that enters our email inboxes, ISPs who use these lists (along with other algorithms or software-based capabilities of their own) succeed in filtering out the vast majority of spam. A study by the U.S. Federal Trade Commission concluded that one ISP effectively prevented 86 percent of spam messages from entering its users' inboxes, and another ISP managed to block 95 percent of spam messages.[18]

These practices exemplify the peer production of security. The information needed to support them is generated by networks of primarily voluntary actors. The blacklist itself does not have the effect of blocking or stopping anyone's email. Being on the list has an effect only if the list is recognized and implemented by the operators of email servers at specific organizations. Every actor thus has the capability of unilateral action, but the exercise of this capability is conditioned and constrained by the possibility of retaliatory action and negative effects on the actor's reputation. The producer of a blacklist has no inherent capability to get negative recommendations taken seriously and implemented by others; adoption by mail administrators is voluntary and can be ended at any time.[19] Because operators of email servers have a built-in incentive to allow all legitimate mail to pass through their systems, the blacklisting of innocent parties would result in a loss of reputation, low adoption rates, and possibly legal retaliation.[20]

Blacklists are not the only form of networked governance used to combat spam. In certain extreme cases, Internet service providers have simply pulled the plug on spam operations. In 2007 and 2008 joint decisions by ISPs to sever their connections to hosting services catering to

18. "Email Address Harvesting and the Effectiveness of Anti-Spam Filters," A Report by the U.S. Federal Trade Commission's Division of Marketing Practices. November 2005, http://www.ftc.gov/opa/2005/11/spamharvest.pdf.
19. It is also interesting to note that from 2003 on, spam blacklists have been subjected to DDoS attacks, presumably from harmed spammers, and at least one ceased operation in response to the pressure. So the peer production process cuts both ways.
20. Cole 2007 discusses several lawsuits against DNBLs. Multiple lawsuits against MAPS were settled, and prompted MAPS to make its lists fee based. ORBS was sued in 2001 over listings that "seemed quite clearly false and seemed to be motivated by the personal finances of the operator of ORBS, who fled from the suits rather than fighting them." An organization calling itself "EMarketers America" sued people it claimed were involved with SPEWS and people who operated and assisted the SpamHaus Project, but the suit was dismissed with prejudice at the request of the plaintiff.

spammers and criminals put a major dent in the global volume of spam. McColo Corp. was a San Jose, California-based Web hosting service that security experts alleged was hosting the command-and-control infrastructure for three of the world's most prolific spam botnets. In mid-November, 2008, the Internet providers that managed most of the company's Internet connections severed them. The move came after a sustained campaign by *Washington Post* reporter Brian Krebs, who compiled information about the "badness at McColo" and relayed it to its ISPs.[21] When McColo was shut down, spam-sending bot computers were disconnected and could not operate. The volume of spam around the world fell by as much as 70 percent afterward, and took months to recover. Krebs's reporting was also instrumental in generating pressure to disconnect two other bad actors.[22]

Note that it was a combination of publicity and unilateral action by Internet service providers that stopped these spammers—not law enforcement action. When asked why private action succeeded where law enforcement did not, Krebs was unable to provide a simple answer. Law enforcement agencies were monitoring these entities, and Krebs was in communication with them. Krebs did say that two weeks before the story that led to the shutdown of McColo was published, he notified the U.S. Justice Department that it would run and that it would not make them look good. He received no response.

Phishing

Phishing is a criminal activity that involves luring Internet users to Web sites that impersonate banks or other online financial services to trick them into revealing passwords and other credentials. An enticement is sent out via email spam, which purports to be a message from a bank or payment system to its customers, asking them to go to a Web site to provide identification information. The email contains a link to a Web site controlled by the criminals, but which looks and feels as if it were the actual bank or other targeted site. Once a customer is tricked into revealing the account

21. Brian Krebs, "Major source of online scams and spams knocked offline," *Security Fix* blog, *Washington Post* (online), November 11, 2008, http://voices.washington-post.com/securityfix/2008/11/major_source_of_online_scams_a.html.
22. Brian Krebs, "Taking on the Russian business network," *Security Fix* blog, *Washington Post* (online), October 13, 2007, http://blog.washingtonpost.com/securityfix/2007/10/taking_on_the_russian_business.html; Brian Krebs, "Spam volumes plummet after Atrivo shutdown," *Security Fix* blog, *Washington Post* (online), October 9, 2008, http://voices.washingtonpost.com/securityfix/2008/10/spam_volumes_plummet_after_atr.html.

information and login information, their accounts can be cleaned out. Sometimes this involves a network of on-the-ground people, known as money mules, who transfer the cash quickly to help the main perpetrators avoid detection. Estimates of the cost of phishing range from $320 million to $3.2 billion annually.[23]

Like spam, phishing underscores the scalability of cybercrime; in other words, the perpetrators' capacity to automate and reproduce their attacks en masse. In the first half of 2008, an organization that tracks phishing reported 47,324 phishing attacks, using 26,678 unique domain names and 3,389 unique IP addresses. An *attack* is defined as a phishing site that targets a specific brand or entity. One study makes a plausible case that one half of all these phishing attacks come from a single organized gang.[24]

The limits on the role of government law enforcement agencies in combating cybercrime apply here. Few phishers have been tracked, prosecuted, and convicted. Instead, the companies harmed by phishing respond primarily by rapidly identifying and taking down the Web sites. To support this reactive strategy, specialized companies maintain up-to-the-minute lists of phishing sites and develop cooperative relationships with the Internet services industry to execute takedowns. As one report noted: "the vast majority of these phishing sites are not removed by the efforts of law enforcement. Site take down is usually accomplished by companies being targeted by the phishers and third parties, generally private security companies, working on their behalf."[25] Takedown is a form of networked governance. It requires "cooperation between many independent actors with conflicting motivations, from the banks impersonated to the ISPs inadver-

---

23. Anti-Phishing Working Group (APWG), "Spear the Phishers Not the Fish" report, 2007. Moore 2008, 108, estimates that phishing takes in about $320 million per year in revenue from about 803,000 victims per year. Florencio and Herley, on the other hand, estimate that there are two million victims. D. Florencio and C. Herley, "Evaluating a Trial Deployment of Password Re-use for Phishing Prevention," in Anti-Phishing Working Group eCrime Researcher's Summit (APWG eCrime), 2007, 26–36. Gartner research estimated that in 2007, 3.6 million adults in the United States were successfully defrauded by phishing emails at a total cost of $3.2 billion.

24. Moore 2008, 108. Moore dubs this group the "rock-phish gang," and documents how they cooperate by pooling hosting resources and by targeting many banks simultaneously.

25. APWG online report, "Advisory on Utilization of Whois Data for Phishing Site Take Down," March 2008, http://www.antiphishing.org/reports/apwg-pc_Advisory _WhoisDataForPhishingSiteTakeDown200803.pdf.

tently hosting the phishing websites."[26] Most of these "independent actors" have no hierarchical authority over each other and are often distributed across jurisdictional lines. The need for speedy joint action requires the development of cooperative communication relationships. The actors targeting a phishing site need to know who to call within an organization, and the organization contacted needs to understand, or be convinced of, the legitimacy of the request and the requestor, and of the need to respond urgently. Obviously this kind of cooperation works most effectively after repeated patterns of exchange succeed in establishing trust. As to "conflicting motivations," it should be obvious that registries, registrars, and ISPs have interests that are structurally distinct from the interests of the banks and the brand protection industry. From the latter's perspective, the domains hosting an attack are customers to whom they have contractual obligations and from whom they receive revenue. Any accusation that the activities of their customers are illegal and need to be shut down must be treated cautiously. This makes common agreement on a hierarchical or more institutionalized relationship difficult. Given these conditions, networked governance fills the void.

A leading organization in the fight against phishing is the Anti-Phishing Working Group (APWG). Formed in October 2003, the APWG is an association of major Internet brand owners, security software and service vendors/researchers, and online financial firms. Initiated by an entrepreneur in the security software field, APWG combines the functions of a trade association that links security firms to their customers,[27] an industry advocacy group that proposes and voices positions on policy, and a resource-pooling vehicle for compiling and sharing information about phishing. It describes itself as "the global pan-industrial and law enforcement association" and claims to have 3,200 members from more than 1,850 information technology institutions.[28]

Phishing takedowns rely heavily on peer production methods for compiling, sharing, and maintaining information. From its inception, APWG

26. Moore 2008, 88.
27. APWG's organizational positions are occupied by persons who appear to have financial stakes with companies in the brand protection or computer security industry, such as Dave Jevans (CEO of Tumbleweed Communications), Rod Rasmussen (Internet Identity, Inc.), Laura Mather (formerly of Mark Monitor, Inc.), and Pat Cain (security consulting firm Cooper-Cain Group). Membership fees are tiered, running from $50 per annum to $50,000, which is typical of trade associations. Premium members ($15,000 or above) are given a seat on the steering committee.
28. APWG Web site, http://apwg.org.

set up a system to track phishing sites. APWG members sent in records of attacks. In return, APWG provided its paying members with access to this collectively generated database. In October 2006, OpenDNS launched a similar project called PhishTank, which made all its data publicly available. In May 2007, PhishTank and the APWG began sharing their databases.[29] Peer production methods are also used in the development of procedures to share data about phishing incidents in a standardized format that can be more readily automated.[30]

Although APWG and the methods of the broader anti-phishing community have emerged in response to the absence of effective transnational governance by governments, they do rely on some features of the ICANN regime. Registrars and registries are key partners in any takedown effort. ICANN has a form of hierarchical authority over registries and registrars; they must obtain contracts from ICANN before entering the market, and these legally enforceable contracts govern various aspects of their conduct.[31] APWG set up a special subcommittee in 2006 to formulate and make recommendations to ICANN and the registration community. In March 2007, at a time when ICANN was seriously considering modifying its Whois policy to shield potentially sensitive private data from indiscriminate Web-based access, APWG weighed in with a policy paper emphasizing the importance of unrestricted access to Whois data in the fight against phishing.[32] APWG and its supporters have also enlisted the ICANN policy-making process in an attempt to counter a new technique used by phishers known as *fast-flux*, which quickly changes the association between IP addresses and domain names. While fast-flux has some legitimate uses, it has been used by the more professional phishing gang(s) to undermine some of the simpler takedown methods and keep their sites up longer.

29. OpenDNS' PhishTank.com and Anti-Phishing Working Group to Share Data, news release, May 21, 2007, http://www.opendns.com/about/announcements/19/.
30. The standards proposal, drafted by APWG's Pat Cain and D. Jevans, and submitted to the IETF Network Working Group, in 2008 can be accessed here: http://www.ietf.org/id/draft-cain-post-inch-phishingextns-07.txt.
31. One registrar that was accused of being a "haven for cyber criminals" was deaccredited by ICANN after it learned that its CEO was a convicted felon. Brian Krebs, "ICANN de-accredits EstDomains for CEO's fraud convictions," *Security Fix* blog, *Washington Post* (online), October 29, 2008, http://voices.washingtonpost.com/securityfix/2008/10/icann_de-accredits_estdomains.html.
32. APWG memorandum, "Issues in Using DNS Whois Data for Phishing Site Take Down," May 2007, http://www.antiphishing.org/reports/APWG_MemoOnDomain-WhoisTake-Downs.pdf (accessed March 5, 2008).

Building on the network of actors converged around the ICANN regime, APWG has developed a plan that attempts to create a formally accredited network of trusted actors who would be authorized to take down Web sites more rapidly. In a September 2007 interview, Laura Mather of APWG described the proposed takedown process: "The APWG would create a body that would ratify organizations known to be experts in phishing site identification and takedown. A committee of the APWG would specify what evidence is required. . . . A check-list would have to be completed to make sure it was a phishing domain." The APWG's proposal for accelerated takedown, however, has been criticized by some on due-process grounds. Critics fear that peoples' domains or Web sites could be yanked out from under them by private actors acting in accordance with private agreements, without any formal recourse. Recall the earlier discussion of the Indymedia takedown. Who would be responsible if there are false positives or collateral damage, and innocent people are harmed? So far, this idea of APWG's has not materialized.

Operations (Not Code) as Law?

Clearly, traditional prosecution of cybercriminals is only the tip of the iceberg. Underneath the surface, there is an intense amount of peer production, networked governance, and thriving markets for security-related products and services.[33] This is a very different kind of governance than that traditionally associated with crime fighting by police. In it, legislative definitions of bad actors matter less than the *operational* definition adopted and implemented by Internet service providers, takedown processes, and blacklist maintainers. Formal criminal prosecution of malefactors is important; but its slow speed and its limitation to a small number of high-priority cases mean that day-to-day governance relies more on rapid transnational cooperative action to identify and take down bad actors. One can also see how these anti-spam and anti-phishing efforts benefit from having a global institutional framework such as ICANN. A positive feedback relationship exists between the globalized institutional capacity ICANN provides and the network of actors who converge around it to solve problems.

33. This chapter was not able to describe in detail another important manifestation of security governance: the efforts of Internet service providers to internalize many of the externalities associated with security problems. Van Eeten and Bauer (2008) have documented this well, contending that "all ISPs we interviewed described substantial efforts in the fight against malware, even though they are operating in highly competitive markets and there is no governmental regulation requiring them to do so."

Confronted with such facts, the common tendency among social theorists is to decry the lack of public law, or its weakness, and to call for the articulation of formal legislative principles and/or rights to regulate the process.[34] These complaints have merit. But they will be irrelevant until and unless the critique takes account of an essential point: laws, principles, and rights are a form of binding collective action that can only emerge from strong institutions. And in this case there is a fundamental misalignment between the relevant collectivity affected by cybercrime and the territorial nation-state. If we succeed in developing new formulations of rights to govern such activities, the most appropriate unit of collective action would not be the nation-state.

States and Internet Security

One might contend that the peer production of security takes place within a "shadow of hierarchy,"[35] where the hierarchy is composed of a mélange of national laws and international treaties. These laws do serve as reference points in the peer production of security. But one could also say that the residues of hierarchy are becoming entirely dependent upon the networked relations of peer production to have any effect. That is, before it becomes possible to even apply and enforce the laws, the agents of hierarchy (e.g., law enforcement) must participate in and become integrated into the looser transjurisdictional, multistakeholder networks of operators. So let us look more closely at the role of the state and formal treaties and laws, as well as the growing securitization of the Internet.

The Convention on Cybercrime

The problem of Internet security has already produced its own international treaty, through the Council of Europe. The drafting of the Convention on Cybercrime was completed in 2001. It articulates a list of crimes that each signatory state must transpose into its own law. It requires the criminalization of such activities as breaking into computer networks, illegal interception, computer-related forgery and fraud, and the production or sale of devices and software designed to commit such crimes. Confirming this book's list of the main drivers of Internet governance, the Convention did not confine itself to computer security breaches per se, but added offenses related to copyright infringement and content regula-

34. For example, Wall 2004.
35. Mayntz and Scharpf 1995.

tion (child pornography, and forms of political expression deemed insulting or racist). It also tried to harmonize certain procedural mechanisms within the laws of signatory states. For example, in order to facilitate surveillance of criminal suspects, it required that law enforcement authorities have the power to compel an ISP to monitor a person's online activities in real time.

The Convention on Cybercrime has been signed and ratified by twenty-three countries; it has not yet been ratified by thirteen countries that originally signed it.[36] Russia and Germany are two of the more notable holdouts. The United States ratified the treaty in August 2006, after a coalition of industry associations, led by the copyright-minded Business Software Alliance (BSA), pushed for its adoption by the Senate.[37] The United States did not, however, accede to the Convention's additional protocol for censoring insulting political speech, due to its constitutional guarantees of freedom of expression.

There are two prongs to the Convention on Cybercrime: the first involves a traditional but still significant form of legal harmonization; the other establishes an infrastructure for networked cooperation.

The convention erects a harmonized standard for defining certain computer crimes as criminal, in order to facilitate international cooperation among law enforcement agencies. This substantive harmonization, however, can occur (and is occurring) incrementally regardless of whether the Convention on Cybercrime itself is ratified. For example, it is happening through a revision of domestic laws or through regional harmonization.[38] In fact, when it comes to relations between the United States and European countries, the Convention on Cybercrime added little or nothing to what was already possible through established Mutual Legal Assistance Treaties.

The other accomplishment of the Convention on Cybercrime, and what some analysts have called its "most useful tool,"[39] is a simple network form of organization. It is a directory of law enforcement agency contact points called for in Article 35 of the convention. This is an operational network

36. As of January 2009. See the Council of Europe Web site for an up-to-date map of country accession: www.coe.int.
37. The coalition included BSA, the Cyber Security Industry Alliance, the American Bankers Association, the Information Technology Association of America (ITAA), Verisign, Infragard, and others.
38. Sixteen developing countries are listed by the Council of Europe as having used the Convention on Cybercrime as a guideline for national legislation
39. Presentation by Pedro Verdelho, Docente, Centre for Judiciary Studies, Portugal, Council of Europe Octopus Interface Conference on Cooperation Against Cybercrime, Strasbourg, April 2, 2008.

of experts on computer crime, with one point of contact for each country, who agree to be available twenty-four hours a day, seven days a week.[40] These contacts are able to "provide help and cooperation very quickly, even if a formal cooperation request must follow this informal way."[41] It is a way to secure quick preservation of perishable electronic evidence on a worldwide basis. "In the case of either a cyber attack or a case where cyber-evidence is involved, they can call another person on the contact list and that person can hopefully at least preserve the data while you take more formal steps."[42]

The network of contact points of the Convention on Cybercrime was not an innovation. It was built upon a prior informal network established by the G8 in 1997, known as the G8 24/7 contact points network.[43] The Convention on Cybercrime's Article 35 merely formalized this earlier network and tried to give it a clearer and more consistent legal underpinning. There is also a network of "National Central Reference Points" run by Interpol. Consolidation vs. diversity among these networks is an interesting aspect of networked governance, and of the evolution of the state's involvement in global Internet security governance. The Council of Europe notes on its Web site that it wants to "avoid a proliferation of networks" and so "it has been agreed that contact points of the G8 and those established under the Convention on Cybercrime be merged into a single Directory of Contact Points maintained by the G8 Sub-group on High-Tech Crime and the Council of Europe." Interpol has also pushed for consolidating its network with the G8 network.[44]

The London Action Plan

The fight against spam has also produced its own transgovernmental network organization: the London Action Plan (LAP). The LAP was originally formed in October 2004, at a meeting in London, as a network of

40. Most contacts are police, but in some countries (including the United States and the Netherlands) it is a prosecutor's office.
41. Verdelho, see note 39.
42. Christopher Painter, principal deputy chief, U.S. Department of Justice, Computer Crime and Intellectual Property Section, interviewed by Jeremy Kirk, IDG News Service, October 23, 2006.
43. "COMMUNIQUÉ." Meeting of Justice and Interior Ministers of The Eight, December 9–10, 1997, Washington, DC, December 10, 1997, http://www.usdoj.gov/criminal/cybercrime/g82004/97Communique.pdf (accessed January 7, 2009).
44. Speech by Interpol Secretary General Ronald K. Noble, 7th International Conference on Cybercrime, New Delhi, India, September 12, 2007, http://www.interpol.int/Public/ICPO/speeches/India20070912.asp.

government agencies fostering international cooperation in the enforcement of anti-spam laws. True to the theory of TGNs (transgovernmental networks), it forged a loose organization out of a diverse group of mid-level government agencies from twenty-five different national jurisdictions with a common interest in spam fighting. Participants included telecommunications regulators, consumer protection agencies, and data protection agencies. The LAP then expanded the network to include "appropriate private sector representatives," making it a multistakeholder TGN. The administrative infrastructure of the LAP and its conference calls is supplied, on a best-effort basis, by the U.S. Federal Trade Commission. The initial energy that prompted the creation of the LAP dissipated by 2009, however, and some of the original supporters drifted away. LAP was faced with a choice many volunteer networks face: either raise money for a full-time staff and become more professionally organized, or disband.

The main effect of the Convention on Cybercrime was simply to facilitate transnational networked collaboration. Compared to the London Action Plan, it represents a difference of degree rather than a fundamental difference of kind. A harmonized legal framework made it marginally easier for the network partners to collaborate. But few law enforcement agencies would disagree with the claim that most of the real security governance work is done by networked governance techniques, and by the market.

The Globalization of Surveillance

In the area of privacy, surveillance, and data protection we see strong assertions of state power. Paradoxically, the effect is to further undermine differences among national jurisdictions; that is, to make the operant policy transnational. Indeed, it is only a small exaggeration to say that law hardly matters any more; in operational terms, governments can and do get access to just about any information they want, at any time, on the Internet. The limits on their data surveillance capacity are governed more by technical limitations than by law. Using the fear of terrorism, governments have pushed for, and have largely gotten, a blanket capability to indiscriminately accumulate, compile, and data mine information moving over electronic networks, including not just the Internet but also financial networks and other forms of telecommunications. As was the case in Internet identifiers and copyright/trademark, we see the pattern of U.S. leadership creating a more or less globalized approach to surveillance, with the 9/11 attacks serving as the stimulus.[45]

45. Biersstecker and Eckert 2008 discuss the institutional innovations around the monitoring of financial networks after 9/11.

The most extreme example is the warrantless wiretap program in the United States, which was instituted through a Bush Administration Executive Order in 2002. It authorized the National Security Agency (NSA) to conduct surveillance of international telephone and Internet communications. With the complicity of some of the telecommunication firms, NSA installed huge data-surveillance capabilities at strategic points in U.S. telecommunication networks that vacuumed in faxes, phone calls, and Internet traffic, both domestic and international. While excoriated by liberal critics, in the end a Democrat-controlled Congress retroactively legalized the program and immunized the telephone companies from legal liability for their breaches of their subscribers' privacy.

The expansion of surveillance was not confined to the United States. The European Commission passed a data retention initiative in 2006 that required Internet service providers to retain and make available to law enforcement extensive information about users' activities.[46] Here again we see a push to harmonize across national boundaries the capability to engage in effective surveillance of the Internet and other forms of electronic communication. According to the directive, "The legal and technical differences between national provisions concerning the retention of data for the purpose of prevention, investigation, detection and prosecution of criminal offences present obstacles to the internal market for electronic communications, since service providers are faced with different requirements regarding the types of traffic and location data to be retained and the conditions and periods of retention."[47]

One can also point to various ways in which the post-9/11 environment of surveillance has wrought havoc with the efforts by the EU to protect and preserve its distinctive approach to data protection while remaining economically integrated with the United States. Time and again, in various contexts, Europe's data protection and privacy authorities have warned that some practice or aspect of Internet policy or surveillance is inconsistent with European data protection standards—and each time they are overruled or ignored. It happened after it was discovered that U.S. authorities had subpoenaed financial data from SWIFT, the Brussels-based finan-

46. Directive 2006/24/EC of the European Parliament and of the Council of 15 March 2006, http://www.bipt.be/en/203/ShowDoc/3015/European_framework/Directive_2006_24_EC_of_the_European_Parliament_an.aspx. On the retention of data generated or processed in connection with the provision of publicly available electronic communications services or of public communications networks and amending Directive 2002/58/EC.
47. Ibid., paragraph 6, page L 105/54.

cial clearinghouse,[48] and in connection with the collection and processing of airline passenger data.[49]

But the most interesting example of this phenomenon is the Whois service, one of the ICANN regime's most significant authoritative features. Publication of this data conflicts with national privacy/data protection laws of the European Union and other countries, because it can be retrieved indiscriminately over the Internet regardless of whether the registrant is a corporation or a "natural person" (i.e., an individual). Battles over privacy and Whois have raged within ICANN for years.[50]

The brand protection interests regard Whois as useful raw material in the production of their private security services. Indeed, the systematic collection and analysis of Whois data is a critical part of the business model of many of the commercial brand protection service providers who comprise APWG.[51] Normally, these private interests would yield to governmental policy and law. Yet the privatized and globalized institutional framework of ICANN makes it possible for many European or non-U.S. law enforcement agencies to give tacit or active support to open-access Whois, even while acknowledging that it would be illegal under their own national law. In the case of Australia, for example, its governmental representative in ICANN vigorously opposed any move away from open-access Whois, despite court decisions in Australia that have explicitly denied law enforcement agencies indiscriminate access to Whois records in the .au domain (the country code top level domain for Australia).[52] Similar situations held for law enforcement officials from Canada and the Netherlands. In this case it is clear that ICANN's Internet governance regime has

48. Press release on the SWIFT Case following the adoption of the Article 29 Working Party opinion on the processing of personal data by the Society for Worldwide Interbank Financial Telecommunication (SWIFT), November, 23, 2006. Archived at Privacy International, http://www.privacyinternational.org/article .shtml?cmd[347]=x-347-546365.
49. A U.S. law passed in the aftermath of the World Trade Center attacks on 9/11 required airlines operating passenger flights to, from, or through the United States to provide U.S. authorities with electronic access to Passenger Name Record data contained in their reservation and departure control systems.
50. For a more complete and detailed analysis of this issue and the history of contention over privacy and Whois, see Mueller and Chango 2008.
51. "Who Is Fighting Phishing: An Overview of the Phishing Lifecycle and the Entities Involved." MarkMonitor White Paper, July 2007.
52. See "Australia's Contribution to the GNSO Council on Whois," a document submitted by Ashley Cross, GAC representative for Australia, in April 2006, http:// gnso.icann.org/correspondence/australia-gac-whois-apr06.pdf.

created a new, global jurisdiction wherein traditional rights to privacy are redefined.

Internet Security as National Security?

Starting in late 2008, the United States witnessed a concerted effort to reframe Internet security as a national security issue. A report from an expert commission assembled by a Washington, DC, think tank with longstanding roots in Cold War dialogue typified the trend.[53] It urged incoming President Barack Obama to proclaim that "cyberspace is a vital asset for the nation and . . . the United States will protect it using all instruments of national power." Rather than conceiving of the Internet as a global space where individuals and organizations interact and routinely confront issues of crime, espionage and vandalism, the CSIS report attempted to make *national* security the basis for a comprehensive revision of all laws, technologies, and organizational structures around cybersecurity. This approach dramatically shapes policy perspectives. It militarizes what are mostly civil problems,[54] and subordinates the protection of people and households to the protection of vaguely defined *national* interests conceived in terms of rarified interstate rivalries. The deeply rooted institution of the nation-state, however, makes this a winning strategy politically. Claims that invoke "national security" can inflate budgets and provide for more effective political mobilization within bureaucracies and the political class. There is already talk of a cybermilitary-industrial complex.[55]

President Obama bowed to the new trend, declaring that "in today's world, acts of terror could come not only from a few extremists in suicide vests but from a few key strokes on the computer—a weapon of mass disruption."[56] What could have been a sensible effort to improve networked cooperation and coordination among government agencies and the private sector—transnationally as well as nationally—was instead dominated by militaristic rhetoric and a state-centric view of security. Legislation in Congress proposed to authorize the president to seize control of private networks in a "cyber-emergency" and dragged ICANN's contractual relationship with the U.S. Commerce Department into the securitization process.[57]

53. Lewis 2008.
54. The Heritage Foundation produced a report arguing that botnets "have the potential to do untold damage and they should be classified as eWMDs (electronic Weapons of Mass Destruction)." Kelly and Almann 2008–2009.
55. Morozov 2009.
56. President Obama remarks on cybersecurity, May 29, 2009.
57. The Cybersecurity Act of 2009, introduced by Senators Jay Rockefeller and Olympia Snowe.

Lost in the stampede to assume a pose of strength was the simple fact that a concentration of hierarchical power in the hands of a state does not, as far as anyone can tell, represent an innovative or effective response to the unique problems of scale, scope, and distributed control raised by the global Internet. Worse, such a response may undermine the stability and security of the Internet by encouraging other states to view it as a weapon that yields strategic advantage in national power competitions. "Undoubtedly," one academic claimed in response to Obama's address on cybersecurity, "his move will trigger an escalation of attack strategies and incidences from adversaries, including Russia and China, who will see the U.S. policy as a ratcheting of threats and a legitimization of such tactics. And we can expect more debilitating attacks on Websites and services, contracted out to third parties to muddy attribution and allow for plausible deniability. Today's announcement does nothing to explain how to secure against the chaos unleashed by that threat. Ultimately the assurance of security for every nation's critical infrastructure must include an international dimension that preserves the openness of global cyberspace."[58]

Identity Online: The Final Frontier

When law enforcement agencies allow phishing incidents to go unprosecuted, it is partly because cyberspace cloaks the origin of the criminal, and the costs and time commitments required to trace and locate the responsible parties are forbidding. When spammers get away with large-scale distribution of annoying or criminal materials, it is because a combination of hijacked IP addresses, botnets, and spoofed email headers allows the origin of the spam and the identity of the spammers to be obscured. When copyright holders push for shifting the burden of enforcement from their own legal actions to Internet service providers, it is because the costs of identifying and tracking down the alleged acts of infringement are too high. When authorities are unable to stop or retaliate against DDoS attacks, it is largely because they do not know who is responsible for them.

Little wonder that so much security discourse converges on the problem of *identity* on the Internet: the problem of authenticating users and uses. But this is not a simple matter of finding an "identity management solution," as the technology purveyors are wont to say. What really matters is

58. Ron Deibert, "Arms control in cyberspace," *New York Times*, May 29, 2009.

the association between an identifier, the identified individual or entity, and an organization or set of organizations that have institutionalized authority over a specific domain of human activity.

Consider the prospect of an Internet "driver's license." An automobile driver's license is, taken in isolation, nothing but a piece of plastic. What makes it an important form of identification is its relationship to a system of government. Its issuance and use are linked to, and expressions of, authoritative institutions at the state, provincial, or national level. Receipt of the license token is contingent upon meeting certain legally defined qualifications (e.g., being of age, passing a test). A huge, state-supplied administrative apparatus of testing and monitoring exists to fulfill that requirement. To be retained, the holder of the token must pay registration fees to the state and follow the rules of the road promulgated by the state. The association between a unique ID on the license and the holder's name allows the relevant authorities to link its holder to stored data that are critical to policing and maintaining accountability: residence address, jurisdiction, age, appearance, insurance carriers, past driving record. This, too, requires extensive back office capabilities, and the political authority required to compel its collection and accuracy. The collection and processing of this data creates enormous privacy and data protection issues. In terms of its contribution to actual, human security, identification goes far beyond the simple matter of getting a unique identifier in someone's hand and authenticating it.

Look back now at the quotation with which this chapter opened. Technical experts working for banks, brand protection services, law enforcement agencies and e-commerce companies are calling for an Internet driver's license. Do they understand that by creating a system of "identification" on the Internet, we are answering fundamental questions about the nature and scope of government? Who issues this "drivers license" in a world of competing states? To whom is the identifier given, and from whom it is withheld? What are the criteria used to issue or withdraw the identifier? What benefits are restricted to holders? Under what circumstances is someone required to produce the identifier to third parties (e.g., opening an ISP or email account)? To what other form of identification or data is it integrated or linked (e.g., birth certificates, proof of residence)? What happens to people to whom such a license is denied—are they completely banned, exiled, from electronic communications?

Establishing such a system of identification on a global scale for cyberspace would involve an incredible degree of transnational cooperation and probably also the creation of a large, even frightening bureaucratic overlay.[59] Would the U.S. government share this authority with the Chinese and Russian states? Set aside for a moment the question whether citizens can trust their own states with such capabilities: can any state trust other states with a shared and globally integrated identification system, when the Great Powers are all intent on developing and using the Internet as an instrument of spying and warfare?

Even assuming that information technology allows for the standardization and automation of many of these functions in a way that reduces the complexity of implementation, the acceptance of automated identification and authentication functions and their incorporation into routine governmental and commercial transactions at lower levels would constitute a transformative change in the way the world works. Think of how something as simple as the Whois record of one's domain name registration has become the focal point for hundreds of thousands of automated cease-and-desist letters sent out by trademark protection firms and the growth of a large industry around the collection and analysis of the data.

When techies and e-commerce firms wish for something like a driver's license for the Internet, do they have any idea what they are really asking for? And if they do, shouldn't we be even more concerned?

Conclusion

The problem of security has probably done more than anything else to shift the ground of Internet governance discourse away from celebratory references to its freedom and openness to calls for regulation and control. This chapter supported a three-step argument about the role of the state: (1) responding to cybersecurity problems involves highly scalable, difficult-to-trace actions and distributed actors and attacks that easily cross national borders, which often exceeds the capabilities of national approaches to

59. Kim Cameron, who has proposed some very useful "laws" or principles that should govern identity systems, came to this pessimistic conclusion about the prospects of universal, compatible implementation of those principles: "In summary, as grave as the dangers of the current situation may be, the emergence of a single simplistic digital identity solution as a universal panacea is not realistic. Even if a miracle occurred and the various players could work out some kind of broad cross-sector agreement about what constitutes perfection in one country, the probability of extending that universally across international borders would be zero." Cameron 2005. I think Cameron underestimates the possibility that strong network externalities might bring about this effect, but he may be right.

Internet governance; (2) the inadequacy prompts the development of new organizational arrangements that reconstitute relationships among business, government, and civil society in this sphere; (3) the successes and failures of these new arrangements pose novel political issues and governance problems that generate institutional change at the transnational level.

There is, in other words, no simple reassertion of the national state and reining in of the global Internet. There is, rather, an adaptation of states to global networks and networks to states. The recent incorporation of cyberspace into national security dynamics, however, has led to calls for harder forms of power and a vigorous reassertion of the traditional logic of competing nation-states. But the more we try to implement these harder forms of power, I suspect, the more we will appreciate the virtues of the softer, networked methods that have already emerged.

Identity and identification is one of the key arenas where this adaptation will take place. But it is not happening yet. Identity on the Internet is a hard problem—one that implies transformative changes in the relationship between government and citizens. As the problem of a globally functional identity on the Internet gets worked out, we can expect to see both new transnational governance arrangements and new technical standards that require altered governance arrangements to back them up. Insofar as these standards create authoritative and effective forms of leverage over Internet users—such as the ability to accurately identify specific individuals or firms and shut them down—they create new kinds of hard power that will need to be carefully regulated and controlled on a global basis.

9 Content Regulation

In the summer of 2008, the British mobile telecommunication service provider Vodafone announced that it would block access to Web sites with child pornography and racist content in the Czech Republic. That content was, Vodafone claimed, so "socially dangerous . . . that we have access to it automatically blocked for all of our customers." Six months later, Czech resident Radim Hasalik, who runs a technology blog, discovered that the carrier's filter was also blocking him. In fact, it blocked several other innocent sites under the .cz (Czech Republic) country domain: a few other tech blogs, a chat server, a business directory, and a site with bus and train schedules. Vodafone's blocklist, the company said, came from the Internet Watch Foundation, a British nonprofit.[1]

Freedom of expression is at the core of the Internet governance debates. Here the tension between networks and states has its most profound consequences and leads to the most wrenching policy debates.

The Internet made a major contribution to global society by disrupting the regulation of media content by nation-states. It took the libertarian principle of "absence of prior restraint" and globalized it: no one had to ask for permission, or be licensed, to make their ideas and publications globally accessible. This open access, sometimes praised as "network neutrality" or the "end-to-end principle," took states by surprise. The explosion of ideas, services, and expression associated with the Internet's growth in the mid-1990s happened because *states weren't prepared for it* and because *states weren't in charge.*

And yet many still want to designate certain kinds of expression as taboo and have public authorities censor its publishers or users. In other

1. Mark Glaser, "Vodafone's child porn filter blocks innocent Czech tech blogs," *Mediashift*, January 15, 2009, http://www.pbs.org/mediashift/2009/01/-vodafones -child-porn-filter-blocks-innocent-czech-tech-blogs015.html.

words, many people are willing to grant the state a role in content regulation even as they acknowledge the tremendous social advances we have made in the past two decades by undermining its authority to do so.

In Internet governance, any concession to states has profound consequences. Once we recognize a state interest in Internet content regulation, we are led inexorably away from the globalized access to information the Internet delivers. As coercive instruments of collective action, different states enforce different rules. Some permit and even encourage scrutiny and criticism of policies and government officials; others actively suppress political dissidents. Some national content policies are extremely local and idiosyncratic: the Turks, for example, strongly forbid casting any aspersions on country founder Ataturk; the Thais are equally sensitive about the public image of their king. There are major variations in standards of obscenity and indecency among Asian, American, Arabic, and European societies. The United States considers Nazis and racists to have the same rights to freedom of expression as the rest of us. Germany and France don't. In a state sovereignty framework, *no* distinctions can be made between these policies, or between liberal–democratic states and authoritarian ones. National laws, no matter their intent, are equally binding within their respective territories. So if one accepts the principle of national sovereignty, one has no choice but to try to force the Internet to abide by *all* local taboos and regulations.

But there is something profoundly retrograde about rebordering the flow of information services, ideas, and expression so that two hundred different states—and perhaps thousands more provinces and localities—can better impose controls on it. And the combination of a global Internet with resurgent national sovereignty runs the risk of allowing objections from one jurisdiction to restrict or intimidate communicators residing in places where that government has no legitimate authority. Legal scholars have documented the repeated use of UK defamation law by forum-shopping litigants trying to silence journalists or critics.[2] That example of globalizing local jurisdiction, however, is small-scale in comparison to ICANN's attempt to define standards of "morality and public order" to regulate the creation of new top-level domains (discussion to follow).

We seem to be confronted with an unpalatable dilemma: either systematically reborder Internet communications, and thereby destroy one of its most valuable features, or develop a globally harmonized system of content regulation that reaches consensus by pulling the freest states into Faustian

2. For example, Deibert et al. 2008, 191.

bargains with the most authoritarian and repressive ones. Or, even worse, stumble into a confused combination of both approaches. None of these options supports a free and robust Internet.

This problem remains intractable until and unless one questions, directly and openly, the legitimacy and inevitability of state sovereignty over Internet-based expression. This chapter does just that. It argues that an emergent form of networked governance can flexibly and effectively regulate access to Internet content without destroying the Internet's global compatibility and openness. There is still a role for national law in this argument, but it must accept strong and just limits on its applicability.

Scale Shift and Networked Governance (Again)

The story of Internet content regulation starts from the same point as our analysis of cybercrime and copyright. There is a massive scale shift that comes with automated information processing; in addition, global networking disperses responsibility across a virtual space encompassing multiple jurisdictions and organizations.

Consider first the obvious scale shift. Networked computers have produced a quantum leap in the scale and speed with which messages and information can be generated. There is no need to belabor this point: most readers witness every day the rapid proliferation in the number of Web sites; the increasingly dynamic, database-driven nature of online content and services; the harnessing of content generated by millions of users; the elimination of geography (but not language) as a factor limiting distribution. That scale shift upended prior methods of regulation, which relied on licensing and regulating a small number of gatekeeper-publishers, who were unambiguously sited in a national jurisdiction and focused primarily on national or local markets.

While the Internet has vastly expanded the scale and scope of interactive public and private expression, it has triggered an equally impressive, if somewhat lagging, development of technical and organizational methods to monitor and regulate online expression. The Internet disperses to millions of private actors the capability to manage and control their own devices and the conditions under which they access other networks. It not only makes every person a potential publisher, it also makes every person a potential censor of whatever network he or she manages. It not only links people into networks where information flows freely and almost without cost, it also can make them participants in a "report abuse" network that flags objectionable messages or information for possible takedown. While Internet communication has given child predators new avenues, it has also enabled nonstate initiatives, such as the Perverted Justice.org, to lure them into traps where their intentions are exposed and they are arrested.[3]

The industrialization of content generation also produces the industrialization of content surveillance, classification, and management.[4] At their most mundane, so-called filtering software and services are purchased by enterprises to prevent their employees from dallying in sports Web sites or porn sites while on the job. There is close integration between these firms' attempts to regulate access to content and the demand for enterprise-level Internet security services. Similar capabilities are developed at the firmware or hardware level by router manufacturers or the producers of deep packet inspection technologies. The capacity for control does not just exist at the endpoints; the servers and routers that constitute the "middle" of the Internet are gradually acquiring the ability to analyze image, sound, and text files in unprecedented quantities and with unprecedented speed and sophistication. Along with this analytical capacity comes an ability to take action on information as it flows through the network: to scan, to sort, to classify, to contain, to border, to censor. These tools are still relatively primitive, and are certainly no substitute for case-specific applications of law to facts. But the nonscalability of traditional legal judgments is precisely why automated decisions are bound to be used as substitutes for them. And inevitably, the same automated tools can also be purchased and applied by repressive governments to reduce citizens' access to information deemed immoral or politically destabilizing.

In this environment, content regulation becomes a dynamic process in which states must respond to rapid content production globally and private

3. Perverted-Justice.com recruits volunteer contributors who pose as underage children in chatrooms. Posing as kids aged ten to fifteen, these contributors simply go into chatrooms with fake online screen names and wait for predators to instigate conversation with them. Contributors post all information in the chat logs to the Perverted-Justice.com database, claiming that they use "careful verification procedures to ensure authenticity."

4. "Classifying content is what Websense is all about," says the promotional material of one of the leading commercial firms in this field. The company boasts of employing more than a hundred researchers worldwide to "apply a vast array of classification techniques to block malicious or unwanted data from entering the network and protect confidential or proprietary data from leaving." These technologies, the company claims, allow it to discover, identify, classify, and adapt to content trends on a global scale.

actors take over most of the responsibility for monitoring and enforcement. Insofar as a pattern of governance can be discerned, the changes bear a strong family resemblance to the responses to spam, phishing, and copyright infringement discussed earlier. There is

• more delegation to private actors;
• the development of transnational peer production methods to identify and take down content;
• a more transnational discourse around regulatory norms;
• more reliance on transnational institutions;
• more reliance on automated techniques, with the technologies supplied by a globally integrated market.

Yet at all times, the impact of this unsystematic system of governance is patchy and subject to circumvention.[5] China's Falung Gong movement and the University of Toronto's CitizenLab, among others, have developed censorship circumvention software and services that can allow Internet users in repressed countries to bypass blocking. Some of this circumvention is even state sponsored or commercially supported.[6]

What does a political and legal commitment to freedom of expression mean in this context? Even some of the most sophisticated theorists of freedom of expression have not fully come to grips with the nature of this change. We need a concept of freedom of expression better suited to the system of large-scale, automated content generation, interconnected autonomous systems, and highly differentiated layers of access characteristic of the global Internet. This is one of the most critical challenges of global Internet governance.

Child Protection and Networked Censorship

The extensive system of Internet surveillance and censorship in the People's Republic of China is the poster child for Internet content regulation.

5. For general information on technical efforts to avoid censorship, see J. Markoff, "Cyberwar: Iranians and others outwit Net censors," *New York Times*, May 1, 2009, A1, New York City edition.
6. The U.S. Congress appropriated $15 million to support Internet censorship circumvention services in 2008 and 2009. The Obama administration doubled that amount to $30 million in 2010. The developers of Psiphon have created a for-profit company that offers media companies the opportunity to deliver digital content and advertising to Web users behind national firewalls. The Global Internet Freedom Consortium, backed by Chinese and American computer scientists backed by Falun Gong, also has developed a suite of censorship circumvention software.

Here, the attempt to create a "nationalized," bordered Internet has been taken about as far as it can go. The system relies not only on an army of about forty thousand censors at regional centers who implement keyword-based URL blocking at the network layer, but also on centralized control of the physical infrastructure and its gateways to the outside world.[7] The Ministry of Culture demands that all online music distributors provide written lyrics for each song, translated into Chinese, and documents to prove they aren't infringing on intellectual property rights.[8] Its Ministry of Information Industry tried to compel the installation of spyware/content filtering software on every personal computer shipped into the country.[9] As one extreme on a spectrum of control, it serves as a useful reference point. But focusing too narrowly on China can distort our understanding of the problem; it is too easy to think of Internet censorship as something that happens "somewhere else" in a few authoritarian regimes. There is, in fact, extensive Internet content regulation in the rest of the world. At least thirty countries engage in content blocking and the number is growing.

The vanguard of Internet content regulation has been the child safety movement. In the war conducted against transmission and consumption of sexual images of children, we see a full-on embrace of all the distinctive elements that characterize attempts to control expression on the Internet: delegation to nonstate actors; a blurry boundary between state action and private action; notice and takedown; and peer production of blacklists and some transnational sharing of the lists (but surprisingly little standardization). We also see evidence of the globalization of the norms governing content regulation. The emergence of a new regime is greatly aided by the fact that the prescribed behavior and content are universally considered to be criminal, which blunts many of the freedom of expression concerns. Indeed, in some cases it is clear that emotional appeals to "the children" have deliberately been exploited as the entering wedge for a broader reassertion of state control over Internet content.

7. As a Freedom House report documents, "All three [of the least free] countries [China, Iran, and Tunisia] have centralized their Internet infrastructure so that all traffic must pass through a limited number of gateways or service providers . . . before connecting to the global Internet. Karlekar and Cook 2009, 6.
8. Loretta Chao, "China sets new rules for music sold online," *Wall Street Journal*, Technology section, September 5, 2009, http://online.wsj.com/article/SB125207664547286713.html.
9. John Leyden, "China not demolishing green dam: Censorware not going anywhere after all," *The Register*, July 2, 2009, at 10:51 GMT, http://www.theregister.co.uk/2009/07/02/green_dam_back_on/.

Two organizations pioneered the institutional form taken by this kind of content regulation: the Internet Watch Foundation (IWF) in the UK and the National Center for Missing and Exploited Children (NCMEC) in the United States. The institutional form of the IWF in particular has been replicated around the world, and a transnational, cooperative arrangement among these entities has emerged. As private foundations, they are not quite government agencies, but they are often funded by governments as well as private donors and may be utilized by governments to develop and enforce censorship policies. These organizations use hotlines to identify and promulgate lists of Web sites that can be taken down or blocked. In many cases, however, the utilization of their blocklists is voluntary—or at least, nominally so. We need to examine this new method of control, and carefully explore both its strengths and its weaknesses.

Internet Watch Foundation (UK)

The Internet Watch Foundation was established in 1996 by the British Internet industry, at the high tide of self-regulation as a norm. The details of its founding are very similar to what happened a few months earlier in the Netherlands.[10] Peter Dawes—owner of Pipex, one of the earliest ISPs in Great Britain—led the effort along with the London Internet Exchange (LINX) and the British ISP Association.[11] IWF was originally charged with two main tasks. The first was to provide a "hotline" for the public and industry professionals to report potentially illegal online content, which would in turn facilitate takedown by ISPs and prosecution by the police. The hotline function was narrowly focused on what was called, at the time, child pornography.[12]

10. A Dutch "Hotline Foundation against Child Pornography on the Internet" [Stichting Meldpunt ter Bestrijding van Kinderporno op Internet] was founded in 1995. Following calls for action and the discovery that normal police work was unable to attack it, Internet providers involved in the formation of the Dutch Association of Internet Providers (NLIP) combined with some Internet users to establish the hotline. The alliance, initially informal, was officially launched in June 1996 by the then minister of justice, Mrs. W. Sorgdrager. As of 1998, the hotline has an agency from which its activities are carried out.
11. Until March 1997, IWF was overseen by a steering group from the two associations (LINX and ISPA), the UK Department of Trade and Industry, the UK Home Office, and the IWF Chief Executive with funding from the Dawe Charitable Trust.
12. The term *child pornography* is now considered inappropriate by this community because, as NCMEC writes, it "implies simply conventional pornography with child subjects." The preferred label now is *images of child abuse* or *sexually exploitive images of child victims*.

The IWF's second primary task was to help develop a rating system to allow users to regulate their own access to Internet content.[13] There was at the time a widespread belief, or hope, that a globally effective ratings system for Internet content could be put into place. The World Wide Web consortium (W3C) had created its Platform for Internet Content Selection (PICS) to facilitate the development and application of ratings.[14] The idea found a well-heeled advocate in the Bertelsmann Foundation of Germany, an instrument of the multinational publishing and media conglomerate.[15] These ideas were institutionalized in the Internet Content Rating Association.[16] The basic paradigm was drawn from motion picture and television content regulation, but also from the Internet/software developers' belief in the complete malleability of social problems to technical solutions. The hope was that all Web site content would carry a hidden label describing that content in predefined codes. Users would then be able to precisely and automatically filter out any content breaching the specified limits that they had set for themselves.

This was an attempt, laudable in some ways and misguided in others, to extend the end-to-end principle to content regulation. Control criteria would be set by the users, at the endpoints. Indeed, the early IWF showed solicitude for freedom of expression that can only make us nostalgic for the 1990s.[17]

But belief in PICS-style ratings as the solution to the problem of Internet content regulation gradually collapsed after 2002. It had two fatal flaws. At the end-user side, it demanded too much effort and knowledge on the part of the public. The techies at W3C who developed the PICS platform just couldn't understand why the typical household user didn't spend hours self-configuring their browsers to tell it how to handle dozens of different kinds of content. (No one else had any trouble understanding this.) But even if users had been willing and able to assume these respon-

13. See the 1998 Web site via the Wayback machine, http://web.archive.org/web/19990127090401/www.iwf.org.uk/rating/rating_r.html.
14. See Resnick and Miller 1996 and Resnick 1997.
15. Bertelsmann Foundation, "Self-regulation of Internet Content," September 1999, http://www.cdt.org/speech/BertelsmannProposal.pdf.
16. The ICRA Web site is at http://www.fosi.org/icra/.
17. "Rating and filtering techniques . . . are capable of providing selective blocking of material, which is controlled by the users according to their own criteria. Introduced and adopted on a voluntary basis, they do not interfere with anyone's right of free speech on the Net, nor do they prevent any adult from viewing anything they wish to see." See the IWF Web site, note 13.

sibilities, there was an even bigger flaw at the content suppliers' end. Internet content rating was undermined by the increasingly dynamic, scalable nature of Internet content generation. There was simply too much content to tag, and too many ambiguities in the classifications of large, dynamic aggregations of content to make the effort worthwhile.[18]

And so the IWF forgot about ratings and developed into one of the more focused and competent hotlines supporting a notice and takedown function for illegal Internet content. Leveraging peer production, the public hotline provides thousands of "tips" or accusations that particular sites are "potentially illegal." IWF is careful to always use the term *potentially illegal* rather than *illegal*. This reflects their ambiguous status as private sector delegate—they are not judges or courts who can make official determinations of legality but they are familiar enough with the legal standards applied to the objectionable material to make what might be characterized as a well-informed accusation or presumptions of illegality. A team of analysts reviews them and identifies ones that they deem to be "potentially illegal child sexual abuse content URLs." Only about one-third of the content reported is eventually deemed by IWF to be "potentially illegal."[19] These are then referred to ISPs for takedown and to the police for prosecution. IWF's annual report speaks of "a sophisticated system to transfer intelligence and information from IWF to the police," and "a very receptive and amenable Internet Content Service Provider community who remove potentially illegal content immediately they are advised of the problem."[20]

When it comes to taking down illegal child images on the Web, one cannot argue with IWF's success within the UK territorial jurisdiction. In 1997, its first full year of operation, 18 percent of potentially illegal content reported to IWF—almost entirely child abuse images—was hosted in the UK. By 2003 that percentage had dropped to one percent. Since then it

18. "For webmasters who wanted to make an honest attempt at correctly rating every single one of their pages, and one was Sylvia Spruck Wrigley at Demon Internet (where I worked in the 1990s), the whole process was extremely time consuming. I recall her spending ages trying to work out how to rate the pages within a Guy Fawkes themed section of the website; what was a suitable rating for a page that mentioned interrogation techniques [in 1605] and the punishment for treason?" Richard Clayton, "Web content labelling," *Light Blue Touchpaper* blog, September 17, 2007, http://www.lightbluetouchpaper.org/2007/09/17/web-content-labelling/.
19. IWF 2003 *Annual Report*, 8.
20. IWF 2007 *Annual Report*.

has fallen to levels consistently below 1 percent. The IWF *2008 Annual Report* makes it clear (contrary to many alarmist reports) that the publication of illegal images of children via the World Wide Web is stable and under control in the UK.[21]

NCMEC (USA)

In the United States, the counterpart to IWF is the National Center for Missing and Exploited Children (NCMEC). Like the IWF, it originated as a private foundation, but unlike IWF, NCMEC predates the Internet's development into a public medium. Impetus for its creation came from a foundation started by John Walsh, whose son Adam tragically was abducted and killed. NCMEC received a mandate from Congress in 1984 amid the media frenzy created by a series of highly publicized child abductions. Initially focused exclusively on missing children, NCMEC has assumed a broader mandate to fight against all forms of child abuse and exploitation. Unlike its British counterpart, it did not have strong ties to the Internet industry or a commitment to industry self-regulation. Indeed, it has been repeatedly criticized for publishing inflated statistics on child abduction with the implication that such tactics build support for its activities among Congress and private donors.[22]

Today, online abuse of children seems to be gradually taking the place of abductions as a fear-inspiring phenomenon that can be invoked to support NCMEC's mission. Since 1998 it has operated a CyberTipline

21. IWF, together with UK police, issued only fifty-nine notices to UK Internet service providers or host companies to take down content hosted on UK networks. From 2007 to 2008 there was a 9 percent decrease in the number of reported domains confirmed to contain indecent images of children (1,536), and a 21 percent decrease since 2006. See IWF 2008 *Annual Report* news release, April 29, 2009, http://www.iwf.org.uk/media/news.archive-2009.258.htm.

22. NCMEC's claims about the number of child abductions by strangers were first challenged in 1985 by Levinson (2002). Yet NCMEC continues to publish suspect numbers. The 2007 *Annual Report* (p. 8) claims that there are 58,000 abductions by nonfamily members per year "primarily for sexual reasons" and cites a government report for support (Sedlak et al., 2002). This statistic simply cannot be found in the actual report. The report estimates the number of reported cases of nonfamily abductions at twelve thousand and projects unreported cases at thirty-three thousand. The report qualifies both estimates with the footnote: "Estimate is based on an extremely small sample of cases; therefore, its precision and confidence interval are unreliable." The report says nothing about whether the purpose was sexual or not. Only an estimated 115 cases qualified as stereotypical kidnapping.

similar to IWF's hotline. In 2007 it created what it calls a "voluntary" program that feeds participating Internet service providers with URLs alleged to contain sexually abusive images of children. It also maintains a database of child pornography images that gives each one a unique identifier (known as a *hash value*) that can be used by ISPs to identify and remove the images.

IWF and to a lesser extent NCMEC pioneered an organizational form that has been replicated internationally. More than two dozen Internet child-abuse-content hotlines around the world are organized around Inhope, the International Association of Internet Hotlines. NCMEC also internationalized its operations in 1997, forming the International Center for Missing and Exploited Children in the wake of the tragic serial killings of young girls in Belgium.

NCMEC, the IWF and its counterpart hotlines span the boundary between public and private authority. The IWF calls itself "an independent self-regulatory body, funded by the EU and the wider online industry, including Internet service providers, mobile operators and manufacturers, content service providers, filtering companies, search providers, trade associations and the financial sector as well as other organizations that support us for corporate social responsibility reasons." NCMEC is a private nonprofit that gets donations from the Internet and computer industries and other corporations. But in 2007, as in most previous years, it got nearly 70 percent of its $43 million annual budget from the U.S. federal government. It has been called by one critic a "wholly owned and controlled subsidiary of the Justice Department's Office of Juvenile Justice."[23] Inhope, incorporated as a Dutch private company, was also initiated by a private nonprofit, but was formally founded in 1999 with funding from the European Commission's Safer Internet Action Plan.

From Hotlines to Block Lists

The child safety movement, aided by ambitious politicians, has evolved into an advocate of ever-stronger forms of content regulation. In both the Netherlands and the UK, the self-regulatory agencies that ISPs helped to create turned against the industry and began to promote forms of censor-

23. The quotation is from testimony by Bill Treanor, executive director of the American Youth Work Center, before the House Subcommittee on Human Resources. He is quoted in the article by Tadd Wilson, "Suffer the missing children," *Reason Magazine*, November 1995, http://www.reason.com/news/show/29778.html.

ship the providers did not want.[24] They moved from a focus on *takedown* of in-country illegal content to the publication of *blacklists* that attempt to restrict access to content hosted outside a country's jurisdiction. Blocking becomes the content regulators' answer to the transnational nature of the Internet. The rationale is that the content source is outside the reach of national law and therefore cannot be taken down. There are also moral reasons asserted for blocking.[25]

Project Cleanfeed in the UK, and similar efforts in other countries, is typical. IWF compiles and distributes a list of banned sites to ISPs in a manner that is quite similar to the way spam blocklists are compiled and distributed. The public hotline provides thousands of "tips" that particular sites are illegal. A team of analysts reviews them and adds ones that they deem to be "potentially illegal" to a list.[26] The list, which is updated twice daily, typically contains between 800 and 1,200 live URLs targeted for child sexual abuse content at any one time.[27] There is a procedure whereby the Web site owner of any blocked URL has the right of appeal, although IWF does not notify a publisher that it is going to be blocked. Details of every URL with alleged child sexual abuse content are passed with accompanying intelligence not only to domestic law enforcement agencies, but also to a global network of hotline associates around the world. The IWF list is picked up by commercial Web filtering companies as well, such as WebSense and SmoothWall.

The same model has been replicated in Canada. Cybertip.ca creates and maintains a regularly updated list of specific foreign-hosted Internet URLs

24. See the press release regarding Meldpunt ter bestrijding van Kinderpornografie op Internet ("Hotline Combating Child Pornography on the Internet"), September 11, 2007, which advocated blocking and criticized "a number of providers" who "indicated that they do not wish to cooperate with the blocking of child abuse images making use of a list of prosecutable websites provided by the KLPD." http://www.meldpunt-kinderporno.nl/EN/default.htm.

25. The arguments are that display of the images revictimizes the children involved; that blocking reduces the ability of commercial Web sites to make money, limits distribution, and prevents innocent users from accidentally confronting such images. See Stol et al. 2009 for a dispute of these results.

26. The URLs are assessed according to UK law, a process reinforced by reciprocal police training with each image categorized in line with criteria set out by the UK Sentencing Advisory Council.

27. Not all ISPs in Britain accurately notify users that sites are blocked; some return false "404" error messages. 404 means that the server cannot be found, a result that normally means that the domain doesn't exist or is offline for some reason.

associated with images of child sexual abuse and provides that list in a secure manner to participating ISPs. Linking into this "Cleanfeed Canada" is voluntary; ISPs are under no legal obligation to participate in the program. While participating ISPs automatically prevent access to addresses on the list, they do not help to create the list nor do they even know what it contains. Like IWF, Cybertip.ca receives complaints from Canadians regarding Web sites hosting potentially illegal images, and analysts assess and validate the reporting person's information. Reports on objects deemed potentially illegal are forwarded to the appropriate law enforcement jurisdiction. In other countries, such as Norway, Denmark, and Sweden, the blacklist is maintained by the police.

Blocking and the Role of the State

Once a blacklist and the organizational arrangements to make it effective are in place, several critical policy issues arise. One has to do with the transparency and accountability of the list of blocked URLs itself. The other is whether the list of blocked materials can expand to include other kinds of illegal content—or, worse, whether it can surreptitiously expand to include content that some may find objectionable but that is not really illegal. Another question is whether use of the list becomes compulsory. Obviously, all of these questions are related to the same fundamental issue: what is the role of the state in these Internet blocking schemes?

To some actors in Internet governance, blocking of child abuse images has provided both an example and a rudimentary infrastructure for national Internet content regulation. More governments and censorship advocates have begun to think that blocking or "filtering" techniques could recreate the kind of control they once had over traditional territorial media. In addition to the UK, Norway, Denmark, Sweden, and Italy are already filtering child pornography with various mixtures of compulsory and voluntary participation; Germany and Australia joined them in 2009, with hierarchical, state-directed content-blocking regimes.[28]

There are four serious problems with blacklists: (1) they undermine transparency and due process; (2) they often lead to structural overblock-

---

28. An Australian ISP stopped cooperating with the government's blocking trial in March 2009, claiming that "the trial was not simply about restricting child pornography or other such illegal material, but a much wider range of issues including what the Government simply describes as 'unwanted material.'" Asher Moses, "iiNet pulls out of net censorship trials," *Sydney Morning Herald*, March 23, 2009, http://www.smh.com.au/articles/2009/03/23/1237656833566.html.

ing; (3) they seem to shift law enforcement priorities away from catching perpetrators; and (4) they often have extraterritorial effects.

Consider first the transparency problem. If the blacklist cannot be independently monitored, how do we know whether it is accurately targeted on truly illegal images? When spam and phishing fighters compile lists of IP addresses and sites to block, transparency is an important part of the process. The information feeds into a commons-based peer production process where the data can be actively shared, monitored, updated, and improved. More important, no one is required to use the lists, so provider and users have alternatives and blacklist producers have incentives to make them narrowly and precisely targeted. With taboo information like child sexual images, admittedly, transparency is more complicated. Regulators may fear that by releasing the list they would be advertising the existence of, and thus possibly facilitating access to, the very content they are trying to suppress.

While that concern is largely hypothetical, there is no doubt that the absence of transparency has had ill effects. Free expression advocates have succeeded in exposing many lists, substantiating warnings about the dangers of state-sanctioned blacklists. The exposures not only revealed overblocking and mission creep, but indicated that blocking may act as a substitute for takedown and prosecution of truly illegal material.

A free expression advocate in Finland who published the list of blocked Web sites maintained by the Finnish police revealed that the banned sites were not confined to URLs with images of children being sexually abused.[29] On the contrary, most were legal gay and straight porn sites. The secret blacklists of Norway, Australia, and Germany also have been published on the anonymous whistle-blower Web site Wikileaks.[30] In Australia, YouTube postings, gambling and euthanasia sites, as well as legal porn were also on the list. There were obvious mistakes: the Australian list somehow included the Web site of a Queensland dentist and a school canteen consultancy.[31] An Australian anticensorship activist deliberately submitted the URL for a Web site run by antiabortion activists that contained disturbing photos of

29. See "Finnish Internet censorship," *Electronic Frontier Finland*, February 18, 2008, http://www.effi.org/blog/kai-2008-02-18.html.
30. From 2007–2009, Wikileaks exposed detailed secret government censorship lists, or plans to create such lists, for at least eight countries, including Thailand, Denmark, the United Arab Emirates, Australia, and Germany.
31. Asher Moses, "iiNet pulls out of Net censorship trials," *Sydney Morning Herald*, March 23, 2009, Technology section, http://www.smh.com.au/articles/2009/03/23/1237656833566.html.

aborted fetuses to the Australian Communication and Media Authority (ACMA), which maintains the blacklist.[32] The submission was made in order to find out whether legitimate political speech would be censored. ACMA readily agreed to censor the site, thus proving that it was easy to get sites that have nothing to do with child sexual abuse added to the list. When this became public ACMA refused to admit its mistake and threatened to fine blogs and discussion sites that hyperlinked to the blacklisted antiabortion site. Similarly, the Finnish free speech activist who exposed the censorship scheme was rewarded by having his own Web site added to the list of blocked sites in Finland. In Germany, the reaction was even more repressive. The office of Wikileaks.de was forcibly raided by the police after it exposed the German list of banned sites.[33]

Worse, a very large portion of the banned URLs were *not* outside the reach of territorial law. In a study commissioned by their Ministry of Justice, Dutch researchers investigated the status of the Netherlands' police blacklist at two different points in time (mid-February and mid-March 2008). Underscoring the need for continual and rapid updating of such a list, 10 percent of the blocked domains no longer existed or had no content, while 4 percent had no child pornography. Of the sites with illegal content, no less than 92 percent of the blocked sites were located either in the Netherlands itself or in other jurisdictions with strong laws against child pornography and well-established forms of international police cooperation with the Netherlands. Most of these sites (77 percent) were in the United States, which the report notes "officially cooperates with [the Netherlands] in fighting child pornography." The report concludes that "the blacklist seems to function as an alternative for tracking and prosecution."[34] Likewise, the overwhelming majority of the banned sites on the Finnish list were located in the United States or in the EU. These facts completely undermine one of the primary rationales for using blocking, as opposed to takedown.

Undeterred by strong evidence of overblocking in the relatively narrow domain of child protection, European and Canadian hotlines are adding, or considering adding, so-called "hate speech" to their blacklists. This refers

32. As of June 2009 the Web site was http://www.abortiontv.com/Pics/AbortionPictures6.htm.
33. John Ozimek, "German police boot down doors of Wikileaks offices; Authorities advance boundaries of Internet censorship," *The Register*, March 26, 2009, http://www.theregister.co.uk/2009/03/26/german_police_raid_wikileaks/.
34. Stol et al. 2009, 258.

to racist, xenophobic, or dogmatically religious forms of political expression. Typically, this kind of expression falls short of criminal incitement—which is already illegal under other bodies of law. The inherent problem with hate speech regulation is that it can be applied, prima facie, to almost any controversial, high-stakes form of political expression that names names and points fingers. Both sides of the abortion controversy, for example, have accused each other of hate speech. In Canada, Jewish groups attempted to use hate speech laws to open police investigations on those using the term *apartheid* to describe Israel's policy toward Palestinians. If lists of illegal child sexual images can be stretched to include legal porn, one can only imagine what will happen when authorities start to block so-called hate speech sites.

Another serious problem with blacklists is the way they can, through economic pressure, extend the jurisdiction of a government beyond its legitimate boundaries. Multijurisdictional Internet service providers forced to block material in one area may have to apply the same filters across the board in order to avoid the burdensome costs of reconfiguring systems to conform to multiple requirements. This has been an issue in the United States, where state-level attorneys general have imposed agreements on nationwide Internet service providers.[35] Thus one state government acquires the power to censor the Internet for an entire country, or even other parts of the world.

The IWF's decision to block the Scorpions' album cover on Wikipedia (discussed in chapter 2) and the Vodafone case in Czechoslovakia (mentioned at the beginning of this chapter) reveal another danger of blacklists: technically induced overblocking or unanticipated side effects. Depending on the techniques used, blocking can target entire domains when it only needs to block a specific page; it can block entire pages when it only needs to block a specific image; it can block IP addresses when address assignments can be shifted from a targeted site to an innocent user; it can create unintended technical disruptions to innocent parties. (In the Wikipedia/Scorpions' album cover case, the blocking technique used disrupted Wikipedia editors' login process as well as access to the controversial image.) More generally, blocking is a unilateral move by one group of network participants against another group; as such it can disrupt the operation of the network in unintended, destructive ways. When private

35. Adam Thierer, "State AGs + NCMEC = The Net's new regulators?" *TechLiberation Front* blog, November 24, 2008, http://techliberation.com/2008/11/24/state-ags -ncmec-the-nets-new-regulators/.

actors with no inherent monopoly power over access make such mistakes it is bad, but correctable and relatively accountable. Spam blacklists that end up blocking email traffic that users want will not be adopted by enterprises and ISPs. This kind of self-enforcing accountability is not possible when blocking is linked to territorial states with more coercive, politically mediated forms of power.

The Internet content regulation that emerged from the child protection movement was originally a relatively benign form of networked governance. It involved a decentralized, pluralistic but effective method of identifying and authenticating objectionable content, then promulgating it to Internet service providers and governments for takedown. There is, however, a growing trend to expand this process from takedown to blocking, and from private, voluntary action to state-based coercion. That trend brings worrisome indications that the toxin of repression will spread in harmful and unintended ways. But on the whole such content regulation is still a fairly distributed process. It involves multiple ISPs, multiple governments, and differing standards, and thus leaves many cracks in the system. The same cannot be said about ICANN's recent foray into content regulation.

ICANN and Content Regulation

ICANN is a centralized, global institution with hierarchical, uniform control over the domain name and address system. We need a global institution to coordinate Internet identifiers, and this coordination is likely to be more narrowly focused and neutral if it is independent of nation-states. But the policies made by today's expansive, state-dominated ICANN are capable of giving us the most limiting combination of a multinational corporation and national regulation: that is, it can apply any and all national governments' standards to everyone in the world.

On the one hand, ICANN's mission and core values imply that its main task is to maintain the uniqueness of Internet identifiers. On the other hand, it has been evident for some time that ICANN also has the ability to make and enforce public policy by attaching conditions to the use of the critical Internet resources it assigns and allocates. A true "technical coordinator" role implies that ICANN would be indifferent to any social goals other than its fundamental one of maintaining the global uniqueness of domain names and hence the interoperability, stability, and security of the domain name and addressing systems. This implies neutrality with respect to social outcomes unrelated to that basic mission. Yet a less neutral, more regulatory role implies that ICANN would exploit its gate-keeping power over access to identifier resources to load social policy criteria unrelated to compatibility onto its coordination decisions.

Beginning in 2006, ICANN began to develop a policy and process for the regular addition of new generic top-level domains (TLDs) to the root. The results were as fascinating for students of globalization as they were alarming to advocates of freedom of expression. ICANN made content regulation a central part of its new TLD policy. It regulated the semantic aspect of top-level domain names as if they were broadcast content; it also restricted the award of new TLDs based on their semantic meaning or the communities that might be associated with them. While the creation of new top-level domain names provides only a limited field for the regulation of Internet-based expression, it sets important precedents for the Internet as a whole.[36]

There is a clear political explanation for this expansion of ICANN's mission: the .xxx incident. The prospect of a new domain devoted to adult content gave governments an opportunity to posture and flex their regulatory muscles, which was attractive to them precisely because they had so little control over pornographic content elsewhere on the Internet. Governments are, for the most part, unable to engage in prior restraint of content generation on the Internet, despite their fervent desires to do so. Using the centralized institutional mechanism of ICANN, however, they saw an opportunity to impose some prior restraint on expression within new domain names.

During the development of ICANN's new TLD policy, the Governmental Advisory Committee (GAC) developed official "advice" containing "public policy principles" that should govern the addition of new TLDs.[37] In the GAC principles governments demanded that the award of new names respect the "sensitivities" around words with "national, cultural, geo-

36. For example, if the content of Web sites or the type of second-level names permitted becomes a focal point of ICANN's relationship to new gTLDs, it could be extended to old gTLDs. If .com, for example, were regulated the way new gTLDs are likely to be, the implications for Internet content regulation would be immense. While vested interests and switching costs would make it more difficult to impose such regulations on well-established registries such as VeriSign, it is not impossible, as registries' right to operate a registry must be renewed after a period of five years or so.

37. "GAC Principles Regarding New gTLDs," presented by the Governmental Advisory Committee, March 28, 2007, http://old.gac.icann.org/web/home/gTLD _principles.pdf (accessed May 7, 2009).

graphic and religious significance." Indeed, in an early version of the GAC principles a single government would have been authorized to veto any proposed TLD it thought objectionable, for any reason.[38]

ICANN's management was even more desperate than the states to avoid another .xxx incident. So it engineered the policy development process to ensure that the policy would prevent the creation of top-level domain names that anyone would find offensive, polarizing, or controversial. ICANN's staff initially proposed that words relating to the following categories should be banned in the new TLD space:

- Criminal connotations
- Religious connotations
- Explicit/taboo signs
- Illegal drug terminology
- Offending accepted principles of morality
- Sexual connotation
- Sacred words
- Words "that undermine religious, family or social values"
- "General matters of taste and decency"

Defending these restrictions against free expression challenges, ICANN sought refuge in international legal standards, including a nineteenth-century international treaty on trademarks that contained proscriptions against official recognition (as trademarks) of any terms that violate standards of "morality and public order." New top-level domain names, according to a staff implementation draft, "must not be contrary to generally accepted legal norms relating to morality and public order that are recognized under international principles of law."[39] These instruments the staff constructed as prohibiting any names that might lead to

- incitement to or promotion of violent lawless action;
- incitement to or promotion of discrimination based upon race, color, gender, ethnicity, religion, or national origin;

38. Section 2.13 of an earlier version said, in part: "If the GAC or individual GAC members express formal concerns about a specific new gTLD application, ICANN should defer from proceeding with the said application until GAC concerns have been addressed to the GAC's or the respective government's satisfaction."
39. As examples of such principles of law, the staff cited the International Covenant on Civil and Political Rights (ICCPR); the Convention on the Elimination of All Forms of Discrimination Against Women (CEDAW); the International Convention on the Elimination of All Forms of Racial Discrimination; and some intellectual property treaties.

• incitement to or promotion of child pornography or other sexual abuse of children.

These proscriptions did not quell the concerns; on the contrary, it became clear that ICANN was moving even more directly into the realm of content regulation. For it was clear that the real concern was not just the domain name per se, but the *content* that might be published under it, and the *ideas* and *beliefs* of the *people who might use it*. It is obviously impossible for a three or four-letter top-level domain name, by itself, to "incite violent and lawless action." Nor can a domain name, by itself, "promote discrimination." Names that seem controversial or troubling on their face, such as *.kill*, *.nazi* or *.jihad*, are simply words, words that can be uttered or printed legally as an identifier in many contexts. The real concern was that such TLDs might be used by "the wrong kind of people" or to publish or disseminate "the wrong kind of content." By banning such terms in the TLD space, ICANN was being used to create and enforce a global set of taboos applicable to Internet content. Those taboos are not limited to domain names; their purpose was to anticipate the type of content that might be published under a TLD.

Here we see not a simple bordering of the Internet, not a simple realignment of the Internet with state sovereignty, but reliance on new, global institutions to create and enforce binding regulations. We can also see the importance of delegation to private actors in achieving global affect. Given the Constitution's clear prohibition on interference with freedom of expression, the U.S. government would not be able to approve anything like ICANN's new TLD policy, nor would it be able to sign any international treaty that followed such a policy.[40]

The ICANN case shows how dangerous the combination of national sovereignty and private global authority can be. As many have feared and predicted, any attempt to satisfy all the world's sovereigns in a global policy is bound to smother diversity, controversy, and freedom. Globalized content regulation by ICANN does not and cannot extend the freedoms of the U.S. First Amendment to the rest of the world; on the contrary, it can only extend the most restrictive forms of content regulation into the lands where they wouldn't otherwise apply.

40. Although ICANN was based in the United States and a contractor of the U.S. Commerce Department, its status as a "state actor" to whom First Amendment constraints could be applied is questionable. See *McNeil v. VeriSign, Inc.*, 2005 WL 741939 (9th Cir., April 1, 2005). But see also Chan 2006, who argues that ICANN is a state actor.

Toward an Open Internet

The analytical literature on Internet content regulation techniques and policy is now over a decade old. The earliest studies came from free expression advocates and focused on exposing absurd mistakes made by the primitive filtering software packages of the time.[41] The emphasis was on the gap between the promise of technology-enabled, individualized control over access to information and the reality of crude over- and underblocking. The role of the private sector and of coregulatory or self-regulatory schemes was also a prevalent theme in early research—and remains so today. As early as 1996 fears were expressed about the possibility of censorship by unaccountable private actors: "When censorship is implemented by government threat in the background, but run by private parties, legal action is nearly impossible, accountability difficult, and the system is not open and becomes undemocratic."[42]

The contemporary literature focuses more on the growing role of the state in Internet censorship, in particular on the successful use of blocking by authoritarian regimes.[43] Academic studies and journalistic accounts show the spread of the practice to many Western, democratic countries. These studies document filtering/blocking as a form of hierarchical control; the emphasis is no longer on voluntary adoption and use of flawed commercial filtering products by end users, but on the mandated use of blocking as an extension of public policy by states. In this new situation, ISPs and domain name registrars are intermediaries that have been reluctantly pressed into service because of their leverage over what users can access. Concerns expressed about the role of private actors shift accordingly. As before, some of the more central private actors, the ones with governance responsibilities, are seen as assuming state-like powers in content regula-

41. Seth Finkelstein's attack on the first-gen blocking software (CyberPatrol, etc.) showed how it overblocked based on crude technical design and highly value-laden assumptions about what was "objectionable"—e.g., feminist discussion groups, gun-rights advocates. According to Finkelstein, "It's a bait and switch maneuver. The smut-censors say they're going after porn, but they quietly restrict political speech." Cyberwire dispatch, archived on the Interesting-People Listserv, July 3, 1996, http://www.interesting-people.org/archives/interesting-people/199607/msg00009.html. See also Shepherd and Watters 2000.

42. Cyber-Rights & Cyber-Liberties (UK) Report, "Who Watches the Watchmen: Internet Content Rating Systems, and Privatised Censorship," November 1997, http://www.cyber-rights.org/watchmen.htm.

43. Deibert et al. 2008; Villeneuve 2007.

tion while being exempt from the state's due process and constitutional constraints (e.g., NCMEC, IWF, ICANN). Others are seen as hapless intermediaries stuck between users' desires for freedom and public and private governance authorities' desire to regulate content (e.g., the Internet service providers). Still others are perceived as accomplices in the task of repression, either snared into complicity by their desire to do business in certain territories (e.g., Yahoo!, Google) or as profiteers in repression (e.g., the equipment and service producers who sell sophisticated content management and blocking tools to states such as Saudi Arabia, Iran, and China).

Much of the new literature is empirical and takes a studied apolitical, academic posture. It purportedly seeks only to understand how state-based blocking works technically, the rationales and policies that support it, and how much content is successfully blocked. Out of this new approach has emerged a process-oriented method of assessing Internet content regulation. This approach does not critique Internet blocking and filtering per se, but focuses on how "fairly" or how "well" it is done. It raises the issue, for example, of how transparent the censors are. Do they openly acknowledge that they are engaged in censoring the Internet? Do they tell users that the site they are trying to reach is banned, or do they merely supply a generic error message that falsely signals a technical problem?

Legal scholar Derek Bambauer has developed a systematic process-oriented framework to apply to the governance of Internet blocking.[44] Conflicts over the substantive issues around censorship and content regulation, he implies, are intractable because of the tremendous variation in standards from state to state. So we should focus instead on applying process criteria to the practice of censorship to make sure it is done in a "legitimate" manner. "Legitimate" censorship, he claims, should meet four criteria:

First, is a country open about its Internet censorship, and why it restricts information? Second, is the state transparent about what material it filters and what it leaves untouched? Third, how narrow is filtering: how well does content actually blocked— and not blocked—correspond to those criteria? Finally, to what degree can citizens participate in decisionmaking about these restrictions, such that censors are accountable? Legitimate censorship is open, transparent about what is banned, effective yet narrowly targeted, and responsive to citizens' preferences (but not overly so).

As a framework for the analysis and assessment of Internet content governance, Bambauer's framework has some value. If we apply the framework,

44. Bambauer 2009.

he claims, we know whether we are objecting to a "poor implementation of filtering" or are actually debating "a country's larger values and policy choices."[45] However, it should be obvious that the biggest, most important Internet governance issues revolve around the fourth criterion. Restated more directly, that criterion asks: *Who decides what is censored; how reflective of actual public preferences are those decisions; how difficult is it for public pressure to change censorship policies; how do we ensure that the preferences of a majority don't suppress individual rights or the legitimate airing of differences among subsections of the population?* Those questions are so big and so fundamental that the other criteria fade to near-triviality next to them. Bambauer's fourth criterion is not really a "process" issue at all—it is a *political* issue of the highest order.

And that is why, if we are not careful, process-oriented approaches to blocking can become a dangerous diversionary tactic. A process-oriented framework actually legitimizes and encourages Internet censorship, because it is based on the assumption that state-based blocking can be done fairly and appropriately. It implies that we should optimize it rather than resist it. Worse, it contains a hidden assumption with huge political consequences: that the *nation-state* is the appropriate institution for making decisions about global access to information. Bambauer's framework tacitly makes the "country" its unit of analysis, as do most other discussions of the issue, which begs one of the most important political questions around Internet content regulation. The "country" is neither the only available decision-making unit, nor is it necessarily the most appropriate one. Other methods and other Internet-based collectivities could be used, and are being used, to make decisions about what information is accessible. (further discussion to follow).

As part of his fourth criterion, Bambauer posits that states make their censorship more legitimate by giving citizens the right to participate in shaping its scope and application. This sounds very democratic, but he has to qualify it with the warning that content regulation should not be "overly responsive" to public preferences. He says this, presumably, because he recognizes that individuals in any society have some right to express ideas and opinions not in accord with those of the majority or dominant view. (If the German Social Democrats win a 53 percent majority in an election it shouldn't mean that the government now has a right to censor the Greens and the Free Democrats.) But this need for "counter-majoritarian constraints" is not a process issue, it is a substantive one. And it indi-

45. Ibid., 8.

cates why the "country" (i.e., the state) cannot be the sole decider of what is allowed. If one adheres strictly to the idea of national sovereignty, to the idea of the state as the supreme authority over communication policy, then minority or individual protections, and even basic democratic methods, are completely subordinate to the question of who is the ruling political authority in a territory. Conversely, if one puts individual rights first, as I believe we should, the scope and authority of sovereignty become subordinate to the human right to communicate.

Bambauer and other proponents of process-oriented approaches have rather naively reversed the order of causality here: countries will make their Internet censorship open, transparent, suitably narrow, and appropriately limited if *and only if* they respect individual rights to self-determination and freedom of expression. States will not suddenly choose to respect such rights in order to make their Internet censorship more respectable and legitimate. States that practice systematic political or cultural censorship typically do so precisely because they don't recognize individual rights and *don't want* certain preferences or ideas to have any effect. Telling them to make their censorship regimes more accountable by making them more transparent, or by granting a suppressed citizenry more influence, is no different and no easier than asking them to change their basic values and policies. The whole idea of deference to individual or minority rights reflects liberal-democratic norms. In practice and in law, many sovereigns don't recognize those norms. Unless we challenge national sovereignty itself on the basis of liberal norms, we cannot apply this criterion to any state.

Just as it is legitimate and necessary to insist on citizens' procedural rights with respect to the exercise of content regulation by their states, so it is legitimate, necessary—and far more important—to insist on eliminating as much censorship as possible in line with substantive free expression rights. We must uphold the concept of freedom of expression, and insist on the right of individuals to access information and communicate with others regardless of what state they reside in. We must, in other words, question the scope of national sovereignty over communications. If citizens have a right to be *informed* that their government is blocking access to external information, then perhaps it is not too crazy to ask whether they also have a right to *get* that information without interference by their national government. If people have rights and expectations regarding the procedural mechanisms by which censorship is exercised, then perhaps they should also have rights and expectations about the minimizing the scope of censorship.

The governance of the Internet needs to explicitly recognize and embrace the principle that there are limits to national sovereignty over the flow of information. This claim is based on the truth that there are many transnational communities or polities, created by global electronic communications, whose individual members have their own intrinsic rights to communicate among themselves. This basic human right transcends states. The principle is already embodied in Article 19 of the UN Declaration, the U.S. First Amendment, and Article 10 of the European Convention of Human Rights, which guarantees "the right to freedom of expression and information without interference by public authorities and regardless of frontiers, irrespective of the means of mass communication used." The only exceptions to these clear protections of freedom are when such communications violate the rights of others.

Against All Blocking

A commitment to these internationally accepted human rights requires states to abandon completely their attempts to impose national blocking on access to Internet content. There is still a role for illegal content regulation, of course. But states should rely on notice and takedown within their own jurisdiction and abstain from trying to interfere with the operation of the network to block things outside their jurisdiction. States can establish clear, explicit guidelines for what constitutes illegal content in their territory; based on that they can establish a lawful process for requiring ISPs and hosting companies to take down such content when it resides in their own jurisdiction.

There is also no reason to object to the development, by states, of binding international agreements that enable cooperation among states in the takedown of content that is jointly deemed illegal, or that enable the transborder prosecution of the creators or users. The saving grace of this option, of course, is that it is only available when a strong international consensus about the status of the content exists, such as those around the sexual exploitation of young children.

What must be strongly opposed is the attempt by states to require ISPs to install filters in the network that preempt efforts to access content. My viewpoint thoroughly rejects—on moral, political, and practical grounds— a realignment of Internet access with territorial states in order to permit all of them to act as information gatekeepers for their populations.

I reject it, first, because state-mandated, compulsory blocking as a method of content regulation fatally undermines the basic operational and architectural principles that made the Internet so productive and successful in the first place. As many others have argued, the stunning success of the Internet as a medium of expression and engine of economic development was based on the end-to-end principle. The network was designed to be as neutral a platform as possible; it is a mover a bits that leaves the definition of applications and content to the end users. A neutral network eliminates gatekeepers and similar barriers to access. This in turn optimizes the chances that an important new idea will be heard, that new collectives can associate and mobilize at will, and that a valuable innovation will have an opportunity to succeed. A neutral network maximizes access to the public and minimizes the ability of an intermediary to substitute its own judgments for those of end users.

The Net neutrality concept is usually associated with policy toward ISPs, but it was also introduced into the ICANN/domain name area during the development of its new top-level domain policy. In reaction to ICANN's more restrictive approach to new TLD authorizations, free expression groups started a campaign to "Keep the Core Neutral."[46] The adoption of the language of "neutrality" was not, initially, derived from domestic Net neutrality campaigns focused on broadband policy. It emerged more from the Internet technical community's belief in the end-to-end principle. An early paper by Michael Palage and Avri Doria argued that "ICANN actions in adding entries into a database should be a politically neutral technical function."[47] Similar to activism promoting network neutrality, opposition to ICANN's new gTLD regulations was based on the belief that imposing a layer of prior review and standards of "morality and public order" on the selection of top-level domains is inimical to freedom of expression and to innovation. Opponents wanted ICANN's coordination of identifiers to be "neutral" in the same way and for the same reasons that Net neutrality advocates want broadband networks to be "neutral." If a central authority or (equally restrictive) a global plebiscite or collective mobilization decides what names, business models, and standards of appropriateness must be applied at a global level, then diversity will be narrowed, unpopular and controversial concepts or people will be suppressed, and innovative ideas will never get a chance.

Even if we recognize that some content will be illegal and that there may be no right to produce or access it, regulation by nation-states should

46. The "Keep the Core Neutral" campaign was organized by the Noncommercial Users Constituency with support from IP Justice and the Internet Governance Project. See the campaign Web site: www.keep-the-core-neutral.org/.
47. Doria and Palage 2007.

stay congruent with the end-to-end principle and target its enforcement activity at the edges as well. If we try to engineer the network itself to police and censor content, we give states and network operators too strong a gatekeeping role.

Blocking is also an inherently less transparent and accountable form of censorship than takedown and prosecution of the responsible parties. The ongoing tension between the need to maintain secrecy around a list of banned sites and the requirements of accountability means the risk of abuse is high. Further, ISP-based blocking can put the entire telecommunications infrastructure on a slippery-slope toward increasing centralization and control. The best way to optimize the effectiveness of national filtering is to institute a costly, comprehensive Chinese-style system that integrates the control of access to Internet content with regulation of the physical telecommunications infrastructure. That is, ISP blocking pushes countries in the direction of creating centralized gateways and more monopolistic or oligopolistic industry structures in order to preserve the network's ability to act as a chokepoint for controlling and monitoring traffic. In summary, the costs, overblocking mistakes, lack of transparency, and potential for abuse inherent in this type of technical intervention outweigh the benefits.

Private Actors and Content Regulation
The impetus to privatize governance or to delegate to the private sector some of the functions of governance has been a common pattern through the different domains of Internet governance. It is a structural response to limitations embedded in the very nature of government. One is a response to scale; the operator of a network is in the best position to manage the huge volume of activity on it. Another is the need for specialized technical knowledge; private operators of networks are more likely to understand the means by which policy can be implemented. A third reason for the ascendancy of private actors is that they provide a way to overcome the boundedness of jurisdictions and organizations. In the transnational context created by the Internet, this is extremely important. The fourth might be called policy buffering or, more pejoratively, policy laundering. When states are confronted with conflicting and controversial demands they can call upon private actors to do indirectly things they would like to do but cannot do legally.

When it comes to content regulation all of these factors are in play. Notice and takedown by Internet service providers and the child protection hotlines are primarily responses to scale. Privatized hotlines also involve legal evasion: states with constitutional proscriptions against censorship cannot easily create an Internet blocking program. ICANN is primarily a response to boundedness, the need for global coordination; but it is also about the need for expertise and the evasion of due process and other legal rights. Given the structural factors pushing in this direction, it makes little sense to object in principle to this trend; rather, the goal should be to identify its pathologies and to isolate and eliminate them as much as possible.

Critics of the role of private organizations in networked censorship often call for their functions to be governmentalized. IWF's activities, some say, should be taken over by, or more closely supervised by, the state; NCMEC should become a government department.[48] These critics are legitimately concerned about the existence of legal rights, such as freedom of information acts, data protection or privacy laws, and free expression guarantees such as the First Amendment. To assume that the content regulation regime that has grown up around NCMEC or IWF would be improved by governmentalizing it, however, seems to this observer to be wrong. Critics who take this line seem to be suffering from an idealized, depoliticized conception of how and why governments act. Yes indeed, it would be nice if one could abstract out the freedom-enhancing aspects of the state from its other features and rely exclusively on that. But along with state involvement comes a number of other, less pleasant things: more direct authority to impose coercion and constraints; a susceptibility to popular mobilizations that are as likely to reduce freedom as to protect it; the organizational interest of the state itself in greater police and military powers; the growth of bureaucracies that become insulated from accountability over time.

48. In a *CNET News* article by Chris Soghoian, John Morris, senior counsel for the Center for Democracy and Technology said: "We have very significant concerns about the outsourcing of prosecutorial and investigative functions to a non-government entity. And we believe that those functions should only be done (by those subject to) the First and Fourth Amendments, the Privacy Act, and The Freedom of Information Act." He also quotes Adam Thierer, a senior fellow at the Progress and Freedom Foundation saying: "[NCMEC] should either be covered by the Freedom of Information Act and other relevant government oversight laws and processes, or it should be converted entirely into a federal agency so that it is accountable for its actions as an Internet regulator." Chris Soghoian, "Editorial: It's time for a child porn czar," *CNET News*, December 9, 2008, http://news.cnet.com/8301-13739_3 -10118923-46.html.

The worst situations arise when governments actively exploit private governance arrangements in order to avoid substantive and due process rights. State attorneys-general, acting through quasi-private foundations such as NCMEC, have been able to impose regulations on expression that could fail to pass constitutional muster. The same is true, obviously, of ICANN. In that case, the most appropriate solution is to have the state take a step away from the situation, so that the level of coerciveness is reduced and the accountability abuses that can come from combining state and private action are reduced. The adoption of a global First Amendment that rigidly protects free expression from interference by states is obviously the best solution. But it is also a highly unlikely one. Short of a militant and popular global social movement for freedom of expression, it is more likely that other states' standards will be imposed on U.S. users than vice versa. If that is true, the gains from governmentalizing private sector content-regulatory activities are minimal to nonexistent, while the risk of losses from doing so are significant.

One of the key questions about privatized governance relates to its accountability. In this regard, the saving grace of privatized governance is that the private actors have less monopoly power than states, which allows users and suppliers to vote with their feet and establish a kind of account-ability through acceptance. The other strength is its diverse and pluralistic character. Self-organizing and self-governing communities can adapt and accommodate to multiple preferences more readily than states, which follow a logic of uniformity and universality.

This suggests a two-tiered system of content governance. Just as in the security domain, most of the fine-grained work of Internet content gover-nance should be done by private actors (a term that embraces both com-mercial and nonprofit organizations, both market and peer production modes of interaction), operating through "report abuse" buttons, notice and takedown, privately developed and voluntarily adopted filtering soft-ware tools, and so on. But there must be a second tier to accountability, in which government intervenes to counteract excessive market power or when basic human rights are violated.

Distributed, networked governance of content coupled with pluralistic, private management of networks gives subsets of the global population the tools they need to regulate their own access to undesired content. Although I have expressed principled opposition to compulsory blocking by states, and prefer never to see blocking implemented in any form, I cannot express a principled objection to its use by private actors in contexts where the effects are limited to the groups that want it. Anti-spam activists have created a reasonably effective and legitimate form of blocking that maintains accountability-in-practice through voluntary utilization decisions and constant adjustments. Private groups should be able to establish a similar system of networked content regulation.

In a network of networks, some kind of authority to accept or reject outgoing or incoming information is an extension of network operators' right to manage their own systems. As there is no difference in principle between blacklists that keep out spam and other kinds of unwanted content, there is no way to deny corporate and individual actors the ability to manage the content coming into and going out of their networks without also denying them some of the very freedoms one is trying to protect. The important distinction here is between public and private actors. As long as the blocking list is voluntarily adopted by a network operator and customers have the alternative of moving to another service provider, there are important checks and balances imposed on content regulation. The role of competition, pluralism, and diversity among network operators becomes even more important, however.

10 Critical Internet Resources

During and immediately after WSIS, the term *critical Internet resources* became the code word for policy debate over the ICANN regime and all that it represented. Insofar as the phrase had any substantive meaning, it referred to the governance of Internet standards, domain names, and IP addresses, and to the interconnection and routing arrangements among Internet service providers.[1] It was recognized that name and number resources provided one of the few points of global leverage over the operation of the Internet—and that these were precisely the aspects of networks that states had almost no control over.

WSIS is already five years gone. More than a decade has passed since ICANN was first recognized by the U.S. Department of Commerce. And yet debate about the institutional arrangements for global governance of Internet name and number resources has not diminished. There is still heated debate over how we might internationalize or eliminate United States government oversight over the ICANN regime.[2] Within the United

1. The term *critical Internet resources* (CIR) is defined in paragraph 13 (a) of the Report of the UN Working Group on Internet Governance, as "administration of the domain name system and Internet protocol addresses . . . , administration of the root server system, technical standards, peering and interconnection, telecommunications infrastructure, . . . as well as multilingualization." The term appears in the Tunis Agenda in three places: paragraphs 58, 70, and 72. Paragraph 70 calls upon international organizations to develop "globally-applicable principles on public policy issues associated with the coordination and management of critical Internet resources." Paragraph 72 (j) explicitly authorizes the IGF to "discuss, *inter alia*, issues relating to critical Internet resources."
2. For example, on May 5, 2009, European Commissioner Viviane Reding proposed reforms to prepare for the September 2009 expiry of the Joint Project Agreement (JPA) with the U.S. Commerce Department. In response to the midterm review of the JPA, ICANN's Presidential Strategy Committee launched a consultation on "Improving Institutional Confidence."

States, each stage in the evolution of ICANN's contractual agreement with the Commerce Department has become the basis for contentious debates about ICANN's accountability and its institutional model.[3] The International Telecommunication Union continues to act as a redoubt for supporters of an intergovernmental solution to that problem. ICANN itself continues to grow its budget and staff, and restlessly reorganize itself like some alien life form in a science fiction movie.

And the issues connected to critical Internet resources continue to widen. Some of the controversies and concerns faced by ICANN are now being extended to its sister institutions, the Regional Internet Registries (RIRs), which govern IP address allocation. The IANA contract was dragged into the U.S. debate over cyberspace and national security.[4] The problem of who controls the DNS root zone file was revitalized by the emergence of Domain Name System Security Extensions (DNSSEC), a new technical standard that tries to make the domain name system more secure, but requires a cryptographic signature for the root zone records.

Some observers are continuously surprised by the longevity and vigor of these controversies. I am not. As noted repeatedly throughout this book, the ICANN regime was the primary institutional expression of the revolution in governance of communication and information required by the Internet. At the very least, the governance of critical Internet resources raises global policy issues on a par with content regulation, security, and intellectual property. But the controversy around the ICANN regime runs deeper than that: it is ground zero for the conflict between global governance and the nation-state system.

This chapter begins by situating the ICANN regime in a network of actors that is independent of and competitive to the traditional state system. It then analyzes the substantive policy issues posed by the management of critical Internet resources.

---

3. See the records of the 2006 midterm review of the JPA and the 2009 Department of Commerce Notice of Inquiry about the possible expiration of the JPA. "The continued transition of the technical coordination and management of the Internet domain name and addressing system," *Federal Register* 71 (102), May 26, 2006, http://www.ntia.doc.gov/frnotices/2006/NOI_DNS_Transition_0506.pdf.
4. The Cybersecurity Act of 2009, sponsored by Senators Jay Rockefeller and Olympia Snowe, contained a measure requiring a White House advisory group to review and approve any changes in the Commerce Department's contracts with ICANN for their "commercial" and "national security" implications.

ODii (Organically Developed Internet Institutions)

The Internet Engineering Task Force (IETF), the Internet Society, the RIRs, and ICANN constitute an interdependent, cohesive complex of organizations and institutions. These institutions grew up alongside the Internet. One of the key integrative organizations among this network of actors is the Internet Society (ISOC). ISOC was formed in 1992 in an attempt to provide a corporate umbrella for the IETF, and now supports the editor of IETF standards documents. This network of actors sometimes refers to itself as "the Internet technical community" or sometimes just "the community."

ISOC and the broader Internet technical community span and blur the boundaries between nonprofit and private commercial sectors. Some key actors are housed in universities or nonprofits, but are board members or regularly consult with technology companies; others are now firmly lodged in commercial companies like Cisco, Google, and IBM. Many receive government and military research funds. These actors, organizations, and institutions are, like the Internet protocols themselves, transnational in outlook but rather weighted toward the West in general and the United States in particular. They use English to communicate. They emerged independently of traditional state-based institutions and were, for their first decade and a half, eager to avoid traditional forms of state power. I use the phrase *organically developed Internet institutions* (ODii) to label this complex. ODii is an actor network—an *associative cluster* to use the terminology laid out in chapter 3—so I will also refer to it as the ODii network.

The growth and development of ODii constituted a major power shift in the global communication and information sector. It also represented an important change in the manner and substance of policy and governance: a movement from state actors to nonstate actors, to more open and participatory processes, and a shift to new kinds of technical expertise. One of the reasons why critical Internet resources remain a focal point of global controversy is that those resources are firmly under the control of the ODii network. By challenging institutions such as ICANN or the RIRs, states are challenging the hegemony of the ODii network itself. That is why the controversy doesn't go away; that is its underlying significance.

The global politics of Internet governance have become so polarized that most participants assume that one must be either "for" or "against" ODii. If one levels criticism at its actors or organizations, or even if one merely explicitly identifies and analyzes it as a factor in Internet governance, one becomes widely perceived by that camp as an enemy and a supporter of states. But the drama of Internet governance is precisely that the network of actors behind ODii constitutes *both* a force for progressive change, *and* an entrenched elite with significant, growing forms of power and wealth. One can be wary and critical of states without giving a blank check to ODii. It is best to explicitly set out the positive and the critical side by side.

Why ODii Is Good for You

The most important factor weighing in favor of ODii is that these are the people who built the Internet and who keep it running. An unrivaled level of technical expertise regarding the Internet and its problems is embedded in this network of actors. This makes them essential resources for the commercial actors who would finance, build, and operate networks, and indispensable to those who want to control them. But there is more to this virtue than expert engineering. The bond holding this network together was a shared vision of a new, open, and global data communications network developed from the bottom up. A unique combination of libertarian and communitarian spirit developed within ODii; it was resistant to centralized state control and favored openness and innovation, yet maintained a strong sense of collective responsibility or stewardship over shared resources and standards. As noted earlier, it pioneered the open source developer model. Through years of dedicated labor, the ODii network put in place seminal standards and protocols and a set of organizations, processes, and guiding principles that would allow the process of Internet development and governance to move forward indefinitely. Additionally, ODii is transnational and sovereignty-free in outlook. From the beginning, its outlook has been global and universalistic. It is on the whole a cosmopolitan group where nationalism has little place and the first loyalty is to networking rather than to countries per se.

Why ODii May Be Bad for You

But ODii is no longer an upstart, a challenger to entrenched forms of power. It is becoming a mature, institutionalized status quo, committed to maintaining itself and its prerogatives. In terms of its politics, the ODii network is not libertarian or liberal per se. Its first commitment is to what it calls *the community*, by which it means: the ODii network itself. *The community* refers to its own people, its own elders, and its own organizations. In some instances, this might involve fending off states; but it might also mean cutting acceptable deals with states or with business interests if that protects and preserves its governance role.

Furthermore, it is clear that the ODii network's position as administrator of critical Internet resources has the potential to make its key organizations, and the people who run them, wealthy. Figure 10.1 illustrates revenue growth for ICANN. From 2002 to 2009 ICANN's revenues and expenditures increased by a factor of about ten. During that period the salaries of key management personnel more than doubled. The revenue of the RIRs grew at a more modest pace but, in aggregate, still more than doubled in the past five years, jumping from about $15 million to $38 million. There is nothing wrong with budgetary growth per se, of course; for the RIRs especially, most of that growth reflects the continuing increase in the size of the communities they serve. But along with these higher economic stakes comes the potential for higher-level politics, corruption, and abuse.

ICANN in particular, with its greater commercialization and politicization and its weaker accountability, has become the nexus for rewarding and enriching its own management and other key players in the ODii network. A glance at ICANN's pay scales shows that its staff is drawing impressive salaries, not the sort typically associated with nonprofits or with regulatory agencies.[5] An accounting of who ICANN funds as consultants

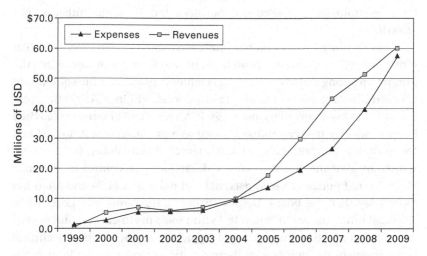

Figure 10.1
ICANN finances: 1999–2009

5. Former ICANN CEO Paul Twomey pulled in about $700,000 per year in 2008; other managers and lawyers made $300,000–$350,000. By way of contrast, the chairman of the U.S. Federal Communications Commission makes $120,000.

reveals a regular flow of cash to ODii network stalwarts.[6] The posh expense-account dinners associated with ICANN managements' visits to Brussels and Washington are known and appreciated by those lucky enough to be included in them. After years of relative penury, the Internet Society achieved financial stability when ICANN awarded it the right to operate the .org registry in 2002. A valuable asset, the .org top-level domain, was divested from arch enemy Network Solutions and given to ISOC, a core ODii organization, over numerous contenders. ISOC now receives around $12 million (U.S.) a year in rents from that relationship, which it uses to fund not only important IETF functions, but also its global recruiting and policy advocacy activities. It recently extended the largesse to the World Wide Web Consortium.

Measured in revenues, the overall size of the critical Internet resources regime (combining ICANN and the RIRs) now tops $100 million per year. The World Trade Organization, with a stable annual budget of about $150 million as of 2008, is about the same size as ICANN. The International Telecommunication Union budget, at about $300 million, is still bigger, but that number has been static or declining for the past five years; another five years of current trends and the ICANN-RIR regime could well be bigger. At $600 million WIPO is much bigger (like ICANN, it derives much of its revenues from fees imposed on industry), but is facing cutbacks, not growth.

As the regime grows, people become uneasy about what was once its chief virtue, namely its autonomy from the state and from public law. While the RIRs retain strong ties to the technical community and its stoic equilibrium between libertarian and communitarian norms, within ICANN "the community" has lost many of its moorings. ICANN's board of directors (advised by its Jones-Day lawyers) thinks of itself as a private corporation first and foremost; it resists both external and internal accountability, fighting constantly to give the board as much discretion and control as possible. ICANN's staff pursues its own personal and political agenda and often has more sway than the board. Despite its public regulatory and governance responsibilities, the organization lacks firm roots in either the communitarian, bottom-up, consensus-oriented approach of the classical technical community, or the due process, bureaucratic procedures, and legal rights guarantees of a government agency. ICANN's board and staff constantly interfere with its supposedly autonomous representative structures in line

6. For example, Lyman Chapin's Interisle Consulting Group or Cisco's Patrik Faltstrom.

with various political and personal agendas. At worst, ODii might become nothing more than an unaccountable private monopoly over essential resources; its global leverage over Internet users could be abused as easily as state power if not properly constrained and held accountable.

Internet Resources: The Policy Issues

What is really at stake in the governance of critical Internet resources? One of the major problems with current dialogue on that topic is that people are so focused on high-level institutional structures and processes that they lose sight of the substantive policy issues. This section provides a descriptive survey of those issues. This analysis will make it clear that domain names and IP addresses, while certainly not the whole of Internet governance, constitute an important part of it that intersects crucially with the other policy domains. Likewise, routing and interconnection, which are almost pure forms of networked governance, constitute the real core of how Internet service is provided.

Address Resources

The Regional Internet Registries are the organically developed institutions that maintain an authoritative registry that ensures that all IP address assignments are unique. They develop policies that conserve address resources while supporting the scalability of the Internet's routing system. The RIRs are private, nonprofit membership organizations. Their membership consists primarily of Internet service providers, organizations with private networks, hosting and Web services providers, and similar direct stakeholders in IP address management. The community they serve is more homogeneous and technical than ICANN's. Unlike ICANN, they have real members with real forms of influence and accountability over the officers.[7] They have developed relatively stable, well-defined methods for developing policies and electing officers. The RIRs wisely detached themselves from direct dependence on ICANN by forming the Number Resource Organization (NRO) in 2003.

After years of relative obscurity, the RIRs now find themselves on the front lines of global Internet governance. They are facing several transformational policy issues: (1) the need to manage scarcity in Internet Protocol version 4 (IPv4) addresses; (2) the need to migrate to a new Internet protocol; (3) intensifying pressure to make the Internet's routing system more

---

7. RIR board members are actually elected by members.

secure and controllable; and (4) pressures to use IP addresses as a basis for law enforcement.

IPv4 Address Scarcity   The basic resource the RIRs manage, IPv4 addresses, is running low. The standards for IPv4, finalized in 1981, created a fixed address field of thirty-two bits. That created a mathematical possibility of about four billion unique addresses. Because of inefficient use and continuing Internet growth, we are running out of those addresses.[8] If the problem is not handled properly it could reduce competition and act as a brake on the growth of the Internet.

In the past, address resource management was based on the assumption that the task of the resource manager is to distribute unused address blocks to organizations for "free," based on "justified need."[9] Needs-based allocation means that a central planner looks at an organization's network design and utilization and decides what quantity of address resources are justified from a technical standpoint.

As the IPv4 free pool nears exhaustion, that approach no longer works. Hundreds of organizations can have equally meritorious technical claims to a certain number of IPv4 addresses, but there might not be enough unused addresses available to satisfy them all. Such a dilemma is not an engineering issue; it is an economic policy issue. In the post-free pool world, any system of IPv4 allocation must

• make decisions about which of two equally justified competing applications should get available addresses;
• move resources from less important, lower-valued uses to more important, higher-valued uses;
• reclaim valuable address resources that have been allocated but remain unused;

8. In the middle of 2009, the last remaining stash of unused address blocks—the so-called unallocated address number pool—had dwindled to only thirty blocks of 16.7 million addresses, which means we have only about a two- to three-year supply left. Hain 2005; Mueller 2008b. DeNardis 2009, chapter 5, contains a very good description of the early years of IPv4 address allocations and how that led to scarcity.
9. The ARIN Number Resource Policy Manual (Version 2009.3–1 June 2009) is typical. "Number resources are issued, based on justified need, to organizations, not to individuals representing those organizations. . . . Examples of assets that justify use of the number resource include, but are not limited to: Existing customer base; qualified hardware inventory; Specific software requirements."

• trim back overly large allocations to organizations that could make do with fewer addresses.

The traditional procedures of the RIRs could not perform any of these functions well. To respond to IPv4 scarcity, they have had to transform their policies and practices.

One innovative response to scarcity was to permit holders of IP address blocks to sell them to other parties who need them. By allowing those who want more IP addresses to pay the existing holders to give up ones they are currently occupying, market transfers will create an incentive to release unused IPv4 resources, and move existing addresses to their most highly valued uses. The emergent price system will also clarify the economic tradeoffs associated with the migration from IPv4 to IP version 6 (IPv6). Equally important, permitting market transfers is intended to prevent the development of a black market or underground trading in address resources. If a black market develops, the RIRs' records will no longer accurately reflect which organization holds which address blocks. A breakdown in the accuracy and universality of the RIRs' registration databases would have severe consequences for the security and orderly management of the Internet's technical infrastructure.

The European regional address registry (RIPE-NCC) was the first to adopt a market transfer policy late in 2008. The North American region (ARIN) followed in early 2009.[10] The Asia Pacific RIR (APNIC) has a proposal before it but at the time of this writing has not implemented it yet. These policies were quite restrictive, however, as they were intended to preserve needs-based allocation. It remains to be seen whether an active market for address resources will develop.

IPv4 scarcity also has led to greater emphasis on reclamation of unused address space. Reclamation has always been one of the biggest weaknesses of the existing regime. Organizations that have been given IP address allocations have very weak incentives to return unused or underutilized address blocks to the RIRs. Nothing bad happens if they don't return them, while an attempt to return them creates administrative and opportunity costs. There is evidence that very large amounts of IPv4 address space are lying fallow.[11] Because some of the holders of large IPv4 address blocks have no

10. See RIPE Policy Proposal 2007–08, http://www.ripe.net/ripe/policies/proposals/2007-08.html, which was passed in December 2008; and ARIN Draft Policy 2009–1: Transfer Policy. https://www.arin.net/policy/proposals/2009_1.html.
11. A large part of the allocated IPv4 address space seems to be unused, especially older allocations in the North American region. An OECD report (Perset 2007,

contractual relationship with an RIR, they lack the authority to recover the resources or regulate their use unless the legacy holders choose to cooperate.[12]

IPv4 scarcity is transformational not only because it commodifies address resources but also because it intensifies the institutionalization of address management. The RIRs become less of a loose industry self-governance arrangement and more like authoritative "title agencies" that must systematically identify, monitor, and track the occupation of address resources and title transfers.

The "Next Generation" Internet?   In theory a new Internet standard, IPv6, solves the problem of address scarcity. IPv6 has a very large address space (2^{128} addresses). But in creating it, the young ODii network was heedless of the economic and political challenges of moving from one deeply embedded technical standard to another. It created a new Internet protocol that is *not natively backward-compatible with the old one*.[13] Anyone who implements IPv6 cannot just throw away their IPv4 capabilities, for that would cut them off from the vast majority of services associated with the old Internet. One must think of the transition from IPv4 to IPv6 as the long-term coexistence of two distinct "Internets."

Migrating to IPv6 promises to be costly. ISPs must use a variety of technical protocols to keep the two Internets talking to each other during the transition. End-user organizations may need to rewrite internally-written

---

26–27) cites surveys that examine the population of visible IPv4 Internet hosts, and finds that "only a low percentage of advertised addresses respond, which could mean that even among routed address space significant address space is unused." Spammers hijacked an entire block of 16.7 million addresses originally allocated to Halliburton in the 1980s, and two address blocks containing tens of thousands of IPv4 addresses were hijacked from NASA and a small software company and used to facilitate spamming. The organizations that were the official holders of those address resources didn't even notice.

12. How big is this problem? Consider that one Internet standards commentary, known as a request for comments (RFC) estimates that about 40 percent of the IPv4 address space was already handed out by 1993 (RFC 1466, May 1993). In the ARIN region, as of 2008 the Whois records associated with 2,357 autonomous systems and 22,718 organizations have not changed since the end of 1997, when ARIN was created. This is a good indication of the large number of entities that are formally outside the governance regime in North America, even though they may cooperate with it.

13. See DeNardis 2009 for the full story of the development of and politics around IPv6.

software programs and scripts; they will be forced to invest in training and in new equipment. These investments bring few near-term benefits to offset the costs. Other than the larger address space, moving to IPv6 does not add any significant new capabilities to one's Internet access.

Assuming that the transition eventually gains traction, it will be fascinating to see how the ODii adapt to the vastness of the IPv6 address space. With 2^{128} addresses in the IPv6 space compared to the 2^{32} addresses of IPv4, the new protocol constitutes a mind-boggling expansion. The address space is so large that it forces us to reassess the economic aspects of Internet addressing and routing.

The *smallest* unit of address allocation in IPv6 is known as the */64 subnet*. It is contemplated that /64 blocks will be assigned to home users or mobile phones.[14] This "smallest" subnet contains 18.4 thousand trillion individual IPv6 addresses.[15] Going up the scale, the basic unit for making allocations to organizations is the /48 subnet. A /48 subnet contains 65,536 subnets of the /64 size. Another step up, and the basic allocation unit for Internet service providers is supposed to be the /32, which yields 4.3 billion /64 subnets. In other words, a /32 block contains as many /64 subnets as there are addresses in the entire IPv4 address space, and each /64 contains many times more addresses than the entire IPv4 address space. There are 2.15 billion /32 blocks in the entire IPv6 address space.

If the IPv6 address space is so indescribably large, do we need to worry about conservation at all anymore? Yes, to some degree. As the previous paragraph explained, the basic units of allocation are also extremely large, and the distribution of such blocks will, without question, result in the "waste" of vast quantities of bit combinations that could be used as addresses. If address blocks are handed out too liberally, and if reclamation is ignored completely as it was last time, it may be necessary to tighten up policies in the future, creating a disadvantage to late-adopting businesses and users. New applications, such as the much-ballyhooed "Internet of things" might push address consumption off the charts. We just don't know.

Once the transition starts to happen—assuming that it does—the RIRs will no doubt learn many new things about the effects of their allocation policies. Perhaps they will not have to charge fees at all. Or perhaps we

14. Internet Architecture Board, "IAB/IESG recommendations on IPv6 address allocations," RFC 3177 (September 2001). This unit was chosen, in part, so that it could incorporate an Ethernet physical address (EUI-64).
15. These decisions were rooted in RFC 2374 and RFC 2450, where the IETF's IPNG working group recommended that the address block given to a single edge network, which may be recursively subnetted, be a 48-bit prefix.

can abandon needs assessment and simply charge (low) recurring fees for holding address blocks. Can a market for transferable leases of IPv6 address blocks eliminate the need for detailed needs assessments by RIRs and make the registries evolve into something more like title agencies? Perhaps we will no longer need to maintain a sharp distinction between the policies we apply to Internet service providers and the policies we apply to end-user organizations.

Perhaps we won't need regional address registries at all anymore, but could rely on a more diverse mix of global ones. IPv6 is so large that thousands of organizations could be administering address spaces many times larger than the entire IPv4 address space.

Routing Security and the RIRs The RIRs face another transformational problem in the near future: routing security. Communication over the Internet is dependent on two things: the ability to identify host computers (using unique IP addresses), and the ability to identify routes that exist between host computers. Routing is currently a kind of loose, self-governed arena in which ISPs, relying mainly on a standard known as Border Gateway Protocol (BGP), work out agreements among themselves bilaterally. Though it has worked remarkably well for 15 years, the Internet's routing system has no systematic security or authentication.

The vulnerability of routing was illustrated dramatically in 2008 when YouTube disappeared from the Internet for about an hour. The national telecommunications authority in Pakistan, acting under the orders of government censors to block YouTube nationally, accidentally propagated the wrong route announcement globally. As the route announcement was picked up by other Internet service providers, it had the effect of blocking YouTube across the entire Internet. But the same openness and flexibility that propagated the error also made it possible for Internet service providers to quickly discover and correct the problem.

In an attempt to prevent such problems, some within the IETF and the RIRs are trying to develop a method of authenticating the allocation of IP address block prefixes to autonomous systems (the technical name for a network operator).[16] Currently, each autonomous system (AS) is assigned a unique number that is used to control routing. Since beginning work in 2005, the Secure Inter-Domain Routing Working Group has published the

---

16. On the Internet, an autonomous system (AS) is the basic unit for establishing router policy. It consists of either a single network or a group of networks that is controlled by a network administrator on behalf of a single administrative entity, such as a university, a business enterprise, or a business division.

Resource Public Key Infrastructure (RPKI) protocol,[17] which proposes to create digital certificates that bind organizational identity (AS numbers) to specific IP address block prefixes. Alongside these standardization efforts, the RIRs are developing the software necessary to support RPKI systems. According to the protocol, authenticating these certificates could rely on one or more trust anchors within the IP address space and AS number allocation hierarchy.

While being able to authenticate the allocation of IP address block prefixes to AS numbers is important, it is only half of securing Internet routing. One must also have accurate, verified information about the interconnections or routes an autonomous system maintains and announces to the rest of the Internet. Sometimes "route objects," which associate Internet routes with AS numbers, are stored in an Internet routing registry. In theory, information in such a routing registry can be used to verify route announcements made by Internet service providers, allowing network operators to filter fake or erroneous routes. However, there is currently no way to globally authenticate the route object data contained in these registries. The system of routing registries is decentralized and voluntary. Several types of organizations (e.g., Internet service providers, RIRs) operate their own routing registries, often mirroring route object data found in other registries. It is a loose form of networked governance similar to spam blacklists in its compilation and propagation. But there is no authoritative, central registry that everyone is required to use.[18]

Here, as in our earlier discussion of address transfers, we see evidence of institutional hardening. In the past year, proposals have been submitted to ARIN,[19] APNIC, and RIPE[20] to develop RIR-based routing registries that combine global RPKI authentication of prefix assignments with route object authorization information. This would provide the ability to authenticate not only which AS was using a particular prefix, but also what routes it announced to the Internet. The RPKI protocol, however, does not

17. Secure Inter-Domain Routing Working Group of the IETF, http://www.ietf.org/dyn/wg/charter/sidr-charter.html.

18. Merit Network's Routing Assets Database maintains a meta-registry of all operating Internet routing registries (IRRs). While it could be considered the de facto authoritative list for the IRR system, it does not have any contractual arrangements with other IRRs to maintain that information, and no one is required to use it.

19. See Randy Bush and David McPherson, "Using the RPKI to Construct Validated IRR Data," http://lists.arin.net/pipermail/arin-ppml/2008-May/010788.html.

20. See RIPE policy proposal 2008–4, "Using RPKI to Construct Validated IRR Data," http://www.ripe.net/ripe/policies/proposals/2008-04.html.

specify which institution (e.g., the United Nations, the International Telecommunication Union, the U.S. Department of Commerce, ICANN, or the RIRs) will maintain the trust anchors that make them globally compatible.

Implementing this kind of system raises major governance issues. Aside from the issue of trust anchor maintenance, it could fundamentally change the role of IANA and the RIRs. As Internet Architecture Board (IAB) member Danny McPherson pointed out, it could be used to link the control of IP number resources to control over what is routed on the Internet. To quote McPherson:

> Upon full employment of such a system, . . . the IP resources allocation hierarchy that exists today, which is sort of an out of band function that has no direct consequence on what's actually routed, now could have direct control over what's actually routed on the Internet, and perhaps most importantly, what's not. So, if you don't pay your RIR membership fees, your address allocations could actually be revoked, and this could trickle its way into the routing system, where filters might be augmented to discard your route announcements, or into a protocol like SBGP where it's actually automated.[21]

The point here is that to "secure" a route, someone must be assigned an exclusive right over the addresses to which a routing announcement refers, and also over the routing announcement of that address prefix. McPherson is warning us that RPKI schemes could be used to make the enforcement of this exclusivity relatively automatic. And because it is likely that the creation of this exclusivity function will rely on a hierarchical chain of certificate authentication, whoever controls the trust anchor(s) at the top of the hierarchy would be in a position to disconnect from the Internet anyone immediately below them in the hierarchy. This kind of power is, obviously, analogous to the control of the DNS root that became so contentious during and after the creation of ICANN. It creates a form of exclusivity and central control over the use of the addresses and routing that simply didn't exist before. It would constitute a fundamental change in the governance status of the RIR regime.

But it is not just the RIRs' role that might change. The concentration of authority within ICANN could also expand. In June 2008, ICANN's Security and Stability Advisory Committee (SSAC) asked the board to budget a specific line item for "Management of certificates for the address-

---

21. D. McPherson, "IPv4 exhaustion: Trading routing autonomy for security," *Arbor Networks* blog, March 2008, http://asert.arbornetworks.com/2008/03/ipv4-exhaustion-trading-routing-autonomy-for-security/.

ing system (RPKI)."[22] Thus, ICANN may be positioning itself to become the centralized trust anchor for the routing system. Also, any newly created centralized point of control might attract the attention of litigants and governments. ICANN's control of the DNS root gave it unavoidable forms of operational leverage over domain name registries and registrars. That control became a magnet for trademark/copyright interests and national governments seeking to assert forms of control over the Internet. In a similar way, secure routing and RPKI could give whoever controls the address assignment and routing authentication hierarchy the ability to exert policy leverage over Internet service providers and their users. This trend could make the RIRs very much like ICANN indeed. There are policy questions to be explored around the hierarchical chain of authentication and trust anchor control in addressing, just as there are in domain names as DNSSEC is introduced (see next section). These issues are only beginning to be discussed outside of the technical community.[23]

Addresses and States   Address space management is very similar to radio spectrum management. It apportions pieces of a scarce virtual resource and assigns them to private users. Those decisions have important collateral affects on standards, equipment design, and services. In the past, radio spectrum management has been a governmental function, handled at the national level by state regulatory authorities and at the international level by the ITU. One could also compare IP address policy to the telephone number allocation and assignment policies of mobile and fixed telephone systems. These policies, too, have been performed by national regulatory authorities, under national law, and coordinated internationally by the ITU.

In the governance of Internet addresses, we see a clear transformation of these regulatory functions; they have moved from national and governmental authorities to transnational, nongovernmental nonprofits. As scarcity and security concerns impinge on this system of transnational governance, we see a hardening and more articulated development of ICANN's and the RIRs' institutional infrastructure. There are pressures for greater monitoring of resource claims, more exclusivity, better definition of property rights, and harder forms of enforcement power.

22. In a June 2008 blog post, Brenden Kuerbis noted that ICANN's Security and Stability Advisory Committee requested a specific line item in the ICANN budget for "management of certificates for the addressing system (RPKI)." "Will ICANN move to control routing security?" *Internet Governance Project* blog, June 25, 2008, http://blog.Internetgovernance.org/blog/_archives/2008/6/25/3762527.html.
23. See Mueller and Kuerbis 2008.

In addition to these internally driven pressures for institutionalization, there are new efforts by national law enforcement agencies and from major private sector firms (Microsoft, the copyright interests) to use addressing to monitor and control bad actors on the Internet. Europe's RIPE-NCC seems to have moved farthest down this path. It formed a special working group for law enforcement agencies early in 2009. It also issued an interesting report on "enhanced cooperation" the same year.[24] With refreshing honesty and directness, the RIPE report recognizes that it is unrealistic to expect governments and other "interested parties outside the traditional RIPE community" to participate in ODii forums such as the RIPE Meetings or mailing lists, "but it is clear that if Internet policy is to have any authority, the policy development process must engage with these parties." Also, since 2004 some member states have been pushing the ITU to either replace or supplement the transnational ODii-based address management regime with nation-state based Internet registries.[25]

Domain Name Industry Regulation
In assessing the relevance of ICANN, set aside for a moment the hype and controversy about its status as a global governance institution and look at what it does. On a day-to-day basis, ICANN occupies the position of an industry regulator for the domain name registration services market. Obviously, its regulation is global rather than national in scope. For the most part ICANN is *not* a loose or networked form of governance. It has direct, hierarchical regulatory authority over registrars and registries in what is called the generic top-level domains (gTLDs). It has more limited, but still important, forms of authority over the country code top-level domains (ccTLDs).

The domain name market has expanded significantly since ICANN was created. As of mid-2009 there were about 185 million domain name registrations in the world. The total number consistently increases at 7–10 percent a year, with short lulls during recessions. Industry revenues are somewhere in the vicinity of $4–5 billion annually.

24. "Report of the RIPE Enhanced Cooperation Task Force," March 2009, RIPE Enhanced Cooperation Task Force Document ID: ripe-464, ftp://ftp.ripe.net/ripe/docs/ripe-464.pdf.
25. On October 21, 2004, Houlin Zhao, director of ITU-TSB, published a memorandum, "ITU and Internet Governance," which contained a proposal to create a new IPv6 address space distribution process based solely on national authorities. In 2009, the ITU proposed a parallel, "competing" system of IPv6 allocation based on country Internet registries (CIRs).

There are many different policy issues raised by domain name regulation. Most of them are pure regulatory economics relating to the way
suppliers are organized and operate. Because of the semantic dimension of
domain names, there are also a whole set of issues related to the tension
between trademark protection and freedom of expression in the appropriation of names. Chapter 9 highlighted the way domain name regulation
overlaps with content regulation. Some ICANN decisions can be considered consumer protection issues.[26] Other policies, notably ICANN's Whois
service, raise privacy issues. Still others are related to the technical and
operational security and stability of the DNS.[27] These are all "public policy"
issues in that they define the techno-economic structure of the Internet
industry in ways that have important economic, legal, political, and cultural consequences for users worldwide.

As an industry regulator, ICANN controls the number and type of new
TLDs and it accredits registrars, which means that it governs both the
economic and technical conditions of entry into the domain name registration services market.[28] The corporation's globally applicable private contracts require the domain name industry to be divided into separate retail
(registrar) and wholesale (registry) segments; this policy is designed to foster
retail-level competition.[29] Vertical separation has been very successful at

26. In the most notorious of these cases, ICANN was forced to suspend the accreditation of RegisterFly, a poorly performing entity that generated almost a hundred
complaints a day during 2007. See records of the *ICANN v. RegisterFly* lawsuit in
United States District Court, Central District of California here: http://www.icann
.org/en/general/litigation-registerfly.htm.
27. See the section on DNSSEC.
28. ICANN's contracts with registries cap the wholesale price that can be charged
to registrars and their assignment must be renewed after a certain period, just like
broadcasting licenses. The corporation accredits registrars, in effect licensing them
to enter the market while requiring them to abide by certain policies. It can withdraw that accreditation to enforce the policies or to punish bad actors.
29. See Mueller 2005 for a more complete discussion of the economics of domain
names. As part of its new gTLD initiative, ICANN commissioned economic studies
to assess whether the vertical separation of registries and registrars could be relaxed
or abolished. Charles Rivers Associates, "Revisiting Vertical Separation of Registries
and Registrars," October 2008, report commissioned by ICANN, http://www.icann.
org/en/topics/new-gtlds/crai-report-24oct08-en.pdf. "Report of Dennis Carlton
Regarding ICANN's Proposed Mechanism for Introducing New gTLDs," June 5, 2009,
http://www.icann.org/en/topics/new-gtlds/carlton-re-proposed-mechanism
-05jun09-en.pdf.

creating effective price competition around the supply of registrations in the legacy .com, .net, and .org domains. It has been much less successful at creating competition among registries. Despite some (limited) new entry, .com, .net, and .org registrations still account for 54 percent of the market, with legacy country code TLDs accounting for 40 percent of the remainder. Thus, new top-level domains so far have gained only 6 percent of the market. Whatever the merits of its policies, the language, concepts, and issues raised by ICANN's regulation of domain names are virtually identical to those faced by any national regulator of a medium-sized industry.[30]

Two issues in particular are highlighted in this chapter because of the way ICANN's regulation of the domain name industry intersects with the authority of national states. The first concerns new, multilingual domains; the second concerns an attempt to implement a new security standard in the DNS.

Multilingual Domain Names and ccTLDs   After ten years, ICANN finally has gotten around to developing a process for the regular addition of new top-level domains to the root.[31] New TLDs reopen all the old battles ICANN faced in 1998, notably conflicts over rights to names and the distributional conflict between the domain name supply industry and trademark holders.[32] But there is a unique twist to the current initiative. The original domain name system used a simplified character set based on the Roman

30. A major economic policy controversy for the ICANN regime began in 2006, when ICANN agreed, as a settlement of litigation brought against it by VeriSign, to allow VeriSign to operate the .com registry indefinitely. VeriSign's control of .com can be withdrawn only if a court or arbitrator issues an order finding VeriSign to be in serious violation of its registry agreement. The settlement also increased the price cap on the .com wholesale price by 7 percent per year. In effect, VeriSign received a property right over the .com domain and an authorization to increase its price cap by a fixed amount every year. In return, VeriSign ceased its litigation against ICANN and promised to become a wholehearted supporter of the ICANN regime, which it did. This agreement was approved by the U.S. Department of Commerce (although the Commerce Department noted that its approval did not exempt either party from antitrust liability). A group of registrars, angered over the higher whole-sale prices they would pay and over the lost prospect of bidding for control of the lucrative .com domain, sued VeriSign on antitrust grounds.
31. The detailed policies are laid out in ICANN's Draft Applicant Guidebook, which is summarized at this URL: http://www.icann.org/en/topics/new-gtld-program.htm.
32. See Mueller 2002, chapter 10, for a discussion of the initial battle over rights to names. The current 2008–2009 ICANN proposal to launch an ongoing new TLD addition process has created even more radical proposals to give trademark owners

alphabet. This meant that languages that relied on non-Roman scripts, such as Arabic, Chinese, Russian, or Japanese, could not be represented as domain names. It required the development of a new domain name standard based on Unicode to enable representation in other language scripts.[33] It is now possible to have domain names in almost any alphabet. These are known as *internationalized domain names* or *IDNs*. In theory, the introduction of IDNs makes Web and email addresses more accessible to people who are not users of the Roman alphabet, thus improving access to the Internet. Aside from this "digital divide" issue, the introduction of IDN top-level domains raises issues of competition policy, trade protectionism, global compatibility, and the bargaining power of states in the ICANN regime.

One of the first issues raised by the prospect of IDN top-level domains was whether incumbent commercial registries should have a right to claim a character string that corresponds to the meaning of their existing name in other language scripts. For example, VeriSign argued that when introducing IDNs, it should get first claim to a string that roughly matches the meaning of its English/Roman .com ("commercial" or "commerce") in all non-Roman scripts. All the incumbent registries argued in favor of such a policy; they claimed that widening their existing top-level domain name to include other scripts would be less confusing to users and less prone to abuse. Users could assume that anyone already registered in .com would have the same name in the different character set. But that argument met resistance based on competition policy and diversity concerns. Opponents felt that such a policy would project the market power of the existing registries into the new IDN spaces, and lock in their dominance forever. That argument carried the day. Incumbent gTLD registries will be required to apply for new IDN strings de novo, and will not benefit from any presumptive right to be assigned similar semantics in other scripts.

That seems reasonable enough. But characteristically, ICANN's board could not implement that principle consistently. It is now entertaining a proposal to give incumbent ccTLD registries new top-level domains

---

new forms of extralegal protection in the domain name space. See Report of the Implementation Recommendation Team, "Final Report on Trademark Protection in New TLDs," May 29, 2009, http://www.icann.org/en/topics/new-gtlds/irt-final -report-trademark-protection-29may09-en.pdf.

33. P. Faltstrom, P. Hoffman, and A. Costello, "Internationalizing Domain Names in Applications (IDNA)," RFC 3490 (March 2003), http://www.ietf.org/rfc/rfc3490 .txt.

representing their country name in local scripts. In other words, it is willing to give the ccTLD registries precisely what it was unwilling to give the gTLD registries: a translation of their existing top-level domain name into other language scripts. Even more discriminatory, ICANN plans to hand out these new IDN top-level domains through a "fast track" process restricted to ccTLD registries. In the normal process for applying for new gTLDs, private sector applicants will pay $185,000 just to apply; they will then go through a complicated and treacherous beauty contest that will cost hundreds of thousands if not millions more to complete. If they are finally successful they will pay hefty annual fees to ICANN and be contractually bound to ICANN policies. In the ccTLD IDN fast track, on the other hand, incumbent registries will not have to pay any application fee; they will not have to pay ongoing registry fees to ICANN; they may not even need to have a contract with ICANN.[34]

Discrimination between ccTLDs and gTLDs has bad implications for competition and service innovation. IDNs offer the world one of the best opportunities it will ever have to introduce more diversity and competition into the registry market. In many parts of the world, especially Asia, the market for domain name registrations is dominated by national ccTLD monopolies, many of which are state owned or state connected. Some ccTLDs use their control of the Internet to regulate and censor the population's Internet access. Because of the switching costs associated with domain name registrations, ccTLD registries that can ride a fast track into the IDN market before anyone else will almost certainly dominate the market for IDN registrations far into the future.

ICANN's decision to give ccTLDs a free lunch reflects the ways in which its policy is shaped by a combination of supplier interests and political bargains designed to preserve and sustain ICANN itself. The fast track policy is strongly supported by a coalition of governments (that participate in ICANN through its Governmental Advisory Committee) and ccTLD registries. ICANN is keen to win political support from those groups precisely because governments and ccTLDs can, under shelter of sovereignty claims, more credibly threaten to opt out of the regime.

A typical ccTLD controls 50–90 percent of the domain name market within their countries, and thus they are at least as dominant as VeriSign in their domestic markets. Originally, ICANN grouped ccTLDs with other registries and registrars in a policy-making organ known as the Domain

34. See "IDNC Working Group Board Proposal," June 25, 2008, http://ccnso.icann .org/workinggroups/idnc-wg-board-proposal-25jun08.pdf.

Name Supporting Organization. Country code registries, however, refused to sign contracts and fully join the ICANN regime. Since they were connected to foreign governments and often enjoyed the backing of states, ICANN was unable to hold any hierarchical power over them, short of disconnecting them from the Internet. So the ccTLDs were given their own supporting organization, the country code Names Supporting Organization (ccNSO). The policies that emerge from the ccNSO are starting to resemble those produced by national telephone monopolies in the International Telecommunication Union during the precompetitive era. The ccNSO seems more and more like the Internet's version of a cozy club of incumbent operators.

Another fascinating indication of the tension between networks and states is the potential of IDNs to create what are, in effect, alternate DNS roots around nation-states. The ODii network resisted IDNs for many years because of its English-Western bias and its concerns about global compatibility. Its unwillingness to embrace IDNs created a political and market opportunity for the non-Western advocates of IDN technology to promote root server systems outside of the ICANN orbit. While this effort started with private, entrepreneurial technical people in organizations such as the Multilingual Internet Names Consortium (MINC), its implications were not lost on the Chinese or Russian states. The Chinese unilaterally created new top-level domains that were the Chinese-character equivalents of .China, .com, .net, and .org. These domain names only work fully inside China; if they are accessed from outside the country they append .cn (the Roman alphabet country code for China) on the end of the domain name so that it is compatible with the ICANN root.[35] Thus, in China Internet users can visit the Web site of Peking University using the Chinese character domain name 北京大学.中国. By taking this approach, China did more than just create a national DNS root; it also effectively preempted the award of the top-level domains for .com, .net, .org, and .China in Chinese characters. With the national market in the Peoples Republic of China using an alternate-root Chinese version of .com, ICANN would not dare assign a similar IDN character string to anyone else, as it would create collisions and incompatibilities on the global Internet. Thus, important checks on ICANN's authority are imposed by the credible threat that states will defect from the network. But that threat also creates issues of trade protectionism and the possibility of Internet fragmentation.

35. This method followed a technological approach pioneered by the short-lived alternate top-level domain supplier New.Net.

Securing the DNS?   The domain name system is not just a market, but is also an important part of the Internet's infrastructure. As such it has become subject to the same concerns about security policy as other critical infrastructure areas. Domain Name System Security Extensions (DNSSEC) is a proposed standard that modifies DNS resource records and protocols to provide security for query and response transactions made between name resolvers and name servers. It introduces public-key cryptographic signed data into the DNS using four new resource records.[36] DNSSEC would provide the following:

• Source authentication: a resolver can determine that a response to a domain name query originated from a zone's authoritative name server.
• Integrity verification: a resolver can determine that a response has not been tampered with in transit.
• Authenticated denial of existence: a resolver can verify that a particular query is unresolvable because no DNS resource record exists on the authoritative name server.

The simplest and most straightforward way to implement DNSSEC is to start with a single trust anchor at the root zone; in other words, to create globally unique digital signatures for root zone resource records. By securing the top of the DNS hierarchy in this manner, these root-level digital signatures would make it easier for all domains at lower levels in the hierarchy to follow a consistent and compatible chain of authorization. But who produces and controls these encryption keys? Whoever does gains an important kind of leverage over the entire domain name system. Quite apart from the political issues regarding control, there are important governance issues regarding the procedures that will be used to make sure that the keys are not compromised, or what to do if they are. In sum, DNSSEC creates a jointly administered critical resource, the cryptographic key. Implementation of root signing involves joint production of trust on a global basis.

A report prepared in late 2006 for the U.S. Department of Homeland Security proposed that a single organization assume the role of Root Key Operator (RKO), and be responsible for the Key Signing Key (KSK) and Zone Signing Key (ZSK) for the Internet's root zone.[37] The most straightforward way to implement this plan would be to preserve the existing roles and

36. See Kuerbis and Mueller 2007.
37. "Signing the Domain Name System Root Zone: Technical Specification," http://mail.shinkuro.com:8100/Lists/dnssec-deployment/Message/553-02-B/061031Root SignSpec.pdf.

responsibilities of VeriSign, the U.S. Commerce Department, and ICANN.[38] But deployment of DNSSEC at the root zone in this manner would further institutionalize and lock in the control the United States and ICANN currently hold over the DNS root. It would do so by creating *globally unique* digital signatures for root zone resource record sets; digital signatures that could not be replicated by anyone else. While another entity would still be able to retrieve and publish the resource records contained in the ICANN root, as they could now, they would not be able to replicate the digital signature(s) generated by the authoritative root zone signing device, and thus could not offer a compatible, secured DNS service.

By now the story may start to sound familiar: any attempt to secure the root via DNSSEC reproduces the conflicts over U.S. unilateral control that animated the WSIS debates. Just as the use of RPKI in routing has the potential to create harder forms of hierarchical power over the more loosely networked form of governance among Internet service providers, so does the use of DNSSEC harden the hierarchical character of the domain name system. As things stand now, if the U.S. government or ICANN abused its control of the DNS root, ISPs could reroute their DNS traffic to an alternate root system. But it would be more difficult and costly for alternate roots to coexist once the root zones are cryptographically signed. The safety valve of defection to an alternate root server system would be shut off if DNSSEC is fully deployed.

That is why Philip Hallam-Baker, former chief scientist at VeriSign and now an independent security consultant, labeled DNSSEC "a profoundly destabilizing technology." "It is well understood that security measures alter the balance of power," he wrote. "In the case of DNSSEC, the security measures would tilt the balance of technical control even further in the direction of ICANN and the U.S. administration."[39]

An even stronger expression of this problem came from Russia at the ICANN meeting in Mexico City (2009). After a demonstration of a possible

38. In explaining VeriSign's proposal for DNSSEC implementation, Pat Kane said, "We thought the best thing to do would be [to] preserve the existing roles and responsibilities within the process today. There are three people that roll through the process today: ICANN, the Department of Commerce and VeriSign. And we thought that from a practicality standpoint and a speed standpoint, that that should remain the way that it is today." Transcript of DNSSEC workshop, Cairo ICANN meeting, November 2008.

39. Phillip Hallam-Baker, chief scientist, Default Deny Security Inc. "Comments on the Upcoming ICANN Joint Project Agreement," June 2009, http://www.ntia.doc .gov/comments/2009/dnstransition/078.pdf.

root-signing procedure by U.S. Department of Homeland Security-funded ODii stalwart Steve Crocker, Dmitry Burkov, an Internet engineer from Russia, identified two problems with those plans from the perspective of his country. First, Russia would prefer not to use the RSA encryption algorithm that the U.S.-based ICANN was assuming would be used for the root, probably because Russia thinks it is familiar enough to the U.S. National Security Agency that it could be broken by them. Second, Russia considered it unacceptable for the Russian ccTLD to be cryptographically signed by any foreign entity. "Imagine," Burkov said," "dot mil [the top-level domain for the U.S. military] will be signed by the North Korean administration. Same for us. Sorry."[40]

These concerns about the links between the root signing process and the U.S. government did not just come from rival great powers. The first qualms were publicly expressed at the March 2007 ICANN meeting in Lisbon by the president of the Canadian Internet Registration Authority (CIRA).[41] Two years later, a representative of the European Union was able to claim, "there's still a significant amount of doubt about the political implications [of signing the root], particularly of a single entity signing the root. Not least because signing the root is viewed as an irreversible step."[42] Whereas the Europeans and Canadians expressed their concern by withholding their support for DNSSEC, the Russians express it in a more precipitous way, by threatening to "build [an] alternative system . . . another, different Internet."[43]

If the tension between global and national creates a problem, it is evident that ICANN—because it is global, already in place and has the required expertise—provides the most likely institutional arena for the development of an acceptable solution. And insofar as ICANN is not perceived as the appropriate arena, it is precisely because it is linked too

40. Dmitry Burkov, transcript of DNSSEC Workshop, ICANN Mexico City Meeting, March 4, 2009, http://mex.icann.org/files/meetings/mexico2009/transcript-dnssec-04mar09-en.txt.
41. "So what if Uncle Sam signs the DNSSEC root?" *Educated Guesswork* blog, March 31, 2007, http://www.educatedguesswork.org/movabletype/archives/2007/03/so_what_if_uncl.html (accessed July 8, 2009).
42. William Dee, European Union, transcript of DNSSEC Workshop, ICANN Mexico City Meeting, March 4, 2009, http://mex.icann.org/files/meetings/mexico2009/transcript-dnssec-04mar09-en.txt.
43. Dmitry Burkov, transcript of DNSSEC Workshop, ICANN Mexico City Meeting, March 4, 2009. http://mex.icann.org/files/meetings/mexico2009/transcript-dnssec-04mar09-en.txt.

strongly to a single national government. Securing the Internet's domain name system thus creates pressure for globally effective, nonnational institutions; or, at minimum, new global institutional arrangements among states. And if that institutional innovation should fail, it could fragment the world into a series of more or less interconnected national Internets.

To conclude our survey of domain name policy issues, governance of the domain name system involves not neutral "technical coordination" but routine forms of economic regulation and some broader questions of public policy. ICANN's centralized and hierarchical control of the DNS root gives it the ability to create global communication and information policy. ICANN's policies are concerned with competition policy, market entry conditions, price caps, and some basic forms of consumer protection in the supply of domain names and related services. Those decisions give the regime leverage over rights to privacy, trademarks, and freedom of expression. Some of its decisions (e.g., the crypto-algorithm used by DNSSEC) impinge on national security.

The Problem of State Authority in the ICANN Regime

We now proceed to focus more specifically on the relationship between states and the Internet, and especially the relationship between states and the organically developed Internet institutions. We focus on the ODii because, as noted before, the ICANN regime is ground zero for the conflict between global governance of communication-information policy and the nation-state system.

As noted repeatedly throughout this book, innovation at the edges combined with open, universal access among all users connected to the Internet, regardless of jurisdiction, is precisely what has made the Internet so valuable. A vital part of that equation is the global coordination of the Internet's names and numbers. A consistent root for domain names and a coordinated IP address allocation regime make it possible to have one Internet that connects everybody, as opposed to a bunch of different Internets, driven by different policies and fenced in by territorial permissions. As part of the evolution of the Internet, policy authority over each network resides in the local network operators themselves; policy authority over names and numbers resides in transnational institutions that are more or less independent of states. Interconnection and routing are even further outside the traditional nation-state regime, as decisions and policies about this are not centralized in the ODii, but are negotiated among ISPs themselves on a bilateral, contractual basis.

As the stakes rise, the basic problématique in the governance of critical Internet resources is that this independence from states is both very good, and very risky. It is good because the ODii transcends the territorial limitations of nation-states, and to some extent insulates key aspects of the Internet from the authoritarian and controlling policies of states and the vagaries of national and international politics. It is of concern because states are still our primary mechanisms for developing and applying public standards regarding individual rights and accountability. Invite states in, and along with them comes their fragmentation and stifling political constraints; shut them out entirely, and there is a risk that accountability will disappear and rights will be lost. This problématique permeates much of Internet governance, but it is felt most acutely in critical Internet resources, where there is almost no role for national legislation and where relatively formal and centralized institutions have emerged to provide globalized coordination and policy.

Thus, increasingly, debate about critical Internet resources revolves around the role of governments. What is the relationship that interconnects law, regulation, public policy, and the ODii network? To what degree should the ODii be subject to "oversight?" What is the role of the nation-state in providing such oversight or accountability? Dialogue about this problématique flows in three channels: (1) the attempt by states to assert a special role for themselves in Internet "public policy"; (2) debates over the Governmental Advisory Committee (GAC) within ICANN; and (3) the controversy over the role of the U.S. government in controlling and supervising ICANN.

Nation-States and Internet Public Policy

As noted in chapter 4, WSIS was motivated by, and made an attempt to resolve, the tension between Internet governance and national sovereignty. But the Tunis Agenda confronted the problem from a backward-looking, conservative point of view. WSIS merely reasserted the old system of national sovereignty by trying to define distinct "roles and responsibilities" for governments, business, and civil society. Specifically, the Tunis Agenda tries to separate Internet "technical and operational matters" from "public policy matters," which paves the way for a claim that "authority for Internet-related public policy issues is the sovereign right of States."[44]

44. Tunis Agenda (TA), paragraph 35a. According to the TA, governments should take responsibility for "international public policy issues pertaining to the Internet," but not the "day-to-day technical and operational matters, that do not impact on international public policy issues."

There are three reasons why this claim, and the analytical division upon which it rests, is invalid and cannot work.

Problem one is that in Internet governance there is no way to separate "public policy" from "technical and operational matters." The two are deeply intertwined. So-called technical management processes, such as the separation of registries and registrars, and the implementation of RPKI or a procedure for allocating address blocks, are constantly raising public policy choices. As the Internet Watch Foundation learned when it attempted to censor a page in Wikipedia, any attempt by external actors to shape the system in accordance with public policies will have a major impact on the protocols and operational procedures. When the Internet regime governs these things through policies developed and implemented by the nongovernmental actors in ICANN or the RIRs, they are making "public policy." That is, they are defining the techno-economic structure of the Internet industry in ways that have important economic, political, and cultural consequences for users worldwide. The same interdependence of technology and policy is found in the way we regulate the radio spectrum or the telecommunications industry, which is why traditional national regulations reach deeply into the technical standards and operational procedures of these industries. *To enforce public policy upon the Internet is to regulate technical and operational matters (and vice versa).*

If this is true, many would then leap to the conclusion that national governments should take over the ODii functions. But that conclusion is based on the premise that national governments and only national governments can establish public policy for communication and information—and that is precisely the assumption the Internet challenges. To state the problem more succinctly, who is "the public" in the "public policy" invoked by states? The Internet creates *transnational* communities, businesses, and publics. The fact that (some) states can legitimately claim to represent a majority national polity and a few dominant national interests does not give them an unqualified right to act for a transnational public in the formation of communications policy. Governance institutions should follow the contours of the shared resources being governed and the community of actors who share in the effects of its governance. In this case the contours are not national and territorial. The interactions among people using the Internet cannot be equated with a collection of distinct national publics, who can be represented indirectly by national governments. Indeed, it is a fairly well-accepted dictum in international relations theory that in the international arena states' pursue their own interests and security as states, not in terms of a broader public interest. Any

legitimate deliberation about the global public interest for the Internet,
therefore, must be based on a wider community of actors. In the ODii, the
global, Internet-using public and the supply industry can and often does
speak for itself. And the voices heard often differ from the official positions
put forward by their states.

A third problem with the Tunis Agenda claim is that in a global policy
arena states do not and cannot have "sovereignty." Globally applicable
Internet policy involves multiple sovereigns. National policies vary tre-
mendously around the world, are interdependent, and can contradict one
another. This rather obvious fact was central to the rationale for making
ICANN a nongovernmental entity in the first place. The idea was to detach
coordination and policy from the territorial jurisdiction of national states
in order to avoid these interjurisdictional conflicts.

Ultimately, the Tunis Agenda's attempt to resolve the problem through
a hierarchically imposed division of labor between states and the rest of
society is both conceptually unsound and impossible to implement.

The GAC

The ICANN Governmental Advisory Committee is another improvised
attempt to bridge national governments and global Internet. It is the
approach clearly favored by the U.S. government and (lacking any better
ideas) the ODii network. GAC situates governments inside the ICANN
regime but limits them to the status of "advisor" to the board of a private
corporation. The GAC (and ICANN's management) have been influenced
by the same thinking that produced the Tunis Agenda's demarcation of
roles and responsibilities. A modification of ICANN's bylaws made in
December 2002 conceded that governments are "responsible for public
policy."[45] This "core value" was given procedural form in Article XI, Section
2(1) of the ICANN bylaws, which requires the ICANN board to provide an
explanation whenever it doesn't follow GAC advice on public policy
matters and to seek a mutually acceptable resolution.[46]

This approach has serious problems. The GAC doesn't *resolve* the risks
and problems attendant upon mixing transnational networks and territo-

45. ICANN Bylaws Article 1, Section 2. ICANN, while remaining "rooted in the
private sector," bound itself to "recognize[e] that governments and public authorities are responsible for public policy and duly tak[e] into account governments' or
public authorities' recommendations."
46. "The advice of the Governmental Advisory Committee on public policy matters
shall be duly taken into account, both in the formulation and adoption of
policies. In the event that the ICANN Board determines to take an action that is not

rial states; it *embodies* those problems. In other words, it exemplifies the dangers of the gray area between private and public authority that the ICANN regime now occupies.

The GAC is an anomalous and inherently unstable institutional arrangement. It neither fully integrates governmental actors into an equal-status, multistakeholder governance regime, nor does it formally grant states a distinctive role with clearly defined and limited authority. As noted before, one cannot disentangle public policy from technical and operational matters in Internet governance. To say that GAC has a special role in advising on public policy matters, therefore, means that GAC can address any issue before ICANN in any way that it likes. But while it claims superior authority over public policy (and can *get* superior authority if the ICANN board goes along with its advice) it is completely separate from ICANN's nonstate actor-based methods for developing public policy.[47] Thus, a policy product of the supporting organizations cannot be assumed to be an accepted output by the GAC, and a policy expressed by the GAC may not have support, much less consensus, in any supporting organization. This means that two parallel, unintegrated policy-making processes exist in ICANN: one led by nonstate actors in the ICANN supporting organizations, the other based on governments in the GAC.

This dual system of policy making can not only lead to conflict with ICANN but also give us the worst of both worlds, as the coercive power of governments is linked to a private corporation with monopoly control of critical Internet resources. In this role, governments do not *supervise* or *regulate* ICANN; they *advise* it and *participate* in its determinations. Thus, the governments are liberated from normal lawful due process and human rights constraints, while the private corporation lacks sufficient external accountability. Normally, international agreements among governments require legislative and judicial checks and balances. Governments must take agreements back to their democratically elected legislatures for ratification. If the agreements are inconsistent with the national constitution,

---

consistent with the Governmental Advisory Committee advice, it shall so inform the Committee and state the reasons why it decided not to follow that advice. The Governmental Advisory Committee and the ICANN Board will then try, in good faith and in a timely and efficient manner, to find a mutually acceptable solution."
47. GAC has no constituency in the Generic Names Supporting Organization (GNSO) or the country code Names Supporting Organization (ccNSO) and no votes in either council; government representatives rarely if ever participate as peers in their policy development processes.

they can be challenged in court. State signatories typically must conform to freedom of information act requests and other due process requirements. None of these checks apply to the ICANN-GAC partnership. What is the legal status of a GAC "Communiqué" or "Policy Advice?" What due process rights do global citizens have in connection with monitoring a GAC "decision"? For its part, ICANN's board has no clear, rule-based criteria for accepting or rejecting GAC advice. It can (arbitrarily) invoke the GAC to overrule its supporting organizations—or vice versa. The effect is to make the board less accountable, and the bottom-up policy development less effective. Confronted with a group of alternative policy proposals from unintegrated processes and bodies allows the board to decide for itself which recommendation it follows.

There is another structural problem with GAC. Putting a bunch of governmental representatives together in a separate organizational silo and asking them to "advise" ICANN on public policy has a predictable effect: GAC becomes the advocate of governments qua governments. It tends to seek more power for states at the expense of nonstate actors. Indeed, despite governments' theoretical claim to be representatives of the general public interest, the GAC rarely if ever addresses public interest objectives in domain name policy. Its interventions in ICANN policy processes, almost without exception, have been to claim special benefits or powers *for its member governments*. GAC's most important communiqués and policy advice statements have claimed special powers over the delegation of country code domains;[48] demanded special reservations for country names or geographic names in new TLDs;[49] and supported the ccTLD fast track.[50] The European Union used GAC as the platform to lobby for a new TLD of its own (.eu).

Unilateral Globalism: The Special Role of the United States
Perhaps the most important link between critical Internet resources and the system of nation-states is the ICANN regime's contractual tether to the U.S. government. This third linkage between networks and states, like the other two, is completely dysfunctional. A recent move by the United States has improved the situation, but most of the key issues remain.

48. GAC Principles on ccTLD Delegation (2000), http://www.icann.org/en/commit tees/gac/gac-cctldprinciples-23feb00.htm.
49. GAC Policy Advice on new gTLDs (2006), http://www.icann.com/en/topics/ new-gtlds/gac-principles-regarding-new-gtlds-28mar07-en.pdf.
50. GAC Communiqué #35 (2009), Sydney, http://gac.icann.org/communiques/ gac-2009-communique-35.

There are now two distinct contractual elements to the U.S. government's oversight of ICANN, as noted in chapter 4. There is the IANA contract, which delegates some of the U.S. government's policy authority over the naming and addressing system to ICANN; and there is the cooperative agreement with VeriSign, which controls how the DNS root is actually operated and ensures that ICANN policies are implemented. Until September 30, 2009, there was also an ICANN-U.S. Commerce Department Joint Projects Agreement (JPA) that established guidelines and milestones for ICANN to demonstrate its progress and adequacy. The new Obama administration allowed the JPA to expire, however, and put into place a new arrangement that will be discussed later.

The first two contractual tethers are holdovers, legacy products of the U.S. government's early role in developing the Internet protocol.[51] It was not until October 1998 that the U.S. government asserted any authority over the contents of the domain name system root. The claim first came in Amendment 11 of the VeriSign cooperative agreement, which required VeriSign's predecessor to "request written direction from an authorized USG official before making or rejecting any modifications, additions or deletions to the root zone file." This assertion of authority came not because the U.S. felt that it was needed to preserve the "security and stability" of the DNS or the global Internet, but for mundane competition policy reasons. At that time, VeriSign's predecessor, Network Solutions Inc. (NSI), was the sole commercial registry of generic top-level domain names. As the official operator of the DNS root, NSI implicitly had the power to add new TLDs to the root, or to refuse to do so. Thus, NSI could decide who would be allowed to compete in the market for domain name registration. Both NSI and the Commerce Department realized that allowing a dominant market player to control who could compete with it was not a viable situation. As long as this situation existed, antitrust lawsuits might force "uncontrolled" market entry upon the regime.[52] Thus the Commerce

51. Performing the IANA function was the basis for support given to Internet pioneer Jon Postel by the U.S. military for many years. It was taken over by the Commerce Department after 1997. The VeriSign cooperative agreement dates back to the original 1991 contract between the U.S. National Science Foundation and Network Solutions, Inc., when the United States moved responsibility for the Internet registry function out of the military and into a civilian agency. This contract, too, was taken over by Commerce Department as part of the creation of ICANN.
52. NSI, VeriSign's predecessor, was in fact being petitioned by a start-up company, Name.space, to add dozens of new top-level domains to the root, and it faced the threat of an antitrust lawsuit if it did not comply with this request.

Department amended the cooperative agreement to ensure that a public authority, not a private market player, controlled the contents of the root.

During the creation of ICANN, the United States repeatedly indicated that its assumption of authority over the DNS was temporary, and would soon be delegated to the entity that eventually became ICANN. The underlying premise of the whole proceeding was that the United States was "privatizing" the management of critical Internet resources; it was conceived as a "transition" away from U.S. government control and toward a "private-sector-led" regime.

What happened to this "transition?" The U.S. government now claims that its authority over the root is indefinite and is needed to ensure the "stability and security of the DNS." If we ask why the United States continues to hold on to this authority, we find only two viable explanations.

One is that the nation-state system itself institutionalizes a self-perpetuating, vicious cycle around the control of critical resources. In a world of two hundred plus sovereign states, giving one state special influence over a shared critical resource is an ongoing provocation that undermines stability and security.[53] A Hobbesian solution to the problem of internationalized authority such as this lacks legitimacy and inherently makes other states, and many of their residents, less secure. The general effect of U.S. control is to undermine the reciprocity that undergirds networking, and to politicize the DNS. Naturally enough, then, the political instability caused by unilateral control of the root has not gone away. As long as the United States government hangs on to the unilateral power, it goads other states into focusing on how that power could be used as an instrument of policy, and into demanding a share of it. But in the context of domestic and interstate politics, these demands from other states only strengthen

53. Other states have made it clear that it is not the privatization of critical Internet resources governance per se that irks them, but the obvious contradiction between the allegedly private governance of the ICANN regime and the special role afforded one government. The government of Brazil, for example, complained publicly that "we should work with the options of either having no governments at all, like the case of IETF, W3C [World Wide Web Consortium], NRO [Number Resource Organization], or we have *all* governments on board, like ITU or UNESCO. But ... please, let's also avoid models driven by one single government, like ICANN." Everton Lucero, Government of Brazil, transcript of the Internet Governance Forum, Hyderabad, India, "Arrangements for Internet Governance, Global and National/Regional," December 5, 2008 http://www.intgovforum.org/cms/hyderabad_prog/AfIGGN.html.

the fears of yielding control in the United States, and heighten the calculus of strategic superiority on the part of the privileged state.

The other explanation for continued U.S. control is ICANN's own failure to create accountability and trust. This has made it difficult even for people who approve of its nonstate governance model to embrace its independence. This chapter has documented the highly centralized and potentially hierarchical forms of power over the Internet that can be exercised through control of names and numbers. If this authority is not checked or subject to some higher legal standards, then to whom is it accountable? To whom can wronged parties appeal? What chain can be yanked if it goes off course? This problem is one of ICANN management's own making.

ICANN is a private corporation. For-profit private corporations are held accountable in three distinct ways: their boards and management are directly accountable to the shareholders, who can literally throw them out for bad performance; equally important, their reputation and performance are rewarded or punished in the commercial marketplace; and, finally, governmental laws and regulations prevent them from engaging in theft, deceit, or other forms of abuse.

A nonprofit private corporation such as ICANN lacks the discipline of the market. The name and address roots are unitary, and network externalities confer upon the corporation a very powerful form of insulation from competition. It also doesn't have any shareholders. Accountability for a nonprofit such as ICANN, therefore, can come only from a membership with direct influence over its board and staff, and from legal frameworks that allow it to be sued for abuses. Herein is the fundamental flaw in the way ICANN is currently constituted. Unlike the RIRs, ICANN doesn't have any members. Its articles of incorporation openly declare this. From ICANN's inception, its staff and management have fought to detach the corporation from any kind of defined membership to which the board and staff can be directly accountable. And yet, most of the accountability features of the legal framework under which ICANN was incorporated rest on the notion of a "statutory member."[54] Under its 2002 "reforms" abolishing

54. The California law's strong accountability measures and protections against abuses can be invoked only by statutory members. In 1999, as part of its attempt to create a global "membership" that could elect board members, ICANN's lawyers insisted on denying statutory member status to its members in order to avoid giving them the strong legal rights embodied in California law (including the right to sue the corporation at its own expense). "Analysis: Statutory Members versus Nonstatutory Members for the ICANN At Large Membership," ICANN Staff Report, August 11, 1999, http://www.icann.org/en/meetings/santiago/membership-analysis.htm.

elections and eliminating its already emasculated at-large "membership," the largest portion of ICANN's board is appointed indirectly by a nominating committee composed of ICANN insiders. The rest of the board members come from a variety of heterogeneous communities. All served staggered terms, making it virtually impossible to replace a significant portion of the board if they make bad decisions, or their decisions fail to conform to stakeholders' policy preferences. Additionally, ICANN's review and appeal procedures are comically weak, amounting to nothing more than a nonbinding request for the board to reconsider a decision. The upshot is that ICANN's board lacks strong lines of accountability to any cohesive community of stakeholder-actors.

As a substitute for real accountability, ICANN has created a chaotic mélange of participatory mechanisms, none of which have any real power and all of which can be superseded, manipulated, diverted, or played against each other by the corporation.[55] Instead of real membership, ICANN offers vague notions of "participation" and "consensus" among an open, undefined "community." ICANN as it currently functions is a parody of a bottom-up consensus-building governance institution; the only real accountability comes from the nuclear option of an alternative root system.

Since 2006, debate over the status of the Commerce Department JPA became a kind of proxy for these concerns about accountability in ICANN. Repeated notices of inquiry about the future of the JPA sparked debate about the whether ICANN was ready for independence.[56] Those who supported ICANN (typically, insiders from the ODii network) argued for expiration of the JPA, while those who were critical of ICANN's policy decisions or concerned about its messy and often unfair processes tended to support leaving the JPA in place until ICANN became more "accountable."

55. For a running account of how ICANN staff and board members manipulated the GNSO reform process, see the IGP blog series "Field Guide to the ICANN Reforms," http://blog.Internetgovernance.org. For a well-documented example of an especially acute process violation, whereby ICANN's board agreed to completely upend a policy process after it was completed in order to accommodate trademark interests, see Avri Doria (GNSO chair), "Personal Comments on the Implementation Recommendation Team report," July 6, 2009. http://forum.icann.org/lists/irt-final-report/msg00193.html.

56. For the most recent Notice of Inquiry, see National Telecommunications and Information Administration, Docket No. 090420688–9689–01, "Assessment of the Transition of the Technical Coordination and Management of the Internet's Domain Name and Addressing System," *Federal Register* 74 (78), April 24, 2009.

That pattern was dysfunctional. It forced those who wanted ICANN to become more accountable to rely on the troublesome apparatus of unilateral U.S. control to achieve it. It forced those who wanted ICANN to be independent of U.S. control to advocate eliminating a form of supervision for it, even if they believed that it did not have the proper accountability framework in place. In fact, in ten years the U.S. Commerce Department did next to nothing to improve ICANN's basic accountability problems and often exacerbated them through biased and politicized interventions (such as those concerning .xxx or Whois). The JPA diverted accountability away from the nonstate actors who are supposed to make policy through ICANN, toward the U.S. government and the professional industry lobbyists surrounding it. Worse, it made U.S. national and commercial interests the currency of the debate rather than the global public interest.

The Affirmation of Commitments   On September 30, 2009, a new agreement, called an "Affirmation of Commitments," was released and the JPA was allowed to expire.[57] Wisely deferring to international and domestic pressure to be more global, the Obama administration took one step away from unilateral U.S. oversight and put into place a loose agreement, without any real legal status, designed to keep ICANN committed to certain basic goals. (The IANA contract, of course, remains in place.)

The Affirmation recognizes four areas of concern, one of which is basic accountability and the other three of which are broad policy goals: security, competition, and Whois (yes, Whois!).[58] Note well: the concept of "freedom of expression" is not included as a relevant concern. For each of these four areas, it describes a process by which ICANN will undergo self-reviews every three years. The reviews are to be conducted by *review*

57. The Affirmation of Commitments by the U.S. Department of Commerce and the Internet Corporation for Assigned Names and Numbers, September 30, 2009, http://www.ntia.doc.gov/ntiahome/domainname/Affirmation_of_Commitments _2009.pdf.
58. The presence of Whois constitutes an embarrassingly obvious concession to trademark lobbyists. Security, stability and resiliency, and competition, consumer trust, and consumer choice constitute important generic policy objectives that command widespread assent. But Whois is, at best, a means to those ends; it is a specific approach to handling identification and lookup of domain name information that may or may not be the best way to achieve those basic policy objectives. The idea that one of ICANN's basic governing documents instructs it to "include[e] registrant, technical, billing, and administrative contact information" is a reminder of the lobbying game that underpins U.S. involvement.

panels appointed by the chair of the GAC and the ICANN board chair or president. The review teams develop nonbinding recommendations that the board must act on within six months. Each review panel must include the chair of the GAC, the ICANN board chair or president, and representatives of ICANN's supporting organizations and advisory committees.[59] They can also include a sprinkling of independent experts.

Politically, this was a good move. At a stroke, it eliminated some of the key objections to ICANN coming from Western allies such as the European Union; the GAC has been elevated in status and used to provide a soft internationalization without plunging ICANN into the morass of the United Nations or any other type of intergovernmental agreement. The effect is to institutionalize ICANN as a privatized governance entity and solidify international acceptance of it as such.

As a response to ICANN's accountability problems, however, the Affirmation is far less impressive. The appointment of the review panels is subject to a public comment process, but aside from that they are hand-picked by the leaders of ICANN, the very people who are responsible for what ICANN does. Moreover, the composition of the panel will mirror ICANN's existing policy-making organs. In other words, the people who are being reviewed select the reviewers, largely from among the ICANN subunits already responsible for making policies and decisions. And because of that, any review panel is likely to reproduce the politics of ICANN at any given moment. No new perspectives or checks and balances will be put into place by such a process.

If they are really to supply accountability, a review panel must have specific, well-defined laws, rules, or principles to use as a standard against which to judge ICANN's performance. These rules should be known to all participants and relied upon by all as the basic governing principles. If those rule-parameters don't exist (and they still don't), a "review panel" can become just another layer of politics and second-guessing superimposed upon an already messy and diffuse process.

If the selection process were neutral and impartial, and if the review process were confined to issues of accountability, transparency, and the public interest, the Affirmation would not be so bad. The ICANN bylaws and basic norms of good governance could provide applicable criteria to be applied in the review. Indeed, the Affirmation's charge to provide "an ongoing evaluation of Board performance, the Board selection process, the

59. U.S. reserved a permanent seat for itself on the Accountability, Transparency and Public Interest review panel.

extent to which Board composition meets ICANN's present and future needs, and the consideration of an appeal mechanism for Board decisions" is welcome, as is the idea of "assessing the role and effectiveness of the GAC" and "adequate explanation of decisions taken and the rationale thereof."

But the other three areas constitute policy domains. That is, they pertain to ICANN's outputs rather than to its process and its adherence to predefined rules. There is, therefore, a danger that these top-down review panels could become substitutes or short-circuits for the bottom-up policy making process that is supposed to be conducted by the supporting organizations.

Thus the accountability problem is deferred, not solved. What ICANN needs from states is not the kind of discretionary oversight offered by review panels. What it needs are harder forms of legal accountability that make its board and management accountable to a real membership. It also needs a globally applicable legal framework that ensures that its decisions do not undermine basic human rights and due process rights. The point of a legal framework is not to control or manipulate the policy outputs of ICANN, but to establish the basic human rights and due process constraints under which it operates. If they are to pursue this option, states need to abandon outmoded notions that nation-states have some privileged right to establish public policy for critical Internet resources and concentrate on establishing more general rules. ICANN's status as a public, global governance agency needs to be accepted and recognized, and the job of policy making within that institutional framework ceded to the stakeholders from various sectors—government, business, and civil society—who participate in it.

Whether this problem can be solved transcends in importance the relevance of critical Internet resource policy per se. Finding an effective solution to the accountability problem is a test of our ability to develop global governance institutions that can realize the potential of information and communication technology to meet human needs. An inability to find stable, legitimate institutional solutions indicates that contemporary society is stuck in a suboptimal equilibrium around nation-states.

11 Ideologies and Visions

The World Summit on the Information Society was just the most public symptom of the Internet's profound impact on the global politics of communication and information. While it was the management of critical Internet resources that provided the flashpoint for WSIS, we have seen how the regulation of Internet content, the protection of copyrights and trademarks, and issues of communicative privacy and security are all being transformed by similar forces. We also have seen how new forms of networked governance and peer production have emerged across these policy domains.

Yet even as an Internet-enabled world challenges the state as the preeminent institution for the making of communication and information policy, it also generates strenuous reassertions of national authority. States lay claim to geographic names and the representation of linguistic scripts in cyberspace; they scale up their surveillance capabilities; they make plans to weaponize cyberspace and "secure" their part of it; they try to set themselves up as gatekeepers who can censor content. Most of these assertions of power constitute radically new forms of governmentality rather than a reversion to an old order.

It is clear that nation-states—including the United States of America, not just undemocratic ones—constitute some of the biggest threats to the global character and freedom of networked communications. At the same time, the communication-information sector may need state-like powers to prosecute and incarcerate criminals, ensure due process of law, counter harmful private aggregations of power, or formalize individual rights and sanction violations of them by states or other actors. How to harness power to secure freedom? This is a hard problem.

Ideologies, Old and New

Disruptive technologies shuffle the deck in the short term, but it is only a matter of time before things settle down into a more stable pattern of interaction. While we know that the problems of Internet governance challenge the institutional capacity of nation-states, a core assumption of this book is that there is no deterministic progression to any new form of governance. Those who projected that the state will automatically wither away in this sphere were clearly wrong. Those who rationalize as inevitable a reversion to a bordered and controlled Internet dominated by states are also wrong. Nothing is inevitable. Whatever happens, we will make happen.

When societies are confronted with problems of this level of complexity and novelty, ideas and analysis become especially critical. To make sense of our environment we must be able to name phenomena, come up with explanations, and develop guidelines about how to respond. In such an environment it is not only discrete ideas, but also *ideologies* that become important. Ideologies are systems of ideas that strive to provide coherent explanations across a wide range of social, economic, and political phenomena. Political ideologies tend to fuse the normative and the positive; they provide a framework for analyzing events and evaluating or recommending specific courses of action in line with a set of values.

Europe in the early decades of the twentieth century faced changes as far-reaching as today's. The combination of industrialism, economic depression, nationalism, and war generated political turmoil and structural transformations. In this process, collectivist ideologies such as communism and fascism evolved as critiques of the individualist liberal market order. These distinct worldviews led to different diagnoses of social ills and clashing approaches to the construction of policies and political institutions. After decades of contestation among adherents of these competing ideologies, Western Europe reached equilibrium around social democracy.[1] In the evolution of Internet governance one can see a similar grappling with the interaction of ideas, interests, and institutions. The global transformation of information and communication is producing its own set of competing ideologies.

The term *ideology* has a negative connotation, sometimes justifiably so. It can mean a dogmatic or religious adherence to a set of precepts and predictions regardless of their pragmatic utility or correspondence to

---

1. Ideologies "played an important role in driving events down paths they would not otherwise have taken," linking "people who would not otherwise have been linked" and motivating them to "pursue political goals they would not otherwise have pursued." Berman 2006, 9.

reality. While it is true that ideologies bring those risks, it is also true that any good-faith effort to understand and cope with unprecedented societal developments requires something akin to what I mean by ideology. One's ideas and analysis must strive to make sense of the world in a way that facilitates both private and collective action. People will, in fact, link their perceptions and ideas into relatively consistent, comprehensible principles that can be communicated and understood by a broader public so as to coordinate their response.

The Political Spectrum of Internet Governance

The Internet governance debates already are influenced by ideology. But to anyone steeped in its controversies there is something inadequate about the way they structure discourse and categorize political positions. Most contemporary political ideologies start from the assumption, rooted in the eighteenth to twentieth centuries, that the nation-state is the delivery vehicle for most of society's rules, laws, rights, and policies. Existing political thought arranges viewpoints on a scale of "left" to "right" based on their beliefs about what role this traditional form of the government should play. Yet in the communication-information sector, reliance on the nation-state as the principal institution of governance is precisely what is called into question.

It is possible to conceive of a different kind of political space more suited to the politics of Internet governance. One's position in this space is defined by where one locates oneself in a space defined by two axes. The first pertains to the status of the territorial nation-state in communications governance. The second identifies the level of hierarchy one is willing to countenance in the solution of Internet governance problems (see figure 11.1).

The Nation-State Axis
The nation-state axis has at the rightmost extreme a complete subjection of the Internet to national sovereignty, and at the leftmost extreme a fully globalized domain, with the dissolution of national borders or sovereignty as a relevant factor in governing the Internet. The right favors relying on existing, national political institutions; the left favors creating or evolving new, transnational institutions around the global space for human inter-action the network creates.[2]

2. There are, of course, various spots in between these extremes: from right to left there are bilateral agreements and clubs among sovereign states, formal international

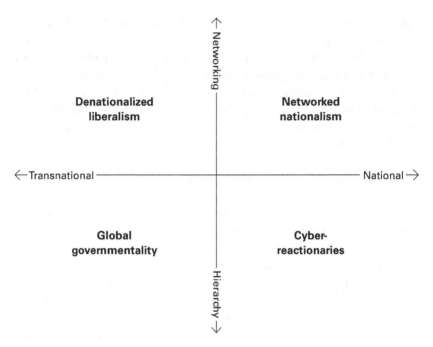

Figure 11.1
The quadrants

The basic factor underlying one's location on this axis is what one considers to be the relevant and legitimate *polity*.[3] A pure nationalist or sovereigntist sees national publics as the most legitimate and important collective actors, and would favor reengineering digital networks to make them conform as much as possible to national law and national authority. A transnationalist, on the other hand, would see the network of people using and supplying Internet services as a distinct polity. Transnationalists would want to more closely align the scope of the governing institutions with the transnational interactions fostered by the Internet, and create around that extended group their own collective deliberation and decision processes for the formation of institutions and policies. Rights would be created and assigned by these transnational institutions.

---

treaties, multistakeholder governance arrangements, delegation to private actors, etc.

3. With origins in the Greek term *politeía*, polity has come to be a generic term for the unit of political organization.

There is also the possibility that one national state (e.g., the United States) will succeed in making its territorial jurisdiction global in scope—a possibility that challenges my linear spectrum but nevertheless can be fit into it. Even though the hegemony of one state could produce globalization, a true transnationalist would reject that as a cyberimperialism that privileges one (national) polity and subjugates others. Transnationalists would be in partial agreement with nationalists in opposing the hegemonist's role. But whereas cybernationalists would favor replacing unilateral power with a multilateral arrangement that shared the power among states, those on the left side of the axis would want to make Internet institutions directly accountable to a global Internet community, and would be as hostile to a multilateral intergovernmental agreement as to unilateral governmental control.

The Networking-Hierarchy Axis
The nation-state axis does not capture all the significant differences over Internet governance. Another dimension, which juxtaposes free association and hierarchy, is required. The networking-hierarchy axis reflects the degree to which one believes the problems associated with Internet governance should be solved using hierarchical mechanisms, or left to the peaceful forms of association and disassociation we have defined as *networking*. On the left side of this axis, most Internet governance would be an aggregate of many unilateral decisions to connect or disconnect, associate or break off links, exchange or not exchange. This is "unilateral action in anarchic fields," or "peer production of governance." On the right, governance emerges from adherence to rules enforced by an authority, where adherence is obtained by force if necessary. Of course, between these two extremes there are many points. A base of private contract law can support a superstructure of more or less free networking; or we can recognize free networking as the primary mechanism of governance but opt for hierarchical intervention when network externalities convey too much power to a private group, or when bottlenecks form around essential facilities.

These two axes form a political space that can provide some structure to the political discourse over the future of Internet governance. In the lower-right quadrant, we have cyberconservatives and outright cyberreactionaries. These are the advocates of forcing the Internet to conform to the authority and parameters of the nation-state. Their intent is to subordinate global communications to established institutions of political authority by realigning its operational units and resources with the jurisdiction of the state. International policy would be handled by intergovernmental institutions, and kept to the bare minimum required to protect or supplement domestic policy. China is an exemplar of this approach. But it would be a mistake to conflate all inhabitants of this quadrant with authoritarian one-party rule; a nationalist might also be democratic and wish to border the Internet and impose high levels of hierarchical control over communications in accordance with a political majority's will.[4]

In the upper-right quadrant, the nation-state is still the dominant governance institution but there is greater willingness to embrace the potential of networking and less of an attempt to impose territorial hierarchies on networked actors and network operations. Public policies and regulations are applied to actors within the territorial jurisdiction but many loopholes and escape valves are left open because of transnational Internet access. States in this quadrant might cope with transnational problems through a mix of transgovernmental networks, delegation to private actors, or formal intergovernmental treaties, but all international institutions would be rooted in states, and any organically evolved Internet institutions would have to be recognized by and subordinated to states. This quadrant is characterized by an acute tension between the boundaries of the polity and the boundaries of networked activity. This may, therefore, be an inherently unstable place, with its adherents eventually migrating to one of the other three quadrants.

The lower-left quadrant encompasses those who advocate global governmentality—namely, hierarchical control of the Internet via new institutions that transcend the nation-state. These new institutions are most likely to be private sector-based and created to advance business interests, though they could be multistakeholder and public-private partnerships. In this realm reside advocates of a globally scoped, corporatist regulatory regime for the Internet, copyright/trademark maximalists, and, at the edge, cyberimperialists who would globalize governance through the extraterritorial application of one state's laws and power.

The upper-left quadrant supports a transnational institutional framework that emerges around nonstate action. It recognizes the individual

4. But these nationalist democrats would have to sacrifice the better part of their liberalism to do so. Moreover, the democratic nationalist empowers and legitimizes the authoritarian nationalist (and vice versa); neither can assert that the norms and policies derived from their national polity should be applied to other national polities. So the power of an authoritarian state to censor and control its citizens' use of the Internet would be left undisturbed by external actors; only people within its jurisdiction could change it.

network participant, not states or corporations, as the fundamental source of legitimate global Internet governance and proposes to create new governance institutions around them. This quadrant combines economic and social liberalism. It proposes to leverage peer production processes, networked governance, and markets to handle the issues of Internet governance as much as possible. It would restrict hierarchical interventions to the function of securing basic protections against theft, fraud, and coercion.

There are of course aspects of the politics of Internet governance not well captured by these axes. Those who believe, for example, that the nation-state is the most suitable unit for political action and discourse can be either democratic or undemocratic; nothing about nationalism per se determines one's position on that. Likewise, those who favor the development of new global governance institutions around the Internet polity also could be democratic or undemocratic; their new institutions could be participatory and inclusive, or elitist and oligarchic. Property vs. commons is a salient issue in Internet governance. While not addressed directly by any of the axes, the definition, recognition, and enforcement of property rights requires some kind of hierarchy or hierarchical law, so it can be incorporated by the second axis. Another key factor affecting one's position in political debates is one's stance toward the competing values of liberty and equality. Because the freedom to exchange information and to associate with other network participants corresponds closely to the upper end of the network-hierarchy axis, and because all forms of egalitarianism require a hierarchical power to level differences and redistribute wealth, the liberty-equality tradeoff is to a large degree captured by the network-hierarchy axis. Public or private ordering is another oft-heard parameter of Internet governance debate. This too can be roughly mapped onto the national—transnational axis because in the current institutional context the boundaries of the "public" are coterminous with the state, and therefore most transnational Internet governance organizations are based on private ordering.

Reimagining Right and Left

The nature of the political spectrum is profoundly changed when we are forced to make the territorial state a variable rather than a constant. Once we have to reconsider the source of authority for the governance of communication and information, the questions that must be answered by a political ideology change. The standard left-right spectrum does not provide reliable guidance on some of the basic institutional questions.

Take the left, first, as an example. Many of the civil society groups that cluster around international institutions, especially UN institutions, are on the left end of the traditional political spectrum. They promote norms of social democracy and articulate demands to redistribute wealth and promote equality.[5] Calling for sustainability, the elimination of poverty, and social justice is one thing; it is quite another to have an ideology that provides a political movement with pragmatic guidance on how to deliver those things to a global polity. Insofar as they are interested in Internet governance, it is clear that contemporary social democrats, in line with their egalitarianism, would locate themselves somewhere near the hierarchical (bottom) end of the network-hierarchy axis. But it is not at all clear where social democrats should locate themselves on the national sovereignty axis.

While many express opposition to free trade and market competition in the ICT sector, few if any advocate a return to a national communications monopoly—even though that institutional arrangement provides the perfect setting for regulating and taxing the industry to promote social goals at the national level. More generally, the left's classic hostility to economic liberalism has a hard problem coping with the liberalization of information and communication services, which has produced the most rapid and sustained growth in the level of communications access in world history while massively expanding the type and diversity of information content and services. While the left often mounts convincing critiques of various failings and market abuses, no systematic institutional alternative is advanced. Would Internet social democrats want to locate themselves in the cyber-reactionary quadrant, alongside conservative nationalists and authoritarian regimes, and attempt to put the Internet genie back into nation-state bottles so that the information economy can be more effectively subject to wealth transfers and social regulation? Probably not.

Does the left, instead, want to enact a global social democracy through existing intergovernmental organizations? On its face, this option is not attractive. International institutions are fundamentally flawed as mechanisms for the realization of social-democratic aims. They are not, at root, democratic at all. They have no citizens; they are collections of nation-

5. "We aspire to build information and communication societies where development is framed by fundamental human rights and oriented to achieving a more equitable distribution of resources, leading to the elimination of poverty in a way that is non-exploitative and environmentally sustainable. To this end we believe technologies can be engaged as fundamental means." From "Shaping Information Societies for Human Needs," Civil Society Declaration to the World Summit on the Information Society, WSIS Civil Society Plenary, Geneva, December 8, 2003, http://www.itu.int/wsis/docs/geneva/civil-society-declaration.pdf.

states. Many of the member states are authoritarian and stubbornly undemocratic, yet as sovereigns they have equal rights under intergovernmental regimes. The politicians who participate in these intergovernmental organizations define and enact their preferences in ways shaped by national politics, not in response to a global population and a global public interest. Simple wealth transfers from one national public to another are unlikely under such conditions.[6] International institutions lack global taxing power. When all is said and done, they simply collect donations from nation-states (and sometimes corporations). More fundamentally, they lack the electoral, democratic deliberative mechanisms and judicial checks and balances that would be required to render global taxation legitimate and lawful. Is it sensible to ask these institutions to enact a gigantic, global wealth redistribution regime for the information economy?

Perhaps, then, latter-day social democrats should be even more radical and mobilize for the creation of a completely new, transnational sector-specific redistributive state for communication-information technology, or move toward the kind of localist anarchism hinted at by the World Social Forum. But where would this institution come from and how would it achieve taxing and regulatory powers over the current system of networked Internet governance, which allows organizations to opt out of financial and technical arrangements that don't suit their interests? What is the strategy for getting out from under nation-states? What kind of a global polity would effectively combine the populations of North and South America, Europe, Africa, Russia, India, and China into a cohesive public? Globalizing the capabilities of social democracy without tempering it with liberalism, and without bringing into being a wide-ranging public sphere that transcends territorially limited cultures and language communities could be quite dangerous.

Social democracy at the national level was originally a step back from harder forms of socialism; it accepted the market's productivity and vitality and tried to harness it politically to promote social aims. Will Internet-era social democrats make a similar concession to liberalism and embrace looser, networked forms of governance at the international level? Will they place themselves in the upper-left quadrant and rely on contractually constructed commons rather than statist redistribution? This path has many positive aspects, but would leave in place a decentralization of power that makes systematic forms of wealth redistribution less feasible.

6. When such transfers occur it will always be conceived as furthering a member state's own national interest or policy in some way.

Whichever path a leftist takes along the nationalism axis, it is evident that the basic character of social democracy will be profoundly affected by the choice. It would be impossible for it to retain its classical program. Contemporary social democrats involved in Internet governance have not even begun to confront this problem. They continue to articulate high-sounding norms and political goals and do not worry much about how to deliver them.

The right side of the standard political spectrum has similar problems. The right now consists of an increasingly strange combination of market liberalism[7] in economics, religious-based social conservatism, and extreme nationalism in international and military affairs. Policy toward Internet governance tends to be dominated by the nationalist element.

The Internet has always posed a problem for the right and its bundle of barely compatible tendencies and constituencies. The Internet makes economic and social liberalism virtually insuperable: if one truly wants to regulate content and conduct in cyberspace to enforce socially conservative values, one must impose severe economic regulations upon it and erect barriers to trade.[8] And if one's political base is animated by fears of foreigners and terrorist attack, and the ideologues and special interest groups within one's coalition exploit those fears to elevate national security and surveillance over civil liberties and privacy, the openness and freedom of the Internet starts to be perceived as an enemy to be attacked.

In the past, market liberals on the right advocated privatization, competition, and liberalization of key infrastructural industries such as telecommunications and energy. In Internet governance, however, an

7. Note that I am using the terms *liberal* and *liberalism* the way Europeans use them (i.e., in their correct, historical sense). *Liberalism* means policies and philosophies that favor individual liberty and choice. In the United States, *liberal* has come to mean almost the same thing as *social democracy*; namely, it is associated with the left rather than the right.
8. The U.S. attempt to control Internet gambling, for example, was sanctioned by the World Trade Organization. China's Ministry of Culture fused trade protectionism, censorship, and copyright protection in a recent ruling. For all music from outside China, including Hong Kong and Taiwan, online music distributors will be required to provide written lyrics for each song, translated into Chinese, and documents to prove they aren't infringing on intellectual property rights. Any company wishing to provide music download services will be required to apply for an Internet culture license. Loretta Chao, "China sets new rules for music sold online," *Wall Street Journal*, Technology section, September 5, 2009, http://online.wsj.com/article/SB125207664547286713.html.

irreconcilable conflict exists between their nationalism and their devotion to the market. Stuck on the issue of U.S. power, they do not fight for liberal ideals in the global Internet polity. Instead, they equate the U.S. nation-state with all the classic virtues of liberal democracy and reduce the politics of global Internet governance to favoring or opposing U.S. preeminence. To these rightists, the U.S. government, when considered as an actor in geopolitics, embodies freedom and democracy. Thus, anyone who challenges its special role in Internet governance is, by definition, an apologist for the enemies of freedom and democracy who also challenge the U.S. role. Sophisticated readers will recognize in this logic the mirror image of the extreme leftist tendency to embrace any political tendency from "the South" that opposes U.S. hegemony (even Islamic theocrats and fascists) and to criticize as domineering, exploitative, and a tool of the United States any political tendencies that embrace market liberalism.[9] Both the conservative apologists for the United States and their anticapitalist counterparts commit the same fallacy: the United States becomes an abstract symbol rather than a real state, and economic liberalism becomes a kind of "market fundamentalism" rather than a set of policies whose effects can be rationally evaluated and used as appropriate. Conservatives both inside and outside the United States are so deeply locked into this dichotomy that they cannot make valuable contributions to the Internet governance debates.

Even the rightwing libertarians of the Ron Paul variety, while more consistent in their liberalism, are completely stuck in the nationalistic rut. They lack any conception of the Internet community as a distinctive polity. They speak reverently of national sovereignty and of their national constitution, revealing that they think of liberty and related political values exclusively within the framework of the nation-state. They seem never to have considered the possibility that liberal rights and freedoms on the Internet cannot be retained if they are only an island in a globally interconnected economy and society. They seem not to understand that the rights they define as "constitutional" might need to be translated into a transnational institutional context to survive for the next fifty years. Mention global governance in the context of the Internet and they hear only "the UN wants to take over the Internet" or "some other state we don't like (China, the EU, whatever) wants to regulate the Internet."

9. See Cohen 2007 for a dissection of the way leftists have embraced Islamic theocrats and fascists along these lines. Note also that Cohen uses the term *liberals* incorrectly.

Because ICANN is viewed as a U.S.-controlled, nongovernmental institution, it is presumed to be good. They never pay attention to the ways the governments of China and the EU influence the Internet via ICANN's GAC. They look the other way when U.S.-based copyright and trademark interests utilize ICANN to regulate and intervene in the market for Internet services, almost always in illiberal ways. They never seem to notice the way ICANN completely nullifies their prized First Amendment in a key area of Internet policy. In short, their conception of the minimal state is confined entirely to the context of domestic politics. These blind spots of conservative idealists are easily manipulated by the corporate and militaristic interests that have less elevated motives for defending and retaining a privileged role for the U.S. government.

New Ideologies?

While it is important to understand the ways traditional left- and right-wing movements respond to Internet governance issues, there are also new ideologies native to the space. This section examines and critiques two such attempts—multistakeholderism and access to knowledge. It then tries to formulate the outlines of a liberal ideology suitable for Internet governance.

Multistakeholderism

In Internet politics, the concept of multiple stakeholder participation threatens to become a new "ism." With its appeals to participatory norms it commands widespread acquiescence, or at least lip service. But as an ideology that can guide change, multistakeholderism is both radically incomplete and flawed.

Multistakeholderism addresses issues of representation and process; it does not provide any guidance on the substantive policy issues of Internet governance. While it does address the problem of democracy and participation, it mostly evades the key axes of national sovereignty and hierarchical power. At best, it tells us to open up existing intergovernmental institutions to participants other than states. The historical importance of this maxim during the WSIS process should be recognized. Still, at best this provides a bridge between an institutional environment dominated by nation-states and . . . something else. It has little to say about what that "something else" is or should be. At worst, it offers a simple-minded communitarianism that implies that all political, economic, and social conflicts can be resolved if everyone involved just sits down and talks about them together. By focusing almost exclusively on the interaction or dialogue among stakeholders, it tends to evade or ignore issues of rights, access, power, and related issues of institutional design. It invites private sector and civil society actors to "participate" in decision-making process, leaving their precise role or authority over the process indeterminate.

One of the chief problems with multistakeholderism is the plasticity and imprecision inherent in the concept of a *stakeholder*. In a democratic polity we know what a citizen is and what rights go with citizenship. But no one knows for sure what a stakeholder is or what rights adhere to that status. Flirting with corporatism, multistakeholderism uses broad categories—private sector, government, and civil society—as the basis for representation in deliberations and decision making. But the political views held within each of these categories are extremely diverse, and real people and real organizations can span more than one of them. This provides ample room for opportunistic and manipulative behaviors.[10] Worse, if not properly institutionalized, multistakeholder processes can give those already holding governance power too much discretion over who is deemed to "represent" different social sectors,[11] or the ability to manipulate the categories of representation. The power to formally designate certain people or organizations as "the" representative of some broad category can be used to disenfranchise the populace as easily as to empower them.[12]

Multistakeholderism often maintains the pretense that nation-states are stakeholders on an equal status with others. But given prevailing institu-

10. Chapter 6 briefly mentioned the debate within civil society over the status of the Internet technical community—should they be given their own category, be classified as civil society, be grouped with the private sector, or even (e.g., representatives of RIRs or ICANN) be considered governmental?

11. In ICANN's latest reform process, civil society groups learned that the ICANN board and staff claimed the right to decide unilaterally whether participants from civil society were sufficiently "representative" or "diverse." Responding to lobbying from business interests, they used no objective standards to determine how "representative" groups were; indeed, a double standard was applied as the levels of diversity and participation demanded of the noncommercial stakeholder group greatly exceeded that of the business interests.

12. The 800-member Election Committee in Hong Kong, which elects the territory's chief executive, is based on a complex division of civil society and business into twenty-eight functional constituencies, six "special" constituencies and religious constituencies, and two governmental bodies. The whole point of this arrangement—under both British and Chinese colonial rule—is to prevent true popular sovereignty and to empower certain constituencies at the expense of others.

tions and power relations, this is a dangerous fiction. States, especially great powers, can pick and choose when to engage in a way that other groups cannot. Moreover, governments are usually not organized in ways that facilitate equal-status deliberation; for example they don't (or sometimes cannot) openly express opinions on public email lists, and can't easily participate in public, free-form discussions of controversial issues without giving the impression that they are taking an official position. ICANN's experience with the GAC, or the IGF's willingness to make governments a bit more equal than the others, attest to some of the problems created by attempts to classify nation-states as "stakeholders" alongside nonstate actors.

If multistakeholderism means only that people who are strongly impacted by policies should be actively heard from, then it is nothing but normal pluralist politics. In any democratic policy-making process, there are numerous opportunities for public hearings and comment and decision makers are open to legitimate forms of persuasion from various interest groups. The critical difference, however, is that pluralist democracy takes place within a legal and institutional framework that gives participating citizens specific civil and political rights, and makes the governmental decision makers formally accountable to them in various ways. Multistakeholder institutions at the global level still lack this rights framework.

A2K

Access to Knowledge (A2K) provides a substantive ideology that is native to digital media. As noted in chapter 7, it is transnational in outlook and founded on an innovative and constructive approach to informational property rights. It provides both a new conception of freedom in the networked environment and a pragmatic appreciation of the capabilities of peer production. It also offers a compelling historical narrative about the clash between an old order and a new order in the information society. Yet A2K suffers from two limitations.

One is that it lacks a clear stance on the nation-state as a governance institution. In general, it does not have anything new or insightful to say about the future of sovereignty. While the A2K movement is not nationalist, neither does it explicitly challenge the nation-state's role in communication-information governance. Aside from the contractual commons, it doesn't offer a vision of an alternative to the nation-state. (The contractual commons may, in fact, be sufficient—but that argument hasn't been made.) A lack of engagement with that problem diminishes the relevance of A2K on some of the key drivers of Internet governance, such as the securitization of the Internet or the formation of new global institutions around critical Internet resources. More significantly, its reflexive support for the public domain in information production isn't grounded in any new, well-developed notion of the proper scope and limits of state action in a globalized information sector. This means that A2K adherents could easily slide down a slippery slope toward old-style socialism, in which taxation dominates the financing of all information production and a protectionist national state reemerges as the dominant actor in the information economy. Under such a regime, the information economy will be organized around national politics rather than local, national, and global sharing and markets. As this happens, advocates of "access to knowledge" will be inexorably drawn toward erecting national fences around themselves—meaning, to restrict access—in order to protect the political and distributional bargains upon which its national information economy is founded.[13]

A deeper problem is that A2K's critique of intellectual property comes from two distinct, sometimes contradictory impulses. On the one hand, A2K as social movement gets a lot of mileage out of a simple appeal to the moral obligation to cooperate and share. Copyrights, trademarks, and patents are oppressive and troublesome, this way of thinking suggests, because *all* property rights are oppressive and troublesome. A deontological claim that sharing is ethically superior to private property threatens to fuse the A2K movement with industrial-era socialist and communist ideologies that oppose property and a market economy as such. This is surely a dead end.[14]

On the other hand, the A2K movement also contains within it a sophisticated critique of the way attempts to institutionalize property rights in the digital environment can create unacceptable restrictions on the freedoms of individuals. Richard Stallman has referred to digital rights management as a "system of subjugation" that extends the owner's control beyond the first sale into a set of ongoing restrictions on human action. It creates a world of publications that can "rat on you";[15] of government-

---

13. We already see hints of this in the cultural diversity movement, where a "diversity" argument is advanced to rationalize protectionist policies toward film, music, and other cultural products instead of the classical economic arguments about infant industries, etc.

14. See Mueller 2008a for a more extensive critique of "info-communism."

15. Boyle 1997a, citing Pamela Samuelson.

mandated technical standards designed to impede what users can do with digital information even when many of the blocked uses are legally and ethically justifiable; a world where Internet service providers might inspect your packets in transit and disrupt them if they use certain protocols associated with copyright violations. This argument is consequentialist rather than deontological; it focuses on the restrictive socioeconomic effects of certain forms of informational property and on the beneficial effects of sharing, commons, and public production under certain conditions. The latter approach to A2K does not assert that sharing is an ethical absolute; it warns us that copyright, patent, and trademark maximalism can turn our technical systems into a Panopticon, undermining the very innovation and creativity intellectual property rights were intended to protect. It is not, or need not be, inherently hostile to property and markets.

A2K as liberal critique of the excesses of intellectual property in the digital age points in a very different direction from A2K as info-communism. That movement has yet to decide which path it will take.

Elements of a Denationalized Liberalism

Cyber-libertarianism is not dead; it was never really born. It was more a prophetic vision than an ideology or "ism" with a political and institutional program. It is now clear, however, that in considering the political alternatives and ideological dilemmas posed by the global Internet we can't really do without it, or something like it. That primal vision flagged two fundamental problems that still pervade most discussions of Internet governance: (1) the issue of who should be "sovereign"—the people interacting via the Internet or the territorial states constructed by earlier populations in complete ignorance of the capabilities of networked computers; and (2) the degree to which the classical liberal precepts of freedom get translated into the context of converged media, ubiquitous networks, and automated information processing.

In the book *Powers of Freedom* (1999), Nicholas Rose observed that liberalism was not the first political movement to proclaim the right of individuals to be free; its innovation was that it was the first to successfully link that claim to a specific system of government. The eighteenth and nineteenth centuries' liberal-democratic state created a particular historical realization of a system of rights and it did this by distributing the responsibility for government to individual citizens qua citizens. The creation of democratic nation-states, however, was limited to bounded territories with more or less shared-culture populations. It should be clear that this kind of a territorial state doesn't scale to global proportions.

The answer to that dilemma may lie in the upper-left quadrant of the political space—a denationalized liberalism.

At its core, a denationalized liberalism favors a universal right to receive and impart information regardless of frontiers, and sees freedom to communicate and exchange information as fundamental and primary elements of human choice and political and social activity. Political institutions should seek to build upon, not undermine or reverse, the limitless possibilities for forming new social aggregations around global communications. In line with its commitment to freedom, this ideology holds a presumption in favor of networked, associative relations over hierarchical relations as a mode of transnational governance. Governance should emerge primarily as a byproduct of many unilateral and bilateral decisions by its members to exchange or negotiate with other members (or to refuse to do so). This networked liberalism thus moves decisively away from the dangerous, conflict-prone tendency of other ideologies to build political institutions around linguistic, religious, and ethnic communities. Instead of rigid, bounded communities that conceal domination with the pretense of homogeneity and a "collective will," it offers governance of communication and information through more flexible and shifting social aggregations.

Although committed to globalism in the communicative sector, it recognizes that, for the time being, people are deeply situated within national laws and institutions regarding such basic matters as contracts, property, crime, education, and welfare. It is characterized not by absolute hostility to national and subnational governments as such, but rather by an attempt to *contain* them to those domains of law and policy suited to localized or territorialized authority. It seeks to detach the transnational operations of Internet infrastructure and the governance of services and content from those limited jurisdictions as much as possible, and to prevent states from ensnaring global communications in interstate rivalries and politico-military games.

Such an ideology needs to answer tough questions about when hierarchical exercises of power are justified and through which instruments they are exercised. A realistic denationalized liberalism recognizes that emergent forms of control will emerge from globally networked communities. It recognizes that authoritative interventions will be needed to secure basic rights against coercive attacks, and that network externalities or bottlenecks over essential facilities may create a concentrated power with coercive effect. It should also recognize the exceptional cases where the governance of shared resources requires binding collective action. Insofar as collective governance is necessary and unavoidable, a denationalized liberalism strives to make Internet users and suppliers an autonomous, global polity. It favors what might be called *neodemocratic* rights to representation and participation in these new global governance institutions. The concept of democracy is qualified by the realization that the specific form of democratic governance associated with the territorial nation-state cannot and should not be directly translated into the global level. However, it does maintain the basic objectives of traditional democracy—to give all individuals the same formal rights and representational status within the institutions that govern them so that they can preserve and protect their rights as individuals. Such a liberalism is not interested, however, in using global governance institutions to redistribute wealth. That would require an overarching hierarchical power that would be almost impossible to control democratically; its mere existence would trigger organized political competition for its levers, which would, in the current historical context, devolve into competition among preexisting political and ethnic collectivities.

Denationalized liberalism embraces both property and commons and seeks to leverage their complementarities. It recognizes the coexistence and interdependence of markets, exclusive property rights, and shared/ unowned resources in communication and information. It rejects the false idea that commons and property are mutually exclusive, totalizing principles for economic organization, seeing them instead as distinct methods of organizing access to resources with their own virtues and failings. Historically, there has been a dynamic interaction between commons and private property; neither could exist in socially productive forms without the other.

The Internet itself embodies an unusually successful example of this complementary relationship between private market and commons. The basic protocols are open, nonproprietary standards that can be freely adopted by anyone. At the same time, the Internet is a network of networks, the constituent parts of which are privately owned and administered. This aspect of the Internet leads to privatization and decentralization of network operations and policies. By facilitating interoperability, the Internet standards commons promotes a private and decentralized market for software applications and information content. Thus, at the endpoints of the Internet, the free market and privatization rule; at the core standards level, a commons is in place. The end-to-end principle has in the past ensured that commons and market complement each other. The sharing and coordinating mechanisms are structured to provide maximum scope for private initiative and innovation at the end points. There is a clear separation between the parts of the system that are subject to private initiative and control, and the parts that are subject to global coordination and nonexclusive access. In short, it is the combination of the private and the common that works.

In short, we need to find ways to translate classical liberal rights and freedoms into a governance framework suitable for the global Internet. There can be no cyberliberty without a political movement to define, defend, and institutionalize individual rights and freedoms on a transnational scale.

References

Adler, P. S. 2001. Market, hierarchy, and trust: The knowledge economy and the future of capitalism. *Organization Science* 12 (2): 214–234.

Anderson, R., R. Boehme, R. Clayton, and T. Moore. 2008. Security Economics and the Internal Market. European Network and Information Security Agency (ENISA). January 31. http://www.enisa.europa.eu/act/sr/reports/econ-sec.

Bambauer, D. E. 2009. Cybersieves. *Duke Law Journal* 59 (3): 377–446.

Banks, K. 2005. Summitry and strategies. *Index on Censorship* 34 (3): 85–91.

Barabási, A. 2002. *Linked: The new science of networks*. New York: Perseus Books.

Benkler, Y. 2006. *The wealth of networks: How social production transforms markets and freedom*. New Haven, CT: Yale University Press.

Benner, T., W. H. Reinicke, and J. M. Witte. 2000. Beyond multilateralism: Global public policy networks. *International Politics and Society* 2:176–188.

Bennett, W. L. 2003. Communicating global activism: Strengths and vulnerabilities of networked politics. *Information Communication and Society* 6 (2): 143–168.

Bennett, W. L. 2004. Global media and politics: Transnational communication regimes and civic cultures. *Annual Review of Political Science* 7:125–148.

Berman, S. 2006. *The primacy of politics: Social democracy and the making of Europe's twentieth century*. Cambridge: Cambridge University Press.

Bernstein, M. H. 1955. *Regulating business by independent commission*. Princeton, NJ: Princeton University Press.

Bhagwati, J. 2004. *In defense of globalization*. Oxford: Oxford University Press.

Biersteker, T. J., and S. E. Eckert, eds. 2008. *Countering the financing of terrorism*. New York: Routledge.

Boerzel, T. A. 1998. Organizing Babylon: On the different conceptions of policy networks. *Public Administration* 36 (1): 3–18.

Borgatti, S. P., and M. G. Everett. 1997. Network analysis of 2-mode data. *Social Networks* 19 (3): 243–269.

Borgatti, S. P., and P. C. Foster. 2003. The network paradigm in organizational research: A review and typology. *Journal of Management* 29 (6): 991–1013.

Boyle, J. 1996. *Shamans, software and spleens: Law and the construction of the information society.* Cambridge, MA: Harvard University Press.

Boyle, J. 1997a. A politics of intellectual property: Environmentalism for the net? *Duke Law Journal* 47:87–116.

Boyle, J. 1997b. *Foucault in cyberspace.* http://www.law.duke.edu/boylesite/foucault .htm.

Brenner, Susan W. 2005. Distributed security: Moving away from reactive law Enforcement. *International Journal of Communications Law & Policy* (Spring): 1–43.

Brock, G. 1994. *Telecommunications policy for the information age.* Cambridge, MA: Harvard University Press.

Bruce, R., S. Dynes, H. Brechbuhl, B. Brown, E. Goetz, P. Verhoest. 2005. *International policy framework for protecting critical information infrastructure: A discussion paper outlining key policy issues* (TNO report 33680). Delft, NL: TNO.

Burk, D. 1995. Trademarks along the Infobahn: A first look at the emerging law of cybermarks. *Richmond Journal of Law and Technology* 1 (1).

Calabrese, A. 2004. The promise of civil society: A global movement for communication rights. *Continuum. Journal of Media & Cultural Studies* 18 (3): 317–329.

Cameron, K. 2005. The laws of identity. May 13. http://www.identityblog.com/ stories/2004/12/09/thelaws.html.

Carlsson, U. 2003. The rise and fall of NWICO: From a vision of international regulation to a reality of multilevel governance. *Nordicom Review* 2:31–68.

Casey, T. D. 2000. *ISP liability survival guide: Strategies for managing copyright, spam, cache, and privacy regulations.* New York: Wiley.

Castells, M. 1996. *The rise of the network society.* Cambridge, MA: Blackwell.

Chan, P. 2006. Safer (cyber)sex with .xxx: The case for first amendment zoning of the Internet. *Loyola of Los Angeles Law Review* 39:1299–1338.

Coase, R. H. 1937. The nature of the firm. *Economica* 4:386–405.

Coase, R. H. 1960. The problem of social cost. *Journal of Law & Economics* 3 (1): 1–44.

Cohen, N. 2007. *What's left: How liberals lost their way.* London: Fourth Estate.

Cole, W. K. 2007. Blacklists, blocklists, DNSBL's, and survival. (Version 1.24.) http:// www.scconsult.com/bill/dnsblhelp.html.

Cowhey, P. 1990. The international telecommunications regime: The political roots of regimes for high technology. *International Organization* 44: 169–199.

Cowhey, P., J. Aronson, and J. E. Richards. 2009. *Transforming global communication and information markets.* Cambridge, MA: MIT Press.

Cowhey, P., and M. Mueller. 2009. Delegation, networks and Internet governance. In *Networks and politics: Agency, structure and power,* ed. M. Kahler, 173–193. Ithaca, NY: Cornell University Press.

Crowston, K., and J. Howison. 2005. The social structure of free and open source software development. *First Monday* 10 (2). http://firstmonday.org/htbin/cgiwrap/bin/ojs/index.php/fm/article/view/1207/1127.

Dean, J., J. Anderson, and G. Lovink, eds. 2006. *Reformatting politics: Information technology and global civil society.* London: Routledge.

Deibert, R., J. G. Palfrey, R. Rohozinski, and J. Zittrain, eds. 2008. *Access denied: The practice and policy of global Internet filtering.* Cambridge, MA: MIT Press.

Deibert, R., and R. Rohozinski. 2009a. *Tracking ghostnet: Tracking a cyber-espionage network.* Toronto: Information Warfare Monitor, University of Toronto.

Deibert, R., and R. Rohonzinki. 2009b. Risking security: Critical trajectories of Internet securitization. Paper presented at the annual meeting of the International Studies Association's 50th Annual Convention, New York, NY, February 15.

DeNardis, L. 2009. *Protocol politics: The globalization of Internet governance.* Cambridge, MA: MIT Press.

Denning, D. E. 2000. Activism, hacktivism and cyberterrorism: The Internet as a tool for influencing foreign policy. *Computer Security Journal* 16 (3): 15–35.

Dimitrov, R. S. 2005. Hostage to norms: States, institutions and global forest politics. *Global Environmental Politics* 5 (4): 1–24.

Doria, A., and M. Palage, 2007. Please, keep the core neutral: An essay on ICANN's proposed policy to introduce new top-level domains. March 25. http://www.bloggernews.net/15463.

Dorogovtsev, S. N., and J. F. F. Mendes 2003. *Evolution of networks: From biological nets to the Internet and WWW.* Oxford: Oxford University Press.

Drahos, P. 2003. *Information feudalism: Who owns the knowledge economy?* New York: New Press.

Drake, W. J. 2000. The rise and decline of the international telecommunications regime. In *Regulating the global information society,* ed. Christopher T. Marsden, 124–177. London: Routledge.

Drake, W. J., and Kalypso Nicolaidis. 1992. Ideas, interests, and institutionalization: "Trade in services" and the Uruguay round. *International Organization* 46 (1): 37–100.

Drezner, D. 2007. *All politics are global: Explaining international regulatory regimes.* Princeton, NJ: Princeton University Press.

Eilstrup-Sangiovanni, M. 2009. Varieties of cooperation: Government networks in international security. In *Networked politics: Agency, structure and power*, ed. M. Kahler, 194–227. Ithaca, NY: Cornell University Press.

Elkin-Koren, N. 2005. What contracts can't do: The limits of private ordering in facilitating creative commons. Unpublished manuscript.

Elliott, M., and W. Scacchi. 2008. Mobilization of software developers: The free software movement. *Information Technology & People* 21 (1): 4–33.

Evron, G. 2008. Battling botnets and online mobs. *Georgetown Journal of International Affairs* 9 (1): 121–126.

Florini, A. 2000. *The third force: The rise of transnational civil society.* Tokyo and Washington, DC: Japan Center for International Exchange; Carnegie Endowment for International Peace. Distributed in the United States by Brookings Institution Press.

Franklin, J., A. Perrig, V. Paxson, and S. Savage. 2007. An inquiry into the nature and causes of the wealth of Internet miscreants. In *Proceedings of the ACM CCS'07 conference*, October 29–November 2, Alexandria, VA. http://www.icir.org/vern/papers/miscreant-wealth.ccs07.pdf.

Fraser, N. 2007. Transnationalizing the public sphere: On the legitimacy and efficacy of public opinion in a post-Westphalian world. *Theory, Culture & Society* 24 (4): 7–30.

Froomkin, M. 2002. ICANN's uniform dispute resolution policy: Causes and (partial) cures. *Brooklyn Law Review* 67 (3): 605–718.

Froomkin, M. 2004. When we say US™, we mean it! *Houston Law Review* 41:839–884.

Goldsmith, J., and T. Wu. 2006. *Who controls the Internet? Illusions of a borderless world.* New York: Oxford University Press.

Goldsmith, S., and W. Eggers. 2004. *Governing by network: The new shape of the public sector.* Washington, DC: Brookings Institution Press.

Hafner-Burton, E., M. Kahler, and A. H. Montgomery. 2009. Network analysis for international relations. *International Organization* 63 (3): 559–592.

Hain, T. 2005. A pragmatic report on IPv4 address space consumption. *Internet Protocol Journal* 8 (3). September. http://www.cisco.com/web/about/ac123/ac147/archived_issues/ipj_8-3/ipv4.html.

Hajnal, P. I., ed. 2002. *Civil society in the information age.* Hampshire, UK: Ashgate.

Halleck, D. 2003. Indymedia: Building an international activist Internet network. *Media Development* 2003 (4). World Association of Christian Communications. http://archive.waccglobal.org/wacc/publications/media_development/archive/2003 _4/indymedia_building_an_international_activist_internet_network.

Heclo, H. 1978. Issue networks and executive establishment. In *The new American political system,* ed. Anthony King, 87–124. Washington, DC: American Enterprise Institute.

Heinz, J. P., E. O. Laumann, R. Salisbury, and R. Nelson. 1990. Inner circles or hollow cores? Elite networks in national policy systems. *Journal of Politics* 52 (2): 356–390.

Hudson, A. 2001. NGOs' transnational advocacy networks: From 'legitimacy' to 'political responsibility'? *Global Networks* 1 (4): 331–352.

Huston, G. 2005. *Just how big is IPv6? or where did all those addresses go?* http://www .potaroo.net/ispcol/2005-07/ipv6size.html (accessed June 20, 2009).

John, P. 2001. Policy networks. In *The Blackwell companion to political sociology,* ed. K. Nash and A. Scott, 139–148. Oxford: Blackwell.

Johnson, D. R., S. P. Crawford, and J. G. Palfrey. 2004. The accountable Internet: Peer production of Internet governance. *Virginia Journal of Law and Technology* 9: 2–33.

Johnson, D. R., and D. Post. 1997. And how shall the net be governed?: A meditation on the relative virtues of decentralized, emergent law. In *Coordinating the Internet,* ed. B. Kahin and J. H. Keller, 62–91. Cambridge, MA: MIT Press.

Jordan, G. 1990. Sub-governments, policy communities and networks: Refilling the old bottle? *Journal of Theoretical Politics* 2:319–338.

Kaeo, Merike. 2007. Cyber attacks on Estonia short synopsis, North American Network Operators Group (NANOG) Presentation, NANOG 40, June 3–6, Bellevue, WA. http://doubleshotsecurity.com/pdf/NANOG-eesti.pdf.

Kahler, M., ed. 2009. *Networked politics: Agency, structure and power.* Ithaca, NY: Cornell University Press.

Karlekar, K. D., and S. G. Cook, eds. 2009. *Freedom on the net: A global assessment of Internet and digital media.* Washington, DC: Freedom House.

Keane, J. 2003. *Global civil society?* Cambridge: Cambridge University Press.

Keck, M., and K. Sikkink. 1998. *Activists beyond borders: Advocacy networks in international politics.* Ithaca, NY: Cornell University Press.

Kelly, John J., and Lauri Almann. 2008–2009. eWMDs. *Policy Review,* no. 152 (December/January). Washington, DC: Heritage Foundation. http://www.modelsoft ware.com/people/152KellyAlmannOffprint.pdf.

Kenis, P., and V. Schneider. 1991. Policy networks and policy analysis: Scrutinizing a new analytical toolbox. In *Policy networks: Empirical evidence and theoretical considerations*, ed. B. Marin and R. Mayntz, 25–62. Frankfurt am Main: Campus Verlag; Boulder, CO: Westview Press.

Klein, H. 2004. Understanding WSIS: An institutional analysis of the UN world summit on the information society. *Information Technology and International Development* 1 (3–4): 3–14.

Kleinwachter, W. 2004. A new diplomacy? Multistakeholder approach and bottom up policy in global ICT governance. *Information Technology and International Development* 1 (3–4). http://cyber.law.harvard.edu/wsis/Kleinwachter.html.

Knight, J. 1992. *Institutions and social conflict*. Cambridge: Cambridge University Press.

Knoke, D. 1990. *Political networks: The structural perspective*. Cambridge: Cambridge University Press.

Knoke, D., and J. Boli. 1997. Comparing policy networks. *Administrative Science Quarterly* 42 (1): 184–187.

Knoke, D., F. U. Pappi, J. Broadbent, Y. Tsujinaka, and R. V. Gould. 1997. Comparing policy networks: Labor politics in the U.S., Germany, and Japan. *American Journal of Sociology* 102 (6): 1745–1747.

Kooiman, J. 2003. *Governing and governance*. London: Sage.

Koops, B., and S. W. Brenner, eds. 2006. *Cybercrime and jurisdiction: A global survey*. The Hague: T. M. C. Asser Press.

Koven, R. 2003. Governments reach out to control cyberspace. In *Press freedom on the Internet, Presented by the World Press Freedom Committee and the Communications Media Committee of the Association of the Bar of the City of New York*, June 26–28, New York, NY. http://www.wpfc.org/site/docs/pdf/Publications/Working%20Papers-Conf%20Booklet.pdf.

Kranich, N. 2004. *The information commons: A public policy report*. New York: The Free Expression Policy Project, Brennan Center for Justice, NYU School of Law.

Krasner, S. D. 1983. *International regimes*. Ithaca, NY: Cornell University Press.

Kuerbis, B., and M. Mueller. 2007. *Securing the root: A proposal for distributing signing authority*. IGP-07-002. Syracuse, NY: Internet Governance Project.

Landes, W. 2003. Indirect liability for copyright infringement: Napster and beyond. *Journal of Economic Perspectives* 17 (2): 113–124.

Landes, W., and R. Posner. 2003. *The economic structure of intellectual property law*. Cambridge, MA: Harvard University Press.

Lemley, M. A., and L. Lessig. 2000. The end of end-to-end: Preserving the architecture of the Internet in the broadband era. Stanford Law School, John M. Olin Program on Law and Economics, Working Paper No. 207; School of Law, Boalt Hall, UC Berkeley Law and Economics, Research Paper No. 2000-19.

Lessig, L. 2001. *The future of ideas: The fate of the commons in a connected world.* New York: Vintage Books.

Lessig, L. 2005. *Free culture: The nature and future of creativity.* New York: Penguin.

Levinson, D., ed. 2002. *Encyclopedia of crime and punishment,* vols. I–IV. New York: Sage Publications.

Lewis, J. 2008. *Securing cyberspace for the 44th presidency: A report of the CSIS commission on cybersecurity for the 44th presidency.* Washington, DC: Center for Strategic and International Studies.

Libecap, G. D. 1989. *Contracting for property rights.* Cambridge: Cambridge University Press.

Litman, J. 2000. The DNS wars: Trademarks and the Internet domain name system. *Journal of Small and Emerging Business Law* 4:141.

Litman, J. 2001. *Digital copyright.* Amherst, New York: Prometheus.

Malcolm, J. 2008. *Multi-stakeholder governance and the Internet governance forum.* Wembley, Australia: Terminus Press.

Marin, B., and R. Mayntz, eds. 1991. *Policy networks: Empirical evidence and theoretical considerations.* Frankfurt am Main: Campus Verlag; Boulder, CO: Westview Press.

Marres, N. 2006. Net-work is format work: Issue networks and the sites of civil society politics. In *Reformatting politics: Networked communications and global civil society,* ed. J. Dean, J. Anderson, and G. Lovink, 3–18. New York: Routledge.

Mathiason, J., M. Mueller, M. Holitscher, and L. W. McKnight. 2004. *Internet governance: The state of play.* Syracuse, NY: The Internet Governance Project.

Mayer-Schönberger, V., and M. Ziewitz. 2007. Jefferson rebuffed: The United States and the future of Internet governance. *Columbia Science and Technology Law Review* 8:188–228.

Mayntz, R., and F. W. Scharpf. 1995. *Gesellschaftliche selbstregulierung und politische steuerung.* Frankfurt am Main: Campus Verlag.

Millet, S., and G. Huston. 2005. *Proposal to amend APNIC IPv6 assignment and utilisation requirement policy.* No. prop-031-v001. August.

Monge, P., and N. S. Contractor. 2003. *Theories of communication networks.* New York: Oxford University Press.

Moore, T. 2008. *Cooperative attack and defense in distributed networks. UCAM-CL-TR-718.* Cambridge: University of Cambridge Computer Laboratory.

Morozov, E. 2009. Cyber-scare: The exaggerated fears over digital warfare. *Boston Review* 34 (4). http://bostonreview.net/BR34.4/morozov.php.

Mueller, M. 2002. *Ruling the root: Internet governance and the taming of cyberspace.* Cambridge, MA: MIT Press.

Mueller, M. 2005. Toward an economics of the domain name system. In *Handbook of telecommunications economics, Volume 2, Technology evolution and the Internet,* ed. M. E. Cave, S. K. Majumdar and I. Vogelsang, 445–479. Amsterdam: North-Holland/Elsevier.

Mueller, M. 2008a. Info-communism? Ownership and freedom in the digital economy. *First Monday* 13 (4), April 7. http://firstmonday.org/htbin/cgiwrap/bin/ojs/index.php/fm/article/view/2058.

Mueller, M. 2008b. *Scarcity in IP addresses: IPv4 address transfer markets and the regional Internet address registries.* IGP-08-002. Syracuse, NY: Internet Governance Project.

Mueller, M., and M. Chango. 2008. Disrupting global governance: The Internet Whois service, ICANN and privacy. *Journal of Information Technology & Politics* 5 (3): 303–325.

Mueller, M., and B. Kuerbis. 2008. Regional address registries, governance and Internet freedom. Internet Governance Project Paper IGP-08-005. http://internetgovernance.org/pdf/RIRs-IGP-hyderabad.pdf.

Mueller, M., J. Mathiason, and H. Klein. 2007. The Internet and global governance: Principles and norms for a new regime. *Global Governance* 13 (2): 237–254.

Mueller, M., B. Kuerbis, and C. Page. 2004. Civil society and the shaping of communication-information policy: Four decades of advocacy. *Information Society* 20 (3): 1–7.

North, D. C. 1990. *Institutions, institutional change and economic performance.* Cambridge: Cambridge University Press.

Odrats, Ivar, ed. 2006. *Information Technology in Public Administration in Estonia, Yearbook 2006* (English version). Ministry of Economic Affairs and Communications of Estonia. 2007. http://www.riso.ee/en/pub/2006it/index.php?mn=0.

Ostrom, E. 2005. *Understanding institutional diversity.* Princeton, NJ: Princeton University.

Ottaway, M. 2001. Corporatism goes global: International organizations, nongovernmental organization networks, and transnational business. *Global Governance* 7: 265–292.

Piatek, M., T. Kohno, and A. Krishnamurthy. 2008. Challenges and directions for monitoring P2P file sharing networks (or, why my printer received a DMCA take-down notice). Paper presented at HotSec '08 (July). Also Technical Report #08-6-01, University of Washington, Department of Computer Science & Engineering, http://dmca.cs.washington.edu/.

Perset, K. 2007. *Internet address space: Economic considerations in the management of IPv4 and in the deployment of IPv6.* DSTI/ICCP(2007)20/FINAL. Paris: OECD.

Picciotto, S. 1997. Fragmented states and international rules of law. *Social & Legal Studies* 6 (2): 259–279.

Podolny, J. M., and K. Page. 1998. Network forms of organization. *Annual Review of Sociology* 24:57–76.

Powell, W. W. 1990. Neither market nor hierarchy: Network forms of organization. In *Research in Organizational Behavior* 12:295–336.

Price, R. 2003. Transnational civil society and advocacy in world politics. *World Politics* 55 (4): 579–606.

Raboy, M. 2004. The origins of civil society involvement in the WSIS. *Information Technologies and International Development* 1 (3–4): 95–96.

Raustiala, K. 2002. The architecture of international cooperation: Transgovernmental networks and the future of international law. *Virginia Journal of International Law* 43 (1) (Fall): 1–92.

Raymond, E. S. 2001. *The cathedral and the bazaar: Musings on Linux and open source by an accidental revolutionary,* rev. ed. Cambridge, MA: O'Reilly.

Reinicke, W. H. 1997. Global public policy networks. *Foreign Affairs* 76 (6): 127–139.

Reinicke, W. H. 1999–2000. The other World Wide Web: Global public policy networks. *Foreign Policy* 117:44–59.

Resnick, P. 1997. Filtering information on the Internet. *Scientific American* (March): 106–108.

Resnick, P., and J. R. Miller. 1996. PICS: Internet access controls without censorship. *Communications of the ACM* 39 (10): 87–93.

Rheingold, H. 2002. *Smart mobs: The next social revolution.* New York: Perseus Books.

Rhodes, R. A. W. 1990. Policy networks: A British perspective. *Journal of Theoretical Politics* 2 (3): 293–317.

Rhodes, R. A. W., S. A. Binder, and B. A. Rockman, eds. 2006. *The Oxford handbook of political institutions.* Oxford: Oxford University Press.

Rimmer, M. 2005. Hail to the thief: A tribute to KaZaA. *University of Ottawa Law and Technology Journal* 2 (1): 173–218.

Risse, T. 2001. Transnational actors and world politics. In *Handbook of international relations*, ed. R. Carlsnaes, T. Risse, and B. Simmons, 255–275. London: Sage.

Risse-Kappen, T. 1995. *Bringing transnational relations back in: Non-state actors, domestic structures and international institutions*. Cambridge: Cambridge University Press.

Roffe, P. 2004. "Bilateral Agreements and a TRIPS-Plus World: The Chile-USA Free Trade Agreement." TRIPS Issue Paper #4. Ottawa: Quaker International Affairs Programme.

Rose, N. 1999. *Powers of freedom: Reframing political thought*. Cambridge: Cambridge University Press.

Rosenau, J., and O. Czempiel, eds. 1992. *Governance without government: Order and change in world politics*. Cambridge: Cambridge University Press.

Ruggie, J. G. 2004. Reconstituting the global public domain—Issues, actors and practices. *European Journal of International Relations* 10 (4): 499–531.

Sanderson, M. T. 2009. Candidates, squatters, and gripers: A primer on political cybersquatting and a proposal for reform. *Election Law Journal: Rules, Politics, and Policy* 8 (1): 3–29.

Schaefer, B. D., J. J. Tkacik, and J. L. Gattuso. 2005. Keep the Internet free of the United Nations. WebMemo #904. Washington, DC: Heritage Foundation.

Scharpf, F. W. 1993. *Games in hierarchies and networks: Analytical and empirical approaches to the study of governance institutions*. Boulder, CO: Westview Press.

Scharpf, F. W. 1997. *Games real actors play: Actor-centered institutionalism in policy research*. Boulder, CO: Westview Press.

Schneider, V., and R. Werle. 1991. Policy networks in the German telecommunications domain. In *Policy networks: Empirical evidence and theoretical considerations*, ed. B. Marin and R. Mayntz, 97–136. Frankfurt am Main: Campus Verlag; Boulder, CO: Westview Press.

Schryen, G. 2007. Anti-spam legislation: An analysis of laws and their effectiveness. *Information & Communications Technology Law* 16 (1): 17–32.

Sedlak, Andrea J. D. Finkelhor, H. Hammer, and D. J. Schultz. 2002. *National estimates of missing children: An overview*. Washington, DC: U.S. Department of Justice, Office of Juvenile Justice and Delinquency Prevention. http://www.ncjrs.gov/pdffiles1/ojjdp/196465.pdf.

Sell, S. K. 1998. *Power and ideas: North-south politics of intellectual property and antitrust*. Albany: SUNY Press.

Shepherd, M., and C. Watters. 2000. *Content filtering technologies and Internet service providers: Enabling user choice*. Ottawa: Industry Canada.

Shirkey, C. 2008. *Here comes everybody: The power of organizing without organizations.* New York: Penguin Press.

Sikkink, K. 1993. Human rights, principled issue networks and sovereignty in Latin America. *International Organization* 47 (3): 411–441.

Slaughter, A. 2004. *A new world order.* Princeton, NJ: Princeton University Press.

Smith, J. 2001. Globalizing resistance: The battle of Seattle and the future of social movements. *Mobilization: An International Journal* 6 (1): 1–19.

Smith, K. 1985. Implications of value added network services. *Data Processing* 27 (6): 41–45.

Solove, D. J. 2007. *The future of reputation: Gossip, rumor and privacy on the Internet.* New Haven, CT: Yale University Press.

Sørenson, E., and J. Torfing eds. 2007. *Theories of democratic network governance.* Basingstoke, UK: Palgrave McMillan.

Souter, D. 2007. *Whose summit? Whose information society? Developing countries and civil society at the World Summit on the Information Society.* Johannesburg: Association for Progressive Communications. http://www.apc.org/en/pubs/manuals/governance/all/whose-summit-whose-information-society.

Stallman, R. 2002. *Free software, free society: Selected essays of Richard M. Stallman.* Boston: Free Software Foundation.

Stol, W. P., H. K. W. Kaspersen, J. Kerstensa, E. R. Leukfeldta, and A. R. Lodder. 2009. Governmental filtering of websites: The Dutch case. *Computer Law & Security Report* 25:251–262.

Tarrow, S. 2001. Transnational politics: Contention and institutions in international politics. *Annual Review of Political Science* 4:1–20.

Tarrow, S. 2005. *The new transnational activism.* Cambridge: Cambridge University Press.

Thorelli, H. B. 1986. Networks: Between markets and hierarchies. *Strategic Management Journal* 7 (1): 37–51.

Thurner, P. W., and M. Binder. 2008. European Union transgovernmental networks: The emergence of a new political space beyond the nation-state? *European Journal of Political Research* 48 (1): 80–106.

Tichenor, D. J., and R. A. Harris. 2005. The development of interest group politics in America: Beyond the conceits of modern times. *Annual Review of Political Science* 8:251–270.

Turner, D. 2008. Symantec global Internet security threat report: Trends for July–December 07, vol. XIII. Cupertino, CA: Symantec, Inc. http://eval.symantec.com/

mktginfo/enterprise/white_papers/b-whitepaper_internet_security_threat_report
_xiii_04-2008.en-us.pdf.

Urban, J. M., and L. Quilter. 2006. Efficient process or "Chilling effects"? Takedown
notices under section 512 of the digital millennium copyright act. *Santa Clara Computer and High-Technology Law Journal* 22:621–693.

Vaidhyanathan, S. 2001. *Copyrights and copywrongs: The rise of intellectual property
and how it threatens creativity*. New York: New York University Press.

Vaidhyanathan, S. 2004. *The Anarchist in the Library: How the clash between freedom
and control is hacking the real world and crashing the system*. New York: Basic Books.

van Eecke, P., and B. Ooms. 2007. ISP liability and the E-Commerce Directive: A
growing trend toward greater responsibility for ISPs. *Journal of Internet Law* 11 (4):
3–9.

van Eeten, M., and J. M. Bauer. 2008. Economics of malware: Security decisions,
incentives and externalities. OECD Science, Technology and Industry Working
Paper No. 2008/1. Paris: Organisation for Economic Co-operation and Development.

Villeneuve, N. 2007. Evasion tactics: Global online censorship is growing, but so are
the means to challenge it and protect privacy. *Index on Censorship* 4:71–85.

Waever, O. 1995. Securitization and desecuritization. In *On security*, ed. R. D.
Lipschutz. New York: Columbia University Press, 46–86.

Wall, D. S. 2004. Digital realism and the governance of spam as cybercrime. *European
Journal on Criminal Policy and Research* 10 (4): 309–335.

Watson, R. T., M. Boudreau, M. Greiner, D. Wynn, P. York, and R. Gul. 2005. Governance and global communities. *Journal of International Management* 11 (2): 125–142.

Weber, S. 2004. *The success of open source*. Cambridge, MA: Harvard University Press.

Wellman, B., and S. D. Berkowitz. 1988. *Social structures: A network approach*. New
York: Cambridge University Press.

Williams, S. 2002. *Free as in freedom: Richard Stallman's crusade for free software*.
Sebastopol, CA: O'Reilly.

Williamson, O. E. 1975. *Markets and hierarchies, analysis and antitrust implications: A
study in the economics of internal organization*. New York: Free Press.

Williamson, O. E. 1985. *The economic institutions of capitalism: Firms, markets, relational contracting*. New York: Free Press.

WGIG. 2005. Working Group on Internet Governance. Chateau de Bossey, Switzerland. June. http://www.wgig.org/docs/WGIGREPORT.pdf.

Zakaria, N., and D. Cogburn. 2006. Webs of culture: Applying high and low-context theory to understand decision-making behaviors in transnational NGO networks involved in WSIS. Paper prepared for presentation at the 2006 Annual Meeting of the International Communication Association, June 19–23, Dresden, Germany.

Zittrain, J. 2008. *The future of the Internet: And how to stop it*. New Haven, CT: Yale University Press.

Index

312 Index

United States (cont.)
pornography and, 26–30
Section 301 and, 133–134
September 11 attacks and, 176,
178n49
spam and, 165
Trade-Related Aspects of Intellectual
Property (TRIPS) and, 133–135
unilateral globalism and, 244–251
VeriSign and, 63
World Summit on the Information
Society (WSIS) and, 61–65, 69–77, 80
United States v. Bank of Nova Scotia,
21n15
Urban, J. M., 138n20
Utsumi, Y., 77n41

Valenti, Jack, 156n53
Van Eeten, M., 172n33
VANS General License, 55n1
VeriSign, Inc., 63, 232n30, 233–234,
237, 245
Vidéazimut, 84
Vincent, Richard, 84
Virgin Killer (Scorpions), 26–30, 200
Viruses, 151, 159
Vixie, Paul, 166
Vodafone, 185, 200
Voices 21, 85

Wall Street Journal, 147n39, 160n3
War, 22–25, 62n16, 78, 159, 179, 190,
254
Washington Post, 71, 75, 168
Watson, R. T., 36n11
Weapons of mass destruction (WMD),
162n9
Wellman, B., 33n2
Whois service, 139–142, 171, 178, 182,
224n12, 231, 249
Wikileaks, 198–199
Wikipedia, 7, 13, 200
critical Internet resources and, 241

Internet Watch Foundation and,
26–30
network governance and, 26–30,
35–36, 47
pornography and, 26–30
Scorpions and, 26–30
Siegenthaler case and, 47n37
Wired Magazine, 144
Working Group on Internet
Governance (WGIG), 66–68
institutional change and, 67–68
intellectual property and, 130
World Association for Christian
Communication (WACC), 85, 94
World Association of Community
Radio Broadcasters (AMARC), 84, 90,
94
World Commission on Dams, 43
World Intellectual Property
Organization (WIPO), 50
Broadcast Treaty and, 147
civil society and, 89, 91n23
critical Internet resources and, 220
Internet Governance Forum (IGF) and,
117
policy issues and, 130–131, 134,
137–138, 153, 155–156
state-centric view and, 79
Whois service and, 139–142, 171, 178,
182, 224n12, 231, 249
World Press Freedom Committee
(WPFC), 99–100
World Social Forum, 90
World Summit on the Information
Society (WSIS), 3n2, 13
advocacy networks and, 11
assessment of, 78–80
authoritarian states and, 69
battle over soul of Internet and, 10–11
Campaign for Communication Rights
in the Information Society (CRIS)
and, 83–87, 93–96, 98–101
Civil Society Bureau and, 98–100

Printed in the United States
by Baker & Taylor Publisher Services